MEDIA KNOWLEDGE

SUNY Series, Teacher Empowerment and School Reform
Henry A. Giroux and Peter L. McLaren, editors

MEDIA KNOWLEDGE

READINGS IN POPULAR CULTURE, PEDAGOGY, AND CRITICAL CITIZENSHIP

BY
JAMES SCHWOCH
MIMI WHITE
SUSAN REILLY

State University of New York Press

Published by
State University of New York Press, Albany

Printed in the United States of America

For information, address State University of New York Press, State University Plaza, Albany, N.Y. 12246

Production by Christine Lynch
Marketing by Dana E. Yanulavich

Library of Congress Cataloging-in-Publication Data

Schwoch, James, 1955–
Media knowledge: readings in popular culture, pedagogy, and critical citizenship / by James Schwoch, Mimi White, Susan Reilly.
p. cm. — (SUNY series, teacher empowerment and school reform)
Includes bibliographical references and index.
ISBN 0-7914-0826-4 (paper) (alk. paper).
ISBN 0-7914-0825-6 (hardcover) (alk. paper)
1. Mass media—United States. 2. Mass media in education—United States. 3. United States—Popular culture. I. White, Mimi, 1953– . II. Reilly, Susan, 1944– . III. Title. IV. Series: Teacher empowerment and school reform.
P92.U5S58 1992
302.23'0973—dc20

91–93565
CIP

10 9 8 7 6 5 4 3 2

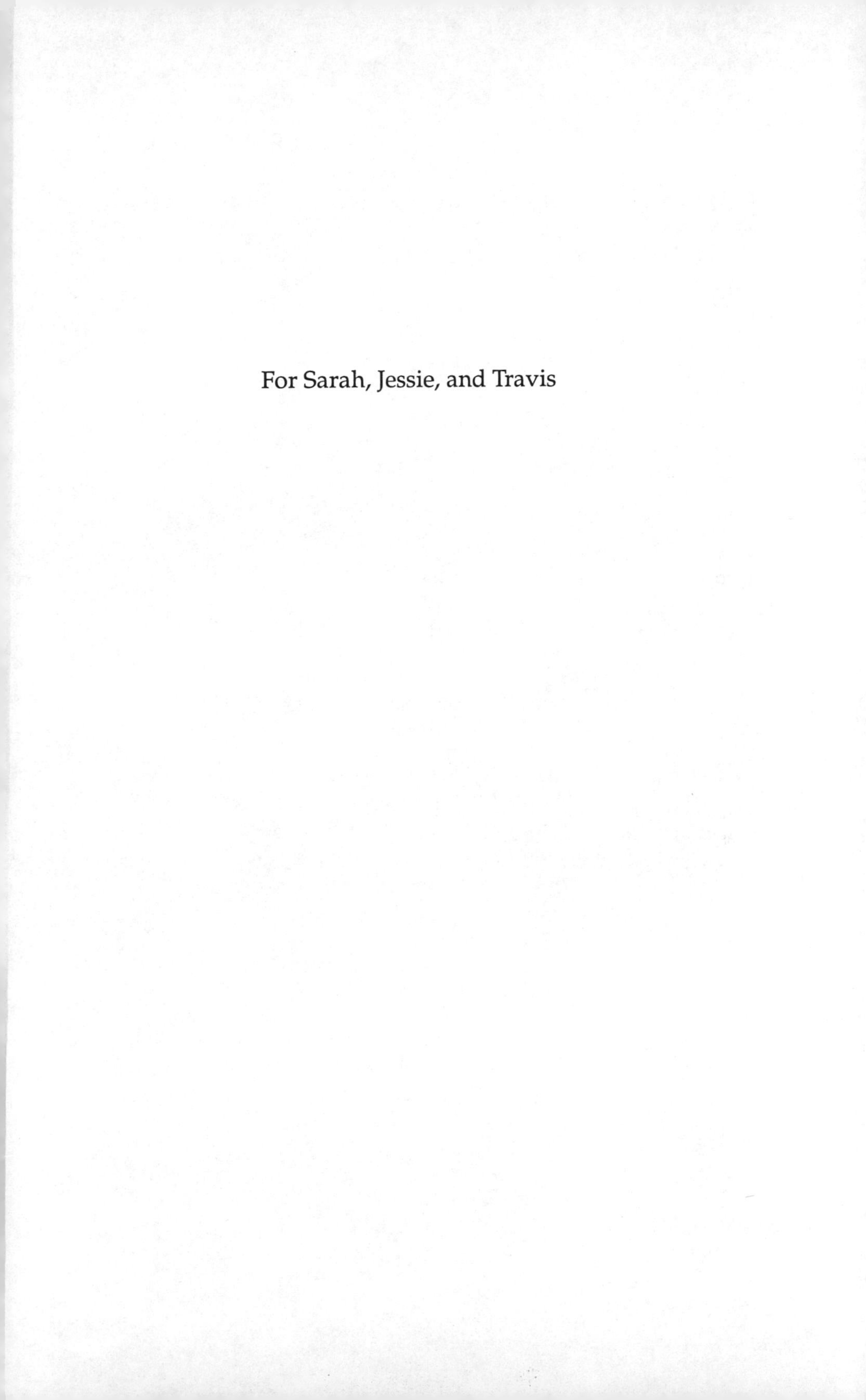

For Sarah, Jessie, and Travis

CONTENTS

FOREWORD

Like any large project, this book has its own history. During the initial discussions with Henry Giroux and Peter McLaren in the summer of 1986 about the series on teacher empowerment and school reform they were beginning to edit, it was clear to all that American media culture was a highly important—and vaguely understood—site of pedagogy. We quickly agreed that a lot of learning, indeed a lifetime of learning, was acquired by consumers of television, radio, film, recorded music, magazines and newspapers, and advertising. But beyond this initial agreement were difficult questions.

What "kind" of learning behavior is this? How does it relate to the conventional pedagogy associated with the American educational system? How does the pedagogy of media culture relate to other social processes of pedagogy outside the sphere of formal education, such as the family or the church? In what ways does the pedagogy of media culture support the American educational system, and in what ways does it undermine that system? Precisely how (and how precisely) could one go about explaining and detailing this pedagogy of media culture?

By the end of that afternoon it had become abundantly clear to all that an examination of contemporary American media culture and its pedagogical processes was an absolutely indispensable project for the new series, and it had become equally clear that the research and writing of such a project was a more slippery and difficult task than had at first appeared. Some of the difficulty, of course, stems from the ability to read individual media texts in multiple and contradictory manners. The image, even more than the written word, has an inherent quality that renders its reading ambiguous. Complicating the issue further is that media texts and messages, when compared to each other, are usually not harmonious but much more often cacophonous. The abundance of media texts and messages encountered on a daily basis amplifies this cacophony. In this maelstrom of media activity, would we be able to discern and reveal the overarching pedagogical functions of contemporary media systems and texts?

As authors, our initial strategy was to divide up the work and begin under the rather general and broad working title of "Media Culture and Information Technology: The Production of Everyday Knowledge." As we each began drafting our individual chapters, the working hypothesis implied in this original title slowly shifted. Halfway through the writing, we realized that the pages produced really did not talk at length about the actual *production* of media culture and pedagogical processes. In other words, we had found that our discussion of the pedagogical experiences of living with contemporary American media culture did not entail examination and analysis of actions and decisions by media creators, or the structure and performance of American media industries. Rather, we concluded that the pedagogy ultimately was in the receiving process rather than the production process of media culture. This decision to emphasize the receiving process does not mean we consider that the study and analysis of the production process is of lesser importance; far from it. Indeed, at several junctures in the book, we touch upon the importance of a critical citizenry beginning to involve itself in the process of media production for its own social community. However, it is our conviction that the media experiences of contemporary everyday life are more often than not those of reception rather than those of production. Therefore, an emphasis on the ways media culture offers meanings that comprise the receiving process are herein offered.

With this in mind, the goal of teacher empowerment and school reform has led us to analyze and explain what it means to be on the consuming or receiving end rather than the creating end regarding media texts and messages. We have done this in a twofold manner. First, the chapters open up their specific objects of analysis to reveal the pedagogical workings of certain aspects of media culture. This includes a discussion of how a mainstream, passive, accepting reception and reading of an array of media texts—such as television news, romance films, or advertising—ultimately supports and reaffirms a dominant ideology in contemporary American culture founded on beliefs in the positive values of consumer capitalism and the rejection of any values perceived as disjunctive to consumer capitalism. Secondly, we have also tried to open the eyes and ears of potential consumers of media culture to a more active, engaging, questioning way of reception and reading—what we call "critical citizenship."

With the term "critical citizenship" we invoke a different way of reading media culture as a part of an alternative theory that opposes current trends in American education, trends that exclusively emphasize excellence, discipline, achievement, and quantitatively verifiable production. Critical citizenship implies a philosophy of pedagogy that instead promotes the teaching of egalitarianism, the value of social difference, and a qualitative concern with individual ability to master the skills needed to gain knowledge throughout life (rather than acquire a set of "facts" without understanding how and why those facts were acquired). We do not object to the acquiring of facts for occupational mobility, or for professional achievement, but feel an educational system with this as its end product does not go far enough. Learning must also include complex intellectual knowledge and skills that enhance the ability of a citizenry to continue to educate itself throughout its social life. An indispensable component of such a lifelong educational experience is an active, engaging, questioning relationship with the social, political, and cultural structures and artifacts that comprise the fabric of everyday life. In this era—the end of the twentieth century—a critical citizenship engaging with media culture is of vital importance.

As a part of the promotion of critical citizenship, students and educators must explore the relationships between the work they do in class and the lives they live outside of class. This includes the incorporation of everyday lived culture into the work of schooling in a manner that does not simply confirm and trivialize what students already know, but instead reveals the workings of how that everyday knowledge is acquired. This is one reason why exploring the pedagogy of media culture is so vital to building a critical citizenship, because contemporary media culture is a major site of everyday learning.[1]

As the above paragraph implies, educators and students of education comprise one major component of the audience for this volume. Although the issues we raise are important for anyone interested in media studies, we have on several occasions specifically developed our arguments to speak to educators and, by extension, their students. We do not mean to imply that the approaches to examining and analyzing media culture in the chapters that follow are the "best" way, or the "only" way; far from it. We do feel that the analytical systems we develop are particularly appropriate for issues of media, culture, and pedagogy. Educators interested in media studies would do well to consider a wide range of approaches for discussing media culture, several of which are briefly discussed in the conclusion of this book.

Furthermore, our discussion of media, culture, and pedagogy is far from exhaustive. Indeed, our chapters examine only a few of the important avenues of inquiry pertinent to this subject. A comprehensive, all-encompassing discussion would probably not be a single book but an entire series unto itself. However, we are convinced that the chapters herein deal not only with crucial aspects of this issue, but do so in such a manner that students and teachers will be able to apply the principles of critical citizenship in their readings of media texts and messages well beyond the examples discussed in this book.

The opening chapter, "Television and its Historical Pastiche," examines the contradictory relationships that television invokes in its representation of the historical. Ranging from news coverage to "golden age" programs to representational practices in current prime time melodrama, this chapter draws in part upon the discourse of postmodernism to provide an analysis of television and media culture's particular appropriations of an established field of intellectual activity—history—and how the conceptions of that field are shaped and reconfigured through television's mediation of the field.

In the next chapter, the focus turns to advertising. Again using television as a case study, this more traditionally based textual analysis of advertising investigates the social construction of consumption for communications services such as telephony. Included are examinations of the various discourses offered through television advertising regarding popular conceptions of the body, time and space, and language. This chapter conjoins two important aspects of media culture: the texts of television advertising on the one hand, and the world of everyday telecommunications services on the other.

Chapter three is the first of two chapters examining broadcast journalism. We felt broadcast journalism, and particularly network television news, to be of vital importance in this project because more Americans receive their daily knowledge of current events from television than any other source. Therefore, the pedagogical implications of television journalism are obvious. The sociological discourse of news analysis serves as a methodology to examine the implications of both domestic and international news coverage.

The next three chapters turn to a more detailed discussion of media pedagogy in the areas of race, gender, and class. Chapter four is a case study of the prime time news special, using the drug abuse story as an example. This chapter also continues the examination of television news begun in the previous chapter. The interweaving of the drug abuse story with concerns of race relations emerges as a central theme. Popular culture and the representation of gender—in this case, feminist theory and the romance genre—is the topic of chapter five. Finally, chapter six draws upon elements of the French school of sociological history to examine technology and everyday life. The chapter raises questions about class formation in relation to the commodification of American culture during the so-called "information age," in a discussion of the acquisition of new communications and information technologies by different segments of American society.

As indicated by this summary of our project, the chapters are disparate in their particular methodologies. At first glance this disparity may seem somewhat unusual to readers unfamiliar with media studies, but those more fully versed in the literature of that field are likely to recognize some familiar ground. Media studies is highly interdisciplinary and has been influenced by a number of methods and approaches in the social sciences and humanities. This book embraces that interdisciplinary impulse in its construction. As stated earlier, the methods and approaches we employ do not encompass the entire range of communications research, but are representative samples of several important trends in the field at this time.

While each of the six chapters takes up pedagogical implications to a certain degree, the conclusion of this book returns to questions of pedagogy and the relationships between media culture and a critical citizenship. Here we more fully elaborate what is implicit in the current debate concerning the world of education, particularly in the American public school system. We also elaborate on how the investigation of media texts and messages within the classroom might eventually transform that debate in political, social, and cultural terms. While we hope readers will examine all of the chapters, individuals reading selectively are encouraged to include the concluding chapter in their examination in order to be more fully informed about the pedagogical implications of the various case studies we undertake in the main body of the text.

*****

Media Knowledge has received encouragement and support from many of our colleagues throughout its journey from concept to publication. We are deeply appreciative of the many contributions from Henry Giroux and Peter McLaren, including their thoughtful introduction. Lois Patton and SUNY Press have done a superlative job of guiding the manuscript through the production process in a timely manner. The insights of Ron Scott, our colleague at Miami University of Ohio, as a co-author of chapter four, significantly enhanced our analysis of race representation. Anne Storer at Miami also helped us in speeding up the drafting and revising of the manuscript, and both Anne and Pat Michell at Northwestern University shuttled numerous mailings, telephone calls, and faxes among the three authors with diligence. The manuscript also benefitted from the ongoing dialogues among the three authors and our colleagues and students at Miami and Northwestern, dialogues that are always an important part of scholarly work.

We also wish to thank the Pembroke Center for Teaching and Research on Women, Brown University, for their support of Mimi White via a fellowship during the 1986–87 academic year; some of the research related to television and historical representation was completed during that period. Thanks also to the National Humanities Center for hosting a symposium at which Mimi White presented that research. Mimi White and James Schwoch also conducted some of the early research while they were associated with the Center for Twentieth Century Studies, University of Wisconsin-Milwaukee, during the 1987-88 academic year; the chapter on telecommunications advertising was a direct result of that association. The College of Arts and Sciences at Miami provided research funds for the purchase of videotapes used in writing some of the chapters. We are especially grateful for the support of Elizabeth Weed and Joan Scott at Pembroke, Bobby Allen at the National Humanitites Center, Kathy Woodward and Pat Mellencamp at the Center for Twentieth Century Studies, and Dean of the College of Arts and Sciences Karl Mattox at Miami. A host of friends and colleagues have also assisted along the way, including Dana Polan, Cecelia Tichi, Andrew Ross, Jane Feuer, John Fiske, Patrice Petro, Pam Falkenberg, Russ Reising, Carole Tennessen, and Helen Sterk. Last, but not least, we especially thank Jack Reilly, whose support and confidence was essential, as always.

We hope the chapters that follow empower teachers, students, and all readers to engage in a lifelong critical citizenship by developing new reading habits in regard to their personal consumption of media culture.

INTRODUCTION
Media Hegemony: Towards a Critical Pedagogy of Representation

Henry A. Giroux and Peter L. McLaren

> Reality is more fabulous, more maddening, more strangely manipulative than fiction. To understand this is to recognize the naivete of a development of cinematic technology that promotes unmediated access to reality.
>
> —Trinh T. Minh-ha[1]

MEDIA AS PERPETUAL PEDAGOGY

When Walter Benjamin wrote about the nineteenth century figure of the *flaneur* or "street reader," the bohemian prototype of the modern intellectual whose method of literary production consisted of strolling the city streets and reflecting upon the everyday production of cultural and social life, he was essentially describing a particular generation of cultural workers whose "object of inquiry was modernity itself."[2] For Benjamin, the poet Baudelaire best embodied the figure of the intellectual *flaneur* as teacher—a socially rebellious cultural worker who is sympathetic to the needs of the proletariat and is able to teach Benjamin's generation of intellectual producers about the social, cultural and economic conditions that informed their lived experience.

The status of the *flaneur* was always precarious: "Unlike the academic who reflects in his room, he walks the street and 'studies' the crowd. At the same time, his economic base shifts drastically, no longer protected by the academic's mandarin status."[3] As capitalism expanded into hitherto uncommodified social and cultural realms, and further implicated itself in the signifying practices of mass communications media, fascism became its afterimage and Benjamin began to notice that the modern role of the *flaneur* was changing to its peril. As cultural producer, the *flaneur* increasingly came under the spell of "the dreaming collective created by consumer capitalism,"[4] which removed him more and more from the historical conditions that produced his own social universe. Susan Buck-Morss writes:

> The reporter, a *flaneur*-become-detective, covers the beat; the photojournalist hangs about like a hunter ready to shoot.... He is the prototype of a new form of salaried employee who produces news/literature/advertisements for the purpose of information/entertainment/persuasion—these forms are not clearly distinguished. Posing as a reporter of the true conditions of urban life, he in fact diverts his audience from its tedium. His mass-marketed products fill the 'empty' hours that time off from work has become in modern cities. At the same time, the *flaneur* as bohemian himself becomes a cafe attraction.[5]

The transformation that the *flaneur* gradually underwent could be seen in the degraded incarnation of the sandwichman. As the structured unconscious of the collective (*Kollektiv*) of the masses (*die Masse*) became porous receptacles for the political phantasmagoria and staged extravaganzas of mass spectacles of the 1930s and 1940s, the most degraded caricature of the *flaneur* was eventually to appear on the streets of Munich in the form of Jews marching through the city bearing placards—barbaric self-advertisements which the Nazis forced upon the Jews as emblems of their ethnic disgrace and which became social hieroglyphs of the most profound evil of the century.[6]

Today we are living in a precarious historical moment in which the intellectual *flaneurs* of the present generation are undergoing even further metamorphosis. The postmodern *flaneurs* of today are corporate individuals cunningly managing and shaping the world of mass-consumed images, superannuated servants of the state whose forms of literary production are most often electronically mediated and fastened securely to the logic of consumption. They still stroll the city streets, as they did in Benjamin's era, but this time they are accompanied by a video crew, production assistants, and armed with a particular format to follow. Often salaried employees of transnational corporations and other standard-bearers of imperialism, the insights served up by the postmodern *flaneur* (to audiences sometimes exceeding millions at one viewing) more often than not serve to mystify and further camouflage class, race, and gender antagonisms, and thereby hinder rather than help viewers to understand the conditions of their everyday existence. As reality increasingly becomes confused with the image, and the mediascape becomes the driving force of our time, the image of the postmodern *flaneur* becomes embodied not in a human presence but in human immanence transmuted and transmogrified through an electronic signal, a satellite beam roaming the earth in search of new spectacles through which to present and contain reality.

Media Knowledge is a book that not only speaks to the political effects of image production, but also to the commodification of those who both produce it and stage it for public consumption—what we have referred to as the postmodern *flaneur.* James Schwoch's, Mimi White's, and Susan Reilly's telling remarks in the opening chapter of analysis set the intellectual tone for the volume:

> the history of everyday life is so accessible—a walk down the street, a glance out the window can show buildings and cars of different ages and eras; a trip to the library can show books and magazines of different generations stacked next to each other on the shelves; if the local community has a folklore festival, historical society, or even something as simple as a farmer's market, we are presented with a kaleidoscopic melange of past and present.... However, the infatuation with television may someday threaten to take away that joy and exercise a monopoly power over it without society's realization of its loss. Unlike the mythic losses promulgated by a televisual past, society's loss of understanding, experiencing, and writing its own everyday history would indeed be painful. (p. 18–19)

Media Knowledge is an attempt to explore the painful loss of everyday history and shared popular memory that has followed the development of media technology since the beginning of this century. More specifically, it is a critique of the relationship between televisual and other mass-produced representations and the logic of consumer capitalism that presently drives media culture. In its attempt to investigate the process, function, and social effects of media production, the authors have been able to provide teachers and students with a clearer understanding of the world of representations, their circuits of production and modes of reception, and the manner in which and the contexts for which they are staged and restaged. In the treatment given by Schwoch, White, and Reilly, media culture becomes "a site of perpetual pedagogy, hierarchy, status, and knowledge-as-power." (p. 106)

The authors maintain that the current state of media knowledge has much to do with an uncritical acceptance of the way in which media knowledge is produced and consumed. Given television's early links to the corporate marketplace, it is hardly surprising that, in the United States and other industrialized societies at that time, the Frankfurt School's insights were not seriously taken up by early pioneers of television programming in order to produce a redemptive social politics; but what remains truly surprising and equally disconcerting is the vastness of the chasm that exists today between the potential role of television as an instrument for social criticism and the deepening of democratic public life and its current ideological role within the social formation. Given the current separation between the role of the intellectual as social advocate, and the production of media knowledge, the authors of this volume are to be congratulated for putting together a work for today's cultural workers whose pedagogical sites go beyond schools and universities, to include theatre, film and television production, alternative presses, and projects in the arts and entertainment fields. The forms of critical analysis offered in this volume are drawn from some of the most advanced work in critical social theory, and we believe the social effects of this work could be an important step in closing the chasm between critical theorizing and popular knowledge.

What Schwoch, White, and Reilly are able to achieve in this volume is to give further critical substance to the idea that media knowledge is more than its seeming facticity, more than the insights brought to us by technologies which possess a privileged and transparent access to the real. Yet they are quick to underscore that neither should such knowledge be dismissed as trivial, nor treated as simply the willful illusions pumped out of the dream factories of entertainment industry moguls or electronic fallout from attempts at state-sponsored ideological management through the airwaves; rather, media knowledge is considered to be productive of the very identities and subjectivities of its viewers. In fact, such knowledge is treated by the authors as the carrier of the culture that is both its ideological precursor and its offspring. In fact, media knowledge as communication is always a form of social practice. As social practice or interaction, media knowledges carry selective ideological investments and interests; as such, they are constitutive of particular forms of associative life:

> Communication is an ensemble of social practices into which ingress conceptions, forms of expression, and social relations. These practices consti-

> tute reality (or alternatively deny, transform, or merely celebrate it). Communication naturalizes the artificial forms that human relations take by merging technique and conception in them. Each moment in the practice coactualizes conceptions of the real, forms of expression, and the social relations anticipated and realized in both. One can unhinge the practice at each of the points. The social forms and relations technology makes possible are themselves imagined in and anticipated by technology. Technique is vectorial and not merely neutral in the historical process. A building, its precise architecture, anticipates and imagines the social relations that it permits and desires. So does a television signal. Social relations of class, status, and power demand both a conceptual structure of persons and a technology to effectuate them. Conceptual structures, in turn, never float free of the expressive forms that realize them or the social relations that make them active agents.[7]

This process is not lost among Schwoch, White, and Reilly, especially as they reveal how television, as a reconstruction and remaking of previous visual and verbal structures, refigures the very concept of history itself. History as presented to viewers through the apparatus of television appears to be unwashed in ideology, a cluster of values that have been sedimented into popular common sense. Such an insight into the ideological production of common sense resonates with those of Stuart Hall, who describes common sense as "a contradictory ideological structure, which, though thoroughly formed as a 'product of history', presents itself to popular experience as transhistorical—the bedrock, universal wisdom of the ages."[8]

Media Knowledge registers a deep concern with respect to the power of television to transform subjectivities into the ideological service of nationalist, racist, and sexist political constituencies. Hall captures this idea in his notion of popular morality. Popular morality "organizes experience and sorts it into evaluative categories. Under the right conditions, 'the people' in their traditionalist representation can be condensed as a set of interpellations in discourses which systematically displace political issues into conventional moral absolutes."[9] Such a morality appears in the making when, according to Schwoch, White, and Reilly, history is compressed into the televisual moment, into a history-as-presence, a conglomerate simultaneity of copresent options, in which a particular historical subject is created. The authors remark that:

> to be situated in history, and as history, in television requires this conflation of past and present, a conflation which involves a (re)historicization of

> the present as well as (re)presentation of the past. History in its otherness masquerades as something new, while the present simulates itself as history. This in turn has the effect of producing an unstable, dispersed subject of historical consciousness. Such instability has ramifications for the process of reception and popular memory. (p. 13–14)

While situating their research in the historical present of the United States, the authors of *Media Knowledge* do suggest some implicit warning for the future construction of a global subject, particularly considering the electronic media's capacity for cultural maintenance, the means by which current media technologies are able to implicate themselves in the construction of the body, of time, of space, and more specifically, in their ability to both legitimize and reproduce the paired ideologies of technological utopianism and the culture of consumption. The concept of the global subject is further complicated by the fact that, as the authors remind us, the largest single user in the world of the electromagnetic spectrum is the United States, with the military the largest user of all government branches. And as the authors note, by the year 1982, the U.S. government held a total of 3.5 billion personal files in its federal agencies, or an average of fifteen files for every American citizen. Comparing the growing competition over intellectual property rights to the land speculation of the American West during the 1800s, the authors demonstrate that manifest destiny, global expansionism, and increasing communications innovations have given a new and more ominous meaning to technological determinism.

The remarkable insights of Schwoch, White, and Reilly into the issues of television advertising, network prime time news programs, the production of the urban black male subject, the use of telecommunications systems, and the construction of female subject positions within feature films, all raise questions which have a direct bearing on how communication acts, structures, and genres promote changes in the way the subject processes signs into meanings, effectively reconfiguring the subject's relation to the world. This is the case whether they happen to be deflating the myth of objectivity in television journalism or discussing how the last four digits of the telephone system owe their existence to ergonomic studies of the productive capacity of the female body conducted by American Telephone and Telegraph (ATT) earlier this century. Recent questions posed by Mark Poster resonate with those raised by the authors in this volume and are questions which prospective and practicing educators need to confront more directly in their pedagogies:

> What happens in society when the boundaries of linguistic experience are drastically transformed? How are social relations altered when language is no longer limited to face-to-face speech or to writing? What assumptions about the nature of society need to be revised when the already complex and ambiguous aspects of language are supplemented by electronic mediation?[10]

To these questions we would add other questions: How is television implicated in both the decentering of the historical object and the reconstitution of the subject according to normative cultural maps of reality? How is the subjectivity of the viewer narrativized in various ways by different forms of media knowledge? Within the production of media knowledges, how do essentially arbitrary cultural codes come to represent the real, the natural, and the necessary? How do current forms of signification in the media invite students to acquiesce in their social positions in a highly stratified and unjust society and thereby accept the fundamental subject positions constructed within current axes of race/class/gender? How are communicational devices able to reinscribe the human subject into prevailing social relations so that these relations are seen as conventional and uncontested? How is social reality encoded by various forms of media knowledge within familiar grids or frames of intelligibility such that social practices which unwittingly affirm racism, sexism, class domination, and heterosexism are rendered natural and commonsensical?

Schwoch, White, and Reilly take up the challenge of such questions and in so doing provide the reader with a greater awareness of the way in which new modes of information designate the way in which symbols, narratives, and media genres are used to communicate meanings and constitute subjects. They do not merely focus on how texts are taken up—as important as this task happens to be—but also on the importance of the political character of the text itself. Further, they recognize that the parameters of the human subject vary according to the media knowledges that are available in any historical moment. That is, dominant social arrangements are recognized as dominant not because they are the only social arrangements but because these arrangements exist for the advantage of certain social groups within particular configurations of power. They also acknowledge that media knowledges, in whatever form they take, never provide viewers with perspectives—critical or otherwise—which escape the consequences of historical and political practices. In fact, there are no timeless or pristine forms of media knowledge—only knowledge effects. This insight is what provokes Trinh T. Minh-Ha to remark: "to address the question of production relations...is endlessly to reopen the question: how is the real (or the social ideal of good representation) produced? Rather than catering to it, striving to capture and discover its truth as concealed or lost object, it is therefore important also to keep asking: how is truth being ruled?"[11]

If there exists no social self that precedes the social construction of subjectivity through the agency of representation, then the character of current regimes of representation that provide a range of ethical and subject positions necessarily represent the possible futures available to us. But it is important to note that Schwoch, White, and Reilly reject the view that media culture creates an antipodean world in which media representations are able to simply inscribe our values, desires, and behaviors. In other words, they realize that individuals are always already constrained by the forms of media knowledge that they use to think about possibilities for human freedom; in doing so, they transcend the idea that representations can be nothing more than compliant vehicles for the dominant culture. The authors of this volume do not see the human subject as irrevocably determined by media discourses. Such discourses never suspend us placelessly outside of history or lodge us immovably within current constellations of power. True, the character of media knowledge as already populated within prior current configurations of power limits the range of existing knowledge and meanings through which people interpret the relationship between themselves and others. However, this does not give Schwoch, White, and Reilly cause for political inertia or for moral despair. They do not believe that media knowledge simply reproduces cultural dupes, that resistance is impossible, or that identities produced by engagements with various forms of media knowledges are necessarily dependent upon the existing politics of representation. They understand that the experience that historical subjects have of being temporally and spatially fixed in history through the centralizing, regulating, and unifying maps of meaning produced by the media—that is, of being situated and re-situated in a pre-existing continuum of intractable social facts that have ideologically fixed their current disposition of being in the world—deludes them into believing that the present is immune to redemption. Yet the fact that the authors are able to effectively subvert the conventionalized narrativization of identity which lead many to believe that they are autonomous rational subjects for whom electronically channeled communication becomes a direct translation of reality, their critical project does not fall into the same traps which so often befall certain strands of the postmodernist critique. In other words, their position that subjects are to a large extent products of media discourses does not lead them to the conclusion that human agency has nowhere to go except into the theoretical vortex of a never-ending decenteredness. Consequently, media knowledge is not necessarily inimical to the deepening and extension of democratic public life. This enables the authors to speak to a politics of social change through various forms of critical media literacy.

Media literacy, as advocated by Schwoch, White, and Reilly, suggests that students and teachers can discover together different ways of examining the tacit assumptions and unarticulated presuppositions that undergird current cultural and social formations of the subjectivities they foster. In doing so, more attention needs to be given to decanonized forms of knowledge, to the everyday artifacts of popular culture. In the following section we develop the concept of a critical pedagogy of representation which we feel complements the project of media literacy which Schwoch, White, and Reilly have undertaken in this volume.

A CRITICAL PEDAGOGY OF REPRESENTATION

Pedagogy occurs wherever knowledge is produced, wherever culture is given the possibility of translating experience and constructing truths, even if such truths appear unrelentingly redundant, superficial, and commonsensical. On the one hand, there are standardized pedagogies which codify experience and shape meaning production in predictable and conventional ways, and in so doing naturalize meaning and the social structures and cultural forms which help to reproduce such meaning. (In effect, then, all pedagogies produce certain meaning-effects). On the other hand, oppositional pedagogies resist such formalized production of meaning by offering new channels of communication, new codifications of experience, and new perspectives of reception which unmask the political linkage between images, their means of production and reception, and the social practices they legitimate.

A critical pedagogy of representation recognizes that we inhabit a photocentric, aural, and televisual culture in which the proliferation of photographic and electronically produced images and sounds serves as a form of media catechism—a perpetual pedagogy—through which individuals ritually encode and evaluate the engagements they make in the various discursive contexts of everyday life. It is an approach that understands media representations—whether photographs, television, print, film, or another form—as not merely productive of knowledge but also of subjectivity. In this case, critical pedagogy must be understood as a deliberate attempt to influence how and what knowledge and identities are produced within particular sets of ideological and social practices. Students are encouraged to recognize connections among the ideologies and practices that structure pedagogical relations (epistemological assumptions, forms of authority, modes of signification, etc.) and those that structure the production and consumption of various kinds of representations. Students can then move from an examination of pedagogical relations in the classroom to those pedagogical relations in everyday life that influence the way in which media representations are both produced and taken up by individuals. In addition, students are encouraged to examine how the way in which they engage the world of media representations helps to constitute the meanings by which they not only come to understand and negotiate reality, but are constituted as political subjects.

Representations are always produced within cultural limits and theoretical borders, and as such are necessarily implicated in particular economies of truth, value, and power. In relation to these larger axes of power in which all representations are embedded, it is necessary to remind the student: Whose interests are being served by the representations in question? Within a given set of representations, who speaks, for whom, and under what conditions? Where can we situate such representations ethically and politically with respect to questions of social justice and human freedom? What moral, ethical, and ideological principles structure our reactions to such representations?

While it is commonplace for some radical educators to emphasize the importance of understanding culture as the struggle over assigned meanings, identities, and histories, educators and other cultural workers need to find ways of reading texts of popular and mass culture from a perspective that is not limited to ideology critique. It is not enough to limit a critical pedagogy of representation to simply a question of reading ideology from either the perspective of locating commodity forms or discovering contradictory expressions of everyday social relations, but to situate representations in a complex field of rational and effective economies that explore how individuals both construct meanings and make emotional investments in those constructions. Giroux and Simon have explored the implications of this pedagogical approach in their study of popular culture:

> Teachers and students need to find ways of creating a space for mutual engagement of lived difference that does not require the silencing of a multiplicity of voices by a single dominant discourse.... What might teachers need to understand in order to engage in such a struggle? What might they wish to find out? If we take popular culture as that terrain of images, knowledge forms, and effective investments within which meaning and subjectivity function, there are several questions teachers might pursue. What are the historical conditions and material circumstances under which popular culture practices are pursued, organized, asserted, and regulated? Do such practices open up new notions of identities and possibilities? Are they disorganized and excluded? How are such practices articulated with forms of knowledge and pleasure legitimized by dominant groups? What interests and investments are served by a particular set of popular cultural practices and which are critiqued and challenged by the existence of such? What are the moral and political commitments of such practices and how are these related to one's own commitments as a teacher (and if there is a divergence, what does this imply)?[12]

Two important pedagogical issues are at stake here. First, a critical pedagogy of representation needs to highlight and problematize the notion of textual authority at work in any classroom practice. Textual authority, in this case, refers to the power educators use to legitimate both the value of a particular image or text and the range of interpretations that can be brought to bear in understanding it. Second, it is crucial for radical educators to develop pedagogical practices that legitimize the conditions that allow students to speak from their own experiences without simply being invited to romanticize their own voices. For instance, media knowledge should be partly approached from the experiences that students use to produce meaning out of their engagement with it. But such meanings should then be made problematic and theoretically extended for the interests they suggest, the social relations they evoke, the histories they might recover, and the possibilities they might contain for reclaiming a politics of representation as a domain from which to reconstruct notions of emancipatory struggle and critical citizenship.[13] Not to acknowledge the historical and cultural specificity of a representation when attempting an interpretation constitutes an involuntary parody that results in a cannibalization of that representation. This does not mean that there exist "authentic" interpretations of any representation. Rather, we are suggesting that to intentionally or unwittingly dehistoricize or decontextualize the politics surrounding any representation is to cloak its ideological means of naturalizing existing interpretations and the relations of power such interpretations support. In this instance, the struggle over media knowledge becomes central to forms of self and social formation that are constitutive of the conditions for democracy itself. At work here is a pedagogy in which difference, knowledge, power, and politics are integral to what it means to think critically and act with ethical and civic courage.

A critical pedagogy of representation acknowledges that images are neither objective nor transparent but are produced within discursive and material sites of disjuncture, rupture, and contradiction. The world of images is better understood from a pedagogical perspective as a terrain of contestation that serves as the loci of multivalent practical-discursive structures and powers. This suggests not only examining media knowledges in terms of what they include but also examining them in terms of their exclusions. Such a strategy invites students to understand the way background institutions and the routines of everyday life arise and make possible particular discursive formations and social practices. Similarly, this approach also encourages students not to sanctify knowledge or to view it as something to be simply revered and received, and in so doing validates the knowledge that students have acquired from their own personal experiences and struggles for meaning and identity. Consequently, students are more likely to read texts and images productively and critically rather than passively. Images and sounds such as those produced, for example, by radio, television, print, film, and computers can be questioned and challenged through the experiences that students use to give meaning to the world, the language they use to understand such experiences, and in this way the production of knowledge itself can thus become part of the process of a critical pedagogy of representation.

We are emphasizing the idea that the interpretations arising from any given representation are always mutable, contingent, and partial; furthermore, their authority is always provisional and not transcendental. Representations have no meaning other than those rhetorically or discursively assigned to them. Such a pedagogy acknowledges that concept formation is shaped and determined by the forms that are inseparable from it and cannot be characterized by a meta-empirical universality that exists independently of the contingencies of differential relations of power and the sensual particularities of material life.

This perspective involves more than a language which simply mimics or parodies the dehumanizing tendencies of the age of mechanical reproduction; but rather means exposing and reconstituting the political linkages between signs and structures of representation and the technologies of power which underwrite them. In this sense, a critical pedagogy of representation is necessary in order to be able to uncover how the materiality and discursivity of everyday knowledge shapes social existence in certain ways to reproduce hidden economies of power and privilege that legitimize unequal social arrangements.

Central to a critical pedagogy of representation is an interrogation of the multiple ways in which culture is inscribed through the presentations that both produce and legitimate it within particular power/knowledge relations. We are using the term "representation" in a manner similar to that of Stuart Hall, who defines it as the way in which meaning is constructed through the placement, positioning, and situatedness of discourse. Hall writes that "how things are represented and the 'machineries' and regimes of representation in a culture...play a *constitutive,* and not merely a reflexive, after-the-event role." Hall notes that representation is "possible only because enunciation is always produced within codes which have a history, a position within the discursive formations of a particular time and place." By granting the concept of representation a formative and not merely an expressive place in the constitution of social and political life, questions of culture and ideology and what Hall describes as "the scenarios of representation"—subjectivity, identity, and politics—take on an increasing significance.[14] Hall's notion of representation presents us with a multilayered, complex, and contradictory view of subjectivity that recognizes the need to develop rather than erase a notion of human agency, identity, and difference. Rejecting the master narratives of bourgeois liberal humanism, Hall articulates a view of identity which does not "universalize" the subject and refuses to treat "otherness" or "difference" as excess, exotic, or unrepresentable—something outside the placement of history, politics, and power.

Following Hall's analysis, a critical pedagogy of representation can, for example, begin to dissolve the practice of essentializing the historical subject—whether this subject is African-American, Puerto Rican, female, or white, etc.—and to underscore the immense diversity and differentiation of the historical and cultural experiences of such subjects. At issue here is a view of subjectivity constituted within rather than outside of cultural, social, and linguistic determinants. For example, when applied to the politics of racism, a critical pedagogy of representation is able to help educators to retheorize the concept of agency and difference such that, in Hall's terminology, it is able to "decouple" ethnicity from its equivalence with nationalism, imperialism, racism, and the violence of the state. In doing so, it helps educators to recognize, according to Hall, that we are *all* ethnically located and our ethnic identities are important but must be constructed so as not to marginalize, dispossess, or displace the "other." As Kobena Mercer notes, "What is at issue is to acknowledge differences without necessarily ending up in a divisive situation, how to enact an 'ethics of agreement', as Hall says, without recourse to rhetorics that cut off the possibility of critical dialogue."[15]

A critical pedagogy of representation not only denaturalizes the conventions that encode the ideological and makes those ideological contents open to interrogation and contestation; but also explores the preconditions of its own categorizations and categorically provisional assumptions. [16] That is, to a certain extent, our very acts of naming reality always occur from positions of intelligibility which are complicitous with the moral imperatives of the dominant social order and must be interrogated for the limits of their conditions for enabling transformation. In this sense, a pedagogy of representation provides the basis for educators to be attentive to a politics of location, one which recognizes and interrogates the strengths and limitations of those places one inherits, engages, and occupies and which frame the discourses through which we speak and act.

A critical pedagogy of representation must also take up a discourse of possibility. In this context, resistance to domination and oppression must consist of more than a critique of dominant forms of knowledge and social practices—more than moral injunctions against dominative evaluative judgments and cultural forms. As long as resistance is "reactive," it positions itself as "other-centered" discourse.[17] As Trinh T. Minh-Ha remarks:

> The notion of "making strange" and of reflexivity remains but a mere distancing device so long as the division between "textual artifice" and "social attitude" exerts its power. The "social" continues to go unchallenged, history keeps on being salvaged, while the socio-historicizing subject is safely maintained. With the status quo of the making/consuming subject preserved, the aim is to correct "errors" (the false) and to construct an alternative view (offered as a this-is-the-true or mine-is-truer version of reality.) It is, in other words, to replace one source of unacknowledged authority by another, but not to challenge to very constitution of authority. The new socio-historical text thus rules despotically as another master-centered text, since it unwittingly helps to perpetuate the Master's ideological stance.[18]

Within a larger project of possibility, resistance must be an *active*, and not a reactive, transvaluation of dominant perspectives. It must be active if it is to generate new "action-guiding" perspectives that can allow cultural workers to escape the larger logic of domination which continues to underwrite many anti-colonialist struggles and resistances—the very logic such local struggles set out to overturn.

In short, we are arguing that a critical pedagogy of representation must establish the relativity of all forms of representations by situating them in historical and social constructions that both inform their content and structure their ideological parameters. Second, a pedagogy of representation must bring to light the strategies that are used to structure how texts are read, used, and received within particular contexts and practices. At stake here is understanding not only how power is inscribed in a pedagogy of representation, but also how such a pedagogy can be used to disrupt the ideological, cultural, and political systems that both inscribe and contain them. This suggests that the practice of reading ideologies be connected to the production of political strategies informed by transformative ideologies. Third, a critical pedagogy of representation must be able to articulate between representations that operate in particular educational sites and representations that operate in other cultural sites around similar forms of address and relevancies. Fourth, a critical pedagogy of representation must be taken up as a form of ethical address which grounds the relationship between the self and others in practices that promote care and solidarity rather than oppression and human suffering. In this case, a pedagogy of representation cannot be disarticulated from the radical responsibility of both politics and ethics.

The preceding discussion enables us to appreciate that the meanings of media knowledge are always bound by the historical, cultural, and political conditions of their production, the epistemological and interpretive resources available to articulate their meaning as they are received by the viewer, and the reading formations that the viewers bring to the act of reception (which very much depend on the personal histories and experiences that are constitutive of the act of reception). Media knowledges are always products of such constraints just as they can, when understood critically, point to the way such constraints work in the broader arena of the state; they teach us that people do not possess power as much as they produce it and are produced by it.

Within a transformative pedagogy, media knowledges not only reveal to us the way power works corporeally to inscribe its hegemonic certainties into the body, but also how they can serve as dominating forms of cultural power to create, in Lukac's terms, "a charnel house of dead interiorities."[19] Just as the photographs of artists such as Cindy Sherman confront essentialist notions of the self yet retain a point of view, a motivating politics;[20] so too, can a critical pedagogy of representation serve as disturbing provocations against hegemonically articulated understandings of subjectivity and power and dominant understandings of representation yet assume an unambiguous condemnation of structures of brutality and the social logic of fascism. A critical pedagogy of representation presents us with an opportunity for locating power not just in the daily disciplinary and incorporative practices of state life, but in the barbaric conjuncture of colonial power and the growth of the capitalist world state.

A critical pedagogy of representation can help students to question the manner in which they, as individual and collective social actors, are located in history so that to be a servant of state power is often to be its unwitting victim. Furthermore, students can be offered the opportunity to recognize their own socially determined position within the reality they are attempting to describe and understand. A critical pedagogy of representation must provide students with the opportunity of recognizing the limitations of the languages that are made available in helping them to understand their everyday experiences, the categories they use to represent these experiences, and the relationship between such categories and the cultural forms, modes of subjectivity, and social practices that will enable them to speak their own truth and transform those conditions that constrain their capacities for critical reflection and their ability to engage in the work of social transformation.

If critical pedagogy is to be taken seriously as a form of cultural struggle, it must seek to create new forms of knowledge not only by breaking down disciplinary boundaries but also by creating new spaces where knowledge can be produced. This means that pedagogy as a form of cultural production must not be limited to canonical texts and social relations that mediate and produce forms of dominant culture. Knowledge must be reinvented and reconstructed by inviting students to be border crossers, by encouraging them to collapse disciplines that separate high from popular culture, theory from practice, art from life, politics from the everyday, and pedagogy from education.[21] Central to the goal of critical pedagogy is the need to create a public sphere of citizens who are able to exercise power over their lives and especially over the conditions of knowledge production and acquisition. Taking on such a goal means critical educators must demonstrate "that a concern for education is inseparable from issues of geography, race, gender, family, income, law—a myriad of social and political concerns that are often considered irrelevant to the classroom."[22]

Creating new forms of knowledge also suggests creating classroom practices that provide students with the opportunity to work collectively and to develop needs and habits in which the social is felt and experienced as an emanicpatory rather than alienating experience. Put in different terms, a critical pedagogy must reclaim the social as a precondition for collective engagement and struggle. David Trend has described many examples in the arts of pedagogical practices where students are provided with the opportunity to learn how to work collectively in and out of schools, in opposition to the traditional competitive and individualist approaches to pedagogy.[23] This approach suggests that when presenting students with the opportunity of challenging the borders of established disciplines, they should learn to connect the specific and the particular to wider social and historical contexts.[24] At the same time, the reconstruction of knowledge/power relations and classroom social practices must extend the promise and possibility of a critical pedagogy by affirming the importance of struggling, not simply over forms of knowledge and classroom relations but also by creating new public spheres outside the schools where learning is as important as it is inside the classroom. Of course, this is not meant to suggest an opposition between schools and other public spheres as much as it is to suggest their common project in political and pedagogical struggles within broader social and political constructs.

Finally, it is crucial that the very category of educator as cultural worker not be limited to people who work in schools. Critical pedagogy is a form of cultural politics, discourse, and power-sensitive social practices which always presuppose particular forms of citizenship, community, and visions of the future. The implication is that all cultural workers should be actively involved in critical pedagogy, regardless of the sites in which they work. Neither those of us who work in the schools, in the arts, in the social services, or in other initiations can retreat into our sites of work and act as if we have no connection with other public spheres or other cultural workers. If critical pedagogy is to contribute to the multiplication of sites of democratic struggles, sites that affirm specific struggles while recognizing the necessity to embrace broader issues that enhance the life of the planet, then all forms of cultural struggle must assert the primacy of cultural workers as active participants in pedagogical practices that deepen a democratic and transformative politics. Specifically, we need a pedagogy that allows us to see how our work relates as a part of the broader struggle to reclaim democratic public life. This is the challenge all educators have to face regardless of the cultural work in which we engage. This represents more than a call for a new dialogue; it points to new forms of struggle over power, human dignity, and social justice.

Those involved in critical pedagogy do not presume to speak for others or on behalf of others, but in solidarity with others whose concerns they happen to share, concerns for a society unburdened by suffering and social injustice. In forgoing relations with dispossessed groups, it is important that critical educators be able to distinguish claims of moral, ethnic, gender, or political superiority that they exercise as outsiders. A consideration concerning how "cultural others" name experience, place labels on their sense of reality, and use their own history and culture to define their struggle for freedom, should be a primary concern within all forms of critical pedagogy. Critical educators must remember, however, that the experiences of those with whom they engage in a critical pedagogy of representation are never self-evident, since experiences are always the seat of ideology and not the state of unmediated innocence. Consequently, critical cultural workers need to provide conditions for themselves and for others to examine the literalness of their reality, the context in which such a reality is articulated, and how their experiences are imbricated in contradictory, complex, and changing vectors of power. Critical educators need to explore the pervasiveness and complexity of social evil in this current historical juncture and offer a project of possibility for cultural workers—and themselves—so that they have the opportunity to confront such evil. In pedagogical terms, such a project must constitute more than a reversal of power relations—more than the production of social logics and practices prohibited by the master—but rather the creation of new spaces for the reconstitution of the social imagination, for building new modes of sociality, and for reconstituting new articulations of the meaning of human emancipation and freedom. Much of this work necessarily involves not only understanding the disabling and emancipatory potential of the media knowledges that are available to us, but also the importance of struggling to overturn current arrangements or extracommunicational forms of power and social relations that undergird—and in some cases help to overdetermine—the production of such knowledges. In this regard, a critical pedagogy of representation seeks to produce partial, contingent, but necessary historical truths that will provide some of the necessary conditions for the emancipation of the many public spheres that make up our social and institutional life, truths which recognize their social constructedness and historicity and the institutional and social arrangements which they legitimate.

As cultural workers whose pedagogical sites are primarily the universities and public schools, we want to issue a caveat regarding the issue of who speaks for whom, and under what conditions. We make no claim to speak for anyone. But we want to emphasize that we choose to speak to issues that concern us from a specific political and ideological location that is always under analysis. There is, we feel, a certain irony in claims made by some educators who profess a certain political correctness in their so-called direct involvement with those whom they label as working-class. One such claim is that if one is an intellectual or cultural worker within academic settings then this precludes one from speaking at all if the form of oppression addressed is not directly experienced. This position often represents a species of white bourgeois guilt that erases the possibility for political action across and between differences. Given the marginality of most social criticism, we believe that the most urgent issue is not whether you can claim to be spending your time advocating for others by adopting a language of "plainspeak" or the now fashionable discourse of partiality but is rather to explore the following questions: What are the issues that need to be addressed in order to create a more just society? Who is listening? With whom do we form alliances, and for what purposes?

For educators, answering these questions means constructing a hybrid pedagogical space where students do not need the colonizer's permission to narrate their own identities, a space where individual identities find meaning in collective expression and solidarity with other cultural workers, where Eurocentric time and Cartesian anxiety recede into the lived, historical moment of contemporary struggles for identity. A critical pedagogy of representation seeks what Trinh T. Minh-Ha calls "the interval." The interval is a space which simultaneously invites and derides closure—a "Space in which meaning remains fascinated by what escapes and exceeds it"; and it is simultaneously a closure of meaning that "can defy its own closure" thereby "displacing and emptying out the establishment of totality."[25]

The foregoing attempt to chart out the rudiments of a critical pedagogy of representation will, we trust, assist educators and other cultural workers in appropriating the wealth of media literacy contained in the pages of *Media Knowledge* and adapting such perspectives to their respective pedagogical sites. Of course, it is up to cultural workers to adapt such a pedagogy and media literacy to the specific context in which they find themselves. It is our hope that the project of media literacy so brilliantly developed by James Schwoch, Mimi White, and Susan Reilly in *Media Knowledge* not be limited to cultural workers in schools, although schools are perhaps the most obvious and primary sites for such a literacy, but also be extended into projects involving the arts, community-based literacy programs, alternative media broadcasting, and other forms of cultural struggles that are developing across the country at this precarious moment in our cultural history.

CHAPTER ONE

TELEVISION AND ITS HISTORICAL PASTICHE

A cartoon in *TV Guide* shows three rows of bookcases in a library-like setting.[1] One is labelled "History," the second "Fiction," and the third is identified as "Made For TV." Here is a joke to be shared by the mass television audience, engaging a particular consciousness of history. It assumes that the distinction between history and fiction is clear, but it also acknowledges that television involves something else, apart from these familiar, conventional categories. There are various ways to interpret the cartoon. In relation to the dominant rhetoric of *TV Guide*, the "Made For TV" category should probably be taken as an aberration, needlessly and irresponsibly confusing or ignoring the long-standing meaningful distinction between "History" and "Fiction."[2] But the cartoon nonetheless represents the "Made For TV" category as equivalent to the other two; they stand together, each carrying the same potential to produce meaning. Here, television as a medium—as the exemplary mass medium—is understood as having the capacity to produce modes of knowledge that are culturally significant, and thereby to function as a mode of pedagogy. This pedagogy cannot simply be rejected as irrelevant or aberrant, although such reactions are far too often the initial and only responses to whatever it is that television does. No matter the amount of time spent with television, viewers must come to grips with what it means for television to be a part of the fabric of everyday life. This is not restricted to understanding television in terms of the information it carries, or the measurable effects it may or may not have on behavior. Of primary importance is an understanding of how television produces modes of discourse and knowledge that become familiar enough to become fodder for expression in contemporary culture, such as the cartoon in *TV Guide*.

An examination of the ways in which the medium works with

"History" as a conceptual category is important for a number of reasons. Such an examination can serve as a case study demonstrating how television produces modes of knowledge in relation to, but not totally dominated by, more traditional bodies of knowledge. (Other categories could also be examined, for example the family, politics, information, crisis, or childhood.) History is also considered a crucial category of learning—something we must know and understand as the foundation of social and cultural identity. If the very discourses of history as a category of knowledge are being transformed, it is important to come to grips with the new formations of thought that are subsumed by the term on a day-to-day basis. Even a cursory glance at the transformation of discourse about history through television brings up a maelstrom of examples.

What, for example, is the relationship between the "history" in the historical mini-series and the "history" at stake when "a historical confrontation" between the Boston Red Sox and the New York Mets will start in a few days? What of the history of the Red Sox—a constant theme of 1986 World Series reporting—as a team fated to lose the World Series, a historical destiny confirmed with yet another loss? How does the World Series as a historical confrontation, along with all the other historic yet regular confrontations from the world of televised sports—which will take place, are taking place, and are finally "history"—compare with another contemporary, historical confrontations cast in the same series of tenses, this time between Mikhail Gorbachev and Ronald Reagan in Rjeykjavik? In this context how can the references to a history extending back to the 1950s on *Late Night with David Letterman* be understood, when the audience already knows that the program has only been on the air for less than a decade? (This knowledge is explicitly avowed in *Late Night* anniversary specials still numbered in the single digits.) And the examples continue to spin out from the screen faster than they can be described.

At first glance such questions might seem trivial, even prosaic. But the very fact that one can pose such questions about the "history" produced on television on the basis of random viewing has crucial implications. Across an array of programs, genres and events of different orders, television invokes "history" as a meaningful term. Yet it is obvious that the result of this process—of identifying programs, genres and events as historical—is not homogeneous or unified, and indeed hardly conforms to the most common uses of the term "history." In particular in the above examples, television designates events as historical without regard for the temporal order, grammatical tense, and/or referential weight that guide conventional assumptions about history.[3] Rather, television generates a field of discourse under the label "history" that is fragmentary, multiple, and contradictory.

In its insistent (one might say persistent) invocation of the term, television promotes history as a crucial conceptual/experiential category. At the same time television would seem to drain history of its specificity as a term of singular linguistic/temporal distinction. Any event—past, present, or future—can be qualified as "historical" or given a "history," fictional or otherwise. Moreover, this is not a hypothetical potentiality, but an initial description of how history is actually expressed through the material that constitutes television. In this sense, television's production of history can be characterized as an overproduction, or to adapt Jean Baudrillard's term, a hyper-history.[4] It seems as if there is *too much* history, as nearly everything is described as historical at one point or another.

Some of the questions of television and history are thus posed in relation to the problematics of postmodernism, which has been characterized in terms of simulation, pastiche, schizophrenia, non-meaning, the absence of master narratives, and even a "fundamental wierdness."[5] In this context the invocation of "history" as a persistent term of reference is significant. It becomes an anchoring point of television discourse, one of the mythic concepts through which the concatenations of a culture in transition are expressed. Perhaps it is not surprising that a medium of electronic signals and "instant" transmission strives to situate itself and its texts in history—with all its associations with the weight of social, political, and cultural tradition. This chapter takes up the challenging and complex questions of television and history. This includes an analysis of the status of "liveness" in relation to history, the ways in which the history of television is routinely told, the representation of history by the medium in programming practices (a self-representation), and the production of the subject of history.

The relationship between "liveness" and "historicity" offers an overdetermined locus for examining the overproduction of history in television. In most conventional senses, liveness, presence, and immediacy, are implicitly opposed to history as closed, absent, or past.[6] This is the case not only in the common sense of experience and temporality, but also in the linguistic distinction between *histoire* and *discours*.[7] Yet in a variety of ways television correlates paradigms of liveness and of historicity in the form of equivalence, alibi, reversal, or identity. The practices and rhetoric of news and public affairs/documentary programming is one area in particular where the concatenations of liveness and historicity are particularly evident.

The production of news has always been a preeminent focus of television's "social contribution" as well as the arena in which liveness and being up-to-date (even up-to-the-minute) are valorized. The popular ideology of broadcast journalism is an unstable conglomeration of realism, liveness, personality, and immediacy. Yet in the context of television news it is not unusual to hear that something that occurred recently, is occurring now, or will occur soon is historic; or to hear that, through television, the audience is witness to "history-in-the-making." Implicit is the understanding that these invocations of history signify the import of such events in the present; they are *momentous* rather than historic. But the slippage here, in one sense an innocent colloquialism, is symptomatic of the collapse of the distinct temporal and discursive orders that have conventionally distinguished history as a mode of narrative discourse. More importantly it suggests that what is most unpredictable (because it is not yet a closed sequence of events with a beginning, middle, and end) can be—must be—historic if it is in the process of being recorded by television. The institution of television itself thus becomes the guarantor of history, even as it invokes history to validate its own presence at an event. Through this process history becomes a signifier of authority and social responsibility.[8]

The interplay between liveness and historicity is equally apparent in advertisements for news broadcasts (network and local) which variably stress traditions of journalism, historic events at which the news was present, and an ability to cover breaking events at a moment's notice—sometimes in conjunction with one another. The implication is that television news is here, now—where things are happening, so that it will have been there, then—where history was made. Or, conversely, because the news has been then and there, we can rest assured they will be here and now, as needed. In either case history and current events, the past and present become mutually supporting frames of reference, the one serving as the alibi and guarantee of the other.

This logic is not restricted to news programming, even if it is most fully and consistently expressed in this context. It impinges on all aspects of programming and promotion in which historical value—expressed as longevity—and innovation are correlated. For example, advertising campaigns promoting *Miami Vice* for syndicated rerun sales stress innovation and enduring values as coextensive characteristics of the show. "Everything About Miami Vice Is New. Nothing About It Is Temporary."[9] The text that follows this advertising headline elaborates on this.

> Miami Vice is the *most innovative* series on television. But viewers watch it not only for what's *new,* but for what's *permanent.* Viewers keep tuning in because it's got the staying power of *classic entertainment.* Our research shows conclusively that what holds viewers are the *enduring qualities* of superb action, suspenseful plots, the ingenuity of the heroes, and the irresistible chemistry between them. Someday, in the future, Miami Vice may not be innovative. But what it will always be is watched. (emphasis added)

Being merely new or innovative is on the one hand desirable, but is not enough, because it is a transient status. Newness has to secure itself in relation to something else. The threat of evanescence is countered by the guarantee of longevity, and affiliation with the history represented by "classic entertainment."

The unstable, but self-validating relay among positions of contemporaneity, liveness, tradition, and history has pervaded broadcasting from the very start, and fully informs the very writing of the history of the medium. In particular this is inscribed in the designation of the 1950s as the "Golden Age" of live television production. The era of broadcasting thus named (roughly 1948–1958) includes dramatic fiction programming and the tradition of news and public affairs. In popular cultural memory and also in many academic accounts, this period is held up as an era of high quality production that was all too quickly supplanted by mindless, standardized, taped programs. As the putative origins of television, the Golden Age is also characterized in terms of innovation, experimentation and even innocence.[10]

The hallowed nostalgia cast on this period of network broadcasting is overdetermined by the relation of live television production to radio, the New York stage, and Hollywood film production. As a singular event the live production can be identified with theatrical performance; and even films are relatively singular in comparison to television series and serials. Liveness—construed in terms of standards of singularity and repeatability—establishes a hierarchy of cultural value to confirm the superiority of the relatively original or unique product. The promotion of television's historic, "live" productions affiliates the medium with the upper end of the cultural scale of value and confers on the medium an elevated, if lost, tradition of authentic creativity and aesthetic worth. This perspective includes the implication that television could be of higher social and cultural value if it returned to a version of singular or "live" production, concomitant with a willingness to sacrifice "mass appeal" and "mass production" for individuated productions with smaller, and presumably higher quality, audiences while at the same time ruefully acknowledging the economic realities of the television industry mitigate against such a return to the past. (It is significant in this respect that most discussions of the Golden Age attribute the decline of live dramatic programs to the need for economic efficiency in production *and* the development of a mass television audience that did not sustain the ratings for anthology drama. Here, business interests, recorded images, repetitive formats, mass audiences, lower taste, and lesser social value are all associated.)

In heralding the Golden Age as the origin and aesthetic highpoint of the medium, this version of television history offers a view of temporal and causal development valorizing live production by the networks as the period of experimental innovation.[11] In the process, earlier inventions and experimentation—including work in mechanical television in the 1920s and early 1930s, and the search for an all electronic system which began in earnest in 1930—are relegated to the status of "prehistory."[12] But what if this period of technological innovation is included in the story of television?[13] Technological experimentation in television significantly antedates the Golden Age, and the ability to record images for (re)broadcast informed this development from the very start. Even during World War II, often considered a "dormant" period in television (pre)history, the National Broadcasting Company (NBC) commissioned studies on the possibility of filming "live" programs.[14] And while the programs of the Golden Age are relatively rare in comparison to contemporary taped television, they are also remembered precisely because they were preserved in recorded form at the time they were broadcast.[15]

From this perspective the "live" production of the 1950s does not represent an originary purity in television. Rather it can be reconceptualized as a transitional moment in larger, ongoing economic, institutional, cultural, and technological stories, in which the establishment of a nationwide system of television broadcasting by the networks precedes the deployment of standardized, perfected methods of recording, even though recording and transmission were always combined at the level of aspiring invention/conceptualization. In this light, to construe the "live" productions of the Golden Age as an aesthetic ontology (and as the origins of television) fails to consider uneven developments in the innovation and diffusion of the particular technologies and discourses that comprise television.

More specifically, to relegate the pre-World War II period of technological invention and innovation to the status of "prehistory" associates the history of the medium with the rise of network television broadcasting. Perhaps this is not surprising to observers of contemporary American society, for current popular thought often seems to demonstrate a shared base of knowledge that begins with the rise of the USA-USSR superpower conflict and sees its own roots no deeper than World War II. As a part of its own historical representation, television downplays its roots in other aspects of American culture, with the partial exception of network radio. "Television" and its history are thus identified with the network system as it developed out of radio, which is in turn positioned as television's history, reinforcing the view that American television is the way it "had to be," predetermined as it was by an institutional and aesthetic base in radio.[16] The Golden Age of television and pre-television radio can then be subsumed together in a generic media nostalgia. Television thus offers its own history as original; yet its history is largely a history of reconstruction and remaking of previous visual and verbal structures. So television's historical origins are not bound up in something new so much as something reified; yet the historical representation to the viewer (and by extension to society) is that of the new, bold, and innovative. By extension, the links between American society before and after World War II also remain obscured, because television so easily offers up its own history largely cleansed of a prewar cultural past. Many researchers working on television history have found this narrative beguiling, and placed the beginnings of their studies after the war, thus perpetuating this repression. The result is that television's historical self-representation is wholly projected as a postwar phenomena.

The point of all this is not to ignore the specificity of the 1950s as a moment within television history, but rather to suggest that the prevailing view of this era as the Golden Age is determined by an unthought privileging of "liveness" as an aesthetic ontology, which in turn follows the logic of particular cultural ideologies and is not ultimately at odds with industry interests. The discourse that promotes the Golden Age as the initiating moment of television history which is, crucially, characterized by liveness, experimentation, and innovation—and as a period of exceptional quality—functions as a retrospective myth of loss whereby the Golden Age is synonymous with Atlantis. It is a loss that confirms perceptions of contemporary television's inferior cultural status, because there is seemingly not enough "live" production (although paradoxically there are more hours of live production now than ever before, especially if cable networks are included). It also affirms and naturalizes the value of television's institutional and economic base because the networks did once promote "live" production.[17] In this history, "liveness" becomes the alibi to assure that the system is not in itself bad, and in fact is based in the best cultural traditions. History and liveness (and history as liveness) authenticate the social truths and cultural value of television as a whole. The valued history of the medium is the story of its liveness, while the ongoing deployment of signs of liveness and immediacy in broadcast network television confirm its social and historical value. Liveness and history thus emerge as equally mystified, but conflatable concepts. Examining other questions of television and history continues to reveal this process of mystification and conflation.

> I believe that the emergence of postmodernism is closely related to the emergence of this new moment of late, consumer or multinational capitalism. I believe also that its formal features in many ways express the deeper logic of that particular social system. I will only be able, however, to show this for one major theme: namely the disappearance of a sense of history, the way in which our entire social system has little by little begun to lose its capacity to retain its own past, has begun to live in a perpetual present and in a perpetual change that obliterates traditions of the kind which all earlier social formations have had in one way or another to preserve. Think only of the media exhaustion of news: of how Nixon and, even more so, Kennedy are figures from a now distant past. One is tempted to say that the very function of the news media is to relegate such recent historical experiences as rapidly as possible into the past. The informational function of the media would thus be to help us to forget, to serve as the very agents and mechanisms for our historical amnesia.[18]

Television of course offers its own versions of history-as-presence in its flow of programming. History is evoked, rewritten, retransmitted, and reconstructed across television's genres and modes, in the reruns, remakes, compilations, and historical fictions that coexist with—and as—the originals, first runs, current events, and contemporary fictions that comprise television programming. In this conglomerate simultaneity of copresent options, the historical determinations of individual programs and events are at once in full evidence and subsumed in an overwhelming "present text" of television flow. Almost all forms of programming are subject to being rerun in their entirety or in fragments (as segments of another show), over the course of a single season and over time, a process extended with the growth of cable and the use of video recorders.

History is thus preserved in forms of dispersal, as the specificity of temporal anchorage is relativized in the process of repetition. Programs from the 1950s air simultaneously, and consecutively, with shows from the 1960s, 1970s, and 1980s. They are shown precisely because, or if, they are popular enough to draw an audience in the present, a "present" which is constantly in the process of being rewritten. An array of formats hold forth the promise of "life after prime time," including syndicated reruns, revivals, remakes, the made-for-TV movie, and most recently, release on videocassette. For example (one that encompasses several of these variations at once), the continuing popularity of *Leave It To Beaver* (one of the quintessential "old fashioned" family sitcoms) in syndicated reruns led to reassembling the cast for *Still the Beaver,* a network made-for-TV movie that picked up the lives of the fictional characters twenty years later. The relative success of the movie in turn generated the renewal of the series, based on the movie, first by the cable network Disney Channel and then in broadcast and cable syndication.

Many television series have been revived as remakes, with actors in contemporary situations assuming character roles familiar from previous incarnations of a program, or with new characters placed in a familiar context. These "new" programs, extending a program's history, often air while the "original" still shows in reruns. These include *The New Gidget, The New Monkees, The New Sea Hunt, Star Trek: The Next Generation,* and *Gumby* to name only a few. And it is not only "old classics" that are subject to revival in this way, but also programs that have only recently been dropped by the networks, such as *Punky Brewster* and *Fame.* And in the extreme case of *The Honeymooners* the discovery of previously unseen ("lost") episodes allows contemporary audiences to see "new" episodes of the infinitely rerun series. In the case of programs in syndicated rerun that are also still on prime time television (or, through cable, syndicated on more than one channel), it is possible to see multiple stages of fictional development—multiple histories—on the same day (e.g. *The Facts of Life, Knots Landing, M*A*S*H*,* and *Magnum, P.I.,* and so forth). The beginnings of videocassette distribution, rental, and sale of old television shows (*I Love Lucy* and *Outer Limits* are two examples) further clouds the issue.

Television represents its own history in this massive combination of texts that includes old and new, past and present, as equivalent choices. Yet in this equivalence the "historical" differences among shows (as old and new, classic and modern) are maintained. Thus, certain networks have identified themselves as promoters of a classic heritage of old television programs. Nickelodeon's evening lineups of 1950s and 1960s situation comedies is promoted in self-parodic toungue-in-cheek commercials that insist on the high entertainment value (often "scientifically" proven) of "classic" entertainment. The Family Channel (FAM), newest incarnation of Pat Robertson's Christian Broadcasting Network, also promotes its lineup of reruns as embodying enduring values. Television produces a history that is readily present, but perhaps remains unthought in its historicity precisely because it is present. In the process television continually constructs its own "tradition" as an effect of complex temporal overdeterminations. This can be read in a given market's programming schedule, in an individual's selections across a programming paradigm, and also may be enacted in the course of a single program.

It is not uncommon for long running series to periodically include episodes incorporating flashbacks. In some instances the fictional past thus represented is reassembled from earlier episodes (which a given viewer, or any number of viewers, may have seen at another time), while in other cases a fictional history which is not identical to the program's history may be retrospectively constructed. *Dallas: The Early Years,* a made-for-TV movie representing the fictional past of the show *Dallas,* was made after *Dallas* had been on the air for seven years, retrospectively dramatizing the history of the characters in the program. The 1986–87 season of *Knots Landing* included a series of flashbacks depicting a previously unknown "history" for several characters as a motivating factor for current narrative developments on the program. The retrospective reconstruction of a fictional past may or may not involve the re-presentation of a program's history; and an individual viewer is not necessarily in a position to tell the difference. Programs may even engage in both practices over time, offering flashbacks that are recycled footage from previous episodes in some cases, and "new" footage of the past in others. (For example, *General Hospital* has used both approaches in representing its fictional history.)

Anniversary and compilation specials offer yet another version of the medium writing its own history in the context of a single show. Programs of this sort celebrate past and present through the assembly of "old" and "new," or recycled and original images, with an implied future, if only of rebroadcast. Compilation specials have been devoted to particular genres, notably including commercials, sitcoms, and bloopers.[19] An anniversary special for *The Tonight Show* or *Late Night With David Letterman* marks progress, highlighting previous seasons with the repetition of selected segments, thus defining a tradition. It is here now, in the anniversary show in the present, because it has a past. The past guarantees the present which in turn surpasses it because it is, inevitably, more "contemporary" (and "sophisticated") than the "dated" past on which it is built. Thus, for example, the hosts or guests in the relative present tense of recording such specials may joke disparagingly about the clothing and hairstyles they sport in a taped segment from the past.

This mixed attitude, of a present superiority to a past which is nonetheless celebrated, is extended to embrace the larger text of television history when David Letterman makes references to *Late Night*'s origins in the 1950s. The self-conscious joke, shared by the audience, involves a complex set of assumptions about television and/as history. It contributes to *Late Night*'s perceived status as a parodic reduplication of *The Tonight Show,* which does have its origins in the 1950s. By implication it also affiliates *Late Night* with television's Golden Age (a tradition of "liveness"), grounding the program in a tradition of innovation—if only by means of historical fiction. Further, viewing *Late Night With David Letterman* is a similar experience to watching a Golden Age program in that they are both recordings of live stagings. Through a play of association and disjunction this may reinforce the perception of *Late Night* as more modern, more hip than *The Tonight Show* precisely because it did not start in the 1950s; at the same time it may imply that *Late Night* is the "true heir" to this former tradition. Thus the "fictional" history carried by the joke proposes a "real" history to explain the joke, and any particular reading of the joke necessarily confirms the show's status in the overall, present context of the medium.

The very possibility of identifying or delimiting historical context becomes increasingly difficult, perhaps only a reassuring fiction. Historical specificity is redefined as dispersion, partiality, irregularity, and repetition, coalescing in an insistent "nowness" which is continually retransforming and rehistoricizing itself. Rather than situate its texts/events in temporal categories of past and present, television asserts a distinction between things that are on the air and those that are not, and both of these categories include "old" and "new" programs, "historical" and "current" events. History as presence is constructed in direct proportion with a process of commodification, because being on the air is finally a function of saleability—to networks, to stations, to sponsors, and to viewers: history as negotiable tender. In this sense, history represents a different kind of currency in its reception. Anything that is not on the air in this context is not free of the force of commodification, but simply a potential commodity awaiting an opportunity to enter into this history.

Our individual and collective memories offer a reserve of material with the potential to be re-presented. Thus it is not only in historical documentaries, news, docudramas, fiction dramas, and historical fictions that television writes a history, but also in counseling, therapy, advice, and talk shows, with their reconstructions of personal case histories. This might even be extended to include the use of consumer video technology. Thus, for example, a story in the *Weekly World News* (1987) tells of a woman who videotaped her husband's heart attack rather than calling an ambulance. (The "truth value" of this tabloid story—an admittedly unorthodox source—is less important than the symptomatic attitude it demonstrates regarding history and video; it is invoked as a contemporary allegory.) The woman is quoted as saying, "He bought the camera for me so we'd have a record of our family life." The article explains that she continued shooting as medics tried to revive her husband, and even attempted to follow him into the emergency room at the hospital. She is reported to have said, "My husband's dying and I've got to get it on tape." The "present" here is subjected to the scrutiny of a video camera with the record as the alibi; it must be recorded now so that in the future there will be a document, a family history. In the terms of the news story, this woman has mastered the values of broadcast journalism and brought them into her daily life.

If history only exists in its realization in the present text of television, the present can only be realized in something which will be a historical document. In the process of rewriting history in the present, television can hold the most extreme, discrepant modes of representation in simultaneity within its boundaries. (It is only the complete absence of representation, video black and silent audio, which is unacceptable.) A striking example of this in the context of a single episode is offered by *The Waltons*. In the episode in question, John-Boy Walton is working as a journalist and travels to New Jersey to cover the landing of the *Hindenberg*. The story thus implicates a common strategy of historical narrative fiction, setting up a fictional character to be witness to a "famous" historical event which the audience may be in a position to anticipate; historical retrospection generates prospective narrative anticipation.[20] In this case, the viewer familiar with the *Hindenberg* explosion is not disappointed. John-Boy arrives at the landing site just in time to witness the arrival and explosion of the dirigible. At this point in the drama, documentary film footage of the *Hindenberg* explosion is intercut with the characters in the fiction as they react to the horrific turn of events. As the scene develops the actors in the "present tense" of the program's historical fiction, in color, are matted via special effects in front of the black and white documentary footage. This marks the historic event within the fiction as "really having happened"; it was not contrived for the story, but actually did occur, confirmed by the old, black and white images. At the same time the discrepancy between the documentary footage and the program's color images is jarring, to say the least. John-Boy, and the actor who portrays him, are obviously *not* present at the event, though the unity of the fiction purportedly requires that we take him to be an on-the-scene witness.

This sort of representational melange, a pastiche of historical styles and modes of representation, has become a prevailing impulse in contemporary television production. *Moonlighting, Magnum, P.I.,* and *Fame,* for example, have all aired episodes with (at least some) footage in black and white, evincing the visual style and narrative conventions of old movies (film noir for *Moonlighting,* the detective film for *Magnum, P.I.,* and the backstage musical for *Fame*—thus confirming the programs in their "proper" generic tradition). Simultaneously, black and white television series are being colorized (e.g. *Wanted: Dead or Alive*) along with the colorization of black and white films for television broadcast. Media history is hereby represented in the present rewriting of a textual past. Simply being old (historical) has no currency, thus "old" movies and television programs are remade as "new" products. But to simulate classic visual and narrative styles in this context becomes a sign of "quality" and prestige. The contemporaneity of *Fame* or *Moonlighting* lies precisely in the self-conscious remodelling of the classic movie genres of which they are the current expression. At the same time old movies and television shows can be revived—brought back to life as circulated commodities—not merely by situating them in current programming flow, but also, and even better (with presumably bigger audiences), by making them look more like current productions with the addition of color.

Contemporaneity and historicity are thus interrelated and coextensive in the present formation of visual and narrative style. To be situated in history, and as history, in television requires this conflation of past and present, a conflation which involves (re)historicization of the present as well as (re)presentation of the past. History in its otherness masquerades as something new, while the present simulates itself as history. This in turn has the effect of producing an unstable, dispersed subject of historical consciousness. Such instability has ramifications for the process of reception and popular memory.

> This is not the world of personal phantasy (and neither, obviously, is it that of reality); this is an oscillating work, in which there is room for the play of forms, a field liberated by the reversal of phantasy, but which still rests upon it. This has nothing to do with aesthetics and it does not necessarily produce hermetic works.[21]

The dispersion of history as a process of rewriting in the present text of television, impinges on all programs and implicates the viewer (all individual viewers) as an agent and effect of selective memory. One forceful expression of this—at once typical and exceptional—can be traced in the narrative development of *Dallas*. In the fall of 1986 at the start of the network prime time television season, *Dallas* premiered with an episode that immediately rewrote—indeed expunged—the whole of the previous year's diegetic narrative. Pam Ewing awoke, apparently the morning after her marriage to Mark Graison (dramatized in the final episode of the previous season) to find Bobby Ewing, her believed-to-be-deceased ex-husband, in the shower.[22] The shock of this discovery was eased by the explanation that Bobby had never actually died; his death as experienced by Pam in the fiction and by the viewing audience was only a dream. In terms of programming time the viewer was thus returned to the final episode of the 1984–85 season, to the moments before Bobby was leaving Pam's house and was fatally hit by a car.[23]

Bobby's death and burial were dramatized at the start of the 1985–86 season, providing significant motivation for new plot developments, along with the continuation of several narrative strands carried over from 1984–85. Bobby's "revival"—carefully anticipated and orchestrated in a massive publicity campaign—signalled the eradication of an entire year of narrative progression on *Dallas*. In popular formulations, a whole season was dismissed as "Pam's dream."[24] But if the program is taken literally (which is perhaps no longer possible, given this turn of events) "Pam's dream" only explicitly includes Bobby's accident, death, and (probably) her subsequent marriage to Mark Graison. What of the rest of the 1985-86 season, including major developments involving J.R. and Jack Ewing, Donna and Ray Krebbs, Cliff and Jamie Barnes, and Pam's kidnapping in Colombia? These and a host of other subplots, culminating in an explosive season finale, were relegated to the netherworld of an unspecified memory.

The events of the 1985–86 season persist. They are part of the program, if no longer part of its fictional continuity or diegetic history. Their status is that of a "memory-effect," an unstable intersection among Pam's unconscious (as parts of her "dream" not brought to conscious recall), the program as a narrational source, and any number of individual viewers of the show who recall events of the 1985–86 season. This memory-effect also carries the potential to infect viewers of another prime time serial melodrama, *Knots Landing,* in which one of the main characters is Gary Ewing, Bobby and J.R.'s brother. Bobby's death provided the presumed motivation for a number of significant plot turns on *Knots Landing* during the 1985-86 season; the program currently proceeds as if uninformed to the fact that Bobby never "really" died. *Dallas* asserts its own version of narrative logic here, including as one possibility an interpretation of *Knots Landing* as the extension of "Pam's dream."

Of course in relation to the genre with which *Dallas* is affiliated—the soap opera—none of this is surprising *per se*. The revival of deceased or disappeared characters—with the same actor resuming a role, or a new actor assuming the part of an established character—is commonplace in daytime serial melodrama; and the prime time soaps, including *Dallas* and *Dynasty,* have readily adopted this convention.[25] By the same token the "revival" of Bobby Ewing on *Dallas* offers a particularly extreme version of this practice. For it is not just the case that Bobby "returned" having never really died. Rather none of the events of the 1985-86 season have the status of diegetic reality. This total rewrite goes far beyond the "reversability" of the soap opera and allows us to characterize *Dallas'* development as excessive in relation to (if exemplary of, as an extreme logical conclusion) the open-endedness of the serial form itself. A general, generically-based narrative mutability and repetitiveness is recast as an absolute repetition of a diegetic time span in complete narrative difference.

This excess may make more sense if situated in relation to television's production of history as rewriting in the present. As a version of history which implicates fictional time and programming time in relation to the audience, it also offers a context for exploring the production of a historical subjectivity. For as *Dallas* rejects, via rewriting, its own fictional history, it simultaneously inscribes history as a space of meaning production specifically in relation to the perspective of the audience. The "new" plot developments promote a forgetting of the previous season by offering a present, alternative version of the story. At the same time the "new" stories exist in the shadow of events as they were previously played out, and as they may be variously remembered by individual viewers. Narrative history, dispensed with as a figment of a single character's imagination (as a dream), is reinscribed as an amorphous imaginary (as memory) that lurks alongside the narrated events of the present season and may be activated by any regular viewer. Here programming history produces a body too much in the form of an "extra" season of narrative.[26]

This logic is subject to extended reproduction in the context of syndicated reruns. To replay the series in continuity will repeat and exacerbate the terms in which it functions. One can imagine the possibility of suppressing (the desire to suppress) the 1985–86 season; it would be easy enough to slightly reedit the scenes involving Bobby's "death" and reappearance, redefining continuity (rewriting the history of *Dallas*), especially since there are no end-of-season cliffhangers in syndicated rerun (that is, syndication reruns are not seasonal). But this fantasy of restored diegetic continuity is immediately contravened by economic considerations. To hold back a whole season of a series from reruns would represent a significant loss of profits for the producers.

Thus in the context of a single program—in this example a contemporary, fiction melodrama—the full force of television's construction of history in relation to subjectivity as a process of imaginary reinscription activated by re-presentation and rewriting becomes recognizable. The subject of this process is singularly indefinite, the effect of an unstable alliance of a fictional character, a (any) regular viewer, and *Dallas* as an impersonal narrating voice. In this overdetermined subjectivity no "one" speaks the historical discourse, though everyone is potentially implicated in its reconstruction. It is produced in the interactions of individual fantasy and commodity circulation (the television program as commodity, the television star as commodity, and the television viewer as commodity; all three also the agency of fantasy), which cannot be collapsed as equivalents nor clearly differentiated.

The viewer's historical knowledge here is delimited, but is not finally determined by the *Dallas*-text, or by Pam Ewing as a functionary, and potential figure of identification, within this text. That is to say, the *Dallas* history can only be known to the extent that it has been represented by the institutional forces that produce and circulate it—not only in the weekly episodes of the show and *Dallas: The Early Years*, but also in the books licensed by the producers (including a series of fiction paperbacks rewriting the program's serial episodes, and a volume detailing the history of the world and characters of *Dallas* as if it were "real," represented as history). But the institution thus defined cannot control how much of this any portion of the audience knows, or remembers, how much of the 1985–86 season it recalls and engages in its current viewing of *Dallas*, or even if that audience continues to watch at all.[27]

Television produces history in an ongoing process of displacements and reinscriptions, as the texts which may activate and engage individual and social memory are always "live"—in the signal flow made present by turning on the television or the video recorder—and yet passing, if not already past. History is represented and reenacted in the ongoing, present dislocations in time, space, and subjectivity continuously reproduced by the medium. It is not just that all history is fiction, as Stephen Heath argues, but also and simultaneously that all fiction is history.[28] From the perspective of postmodern mechanisms of simulacral reduplication, television can easily be understood to participate in the dissolution of "history" as a category of experience, of discourse, and of critical analysis. And yet history seems to haunt the medium; it is both nowhere and everywhere within the discourses that comprise television as a social and cultural apparatus. History is what it does not have, except by virtue of liveness, indeed what it cannot have if it is to celebrate itself in terms of contemporaneity, renovation, innovation, and being up-to-date. History and tradition anchor this discourse of contemporaneity, endowing television and its electromagnetic impulses with substance and weight, offering connections to the social and cultural milieu in which it participates.

Within its multiple discursivity television repeatedly, if variably, invokes "history" in what might be taken as a compensatory struggle to find conventional meaning and order in temporal/social experience, in the very process of revealing the impossibility thereof.

Television has not eradicated the signifying distinction of history as a category once and for all. It can still be, and is, differentiated from its "others," as in the earlier discussed example of the *TV Guide* cartoon represented as "Fiction." But within the current discursive formation that includes television, the understanding of history and of its production cannot be confined to the "same old way" of thinking, whatever that was to begin with. And it is this simultaneity of historical reconceptualization and productivity that the cartoon represents, intentionally or not. In this context it is pointless to simply long for the distinctive clarity of a former signifying order (which is itself, possibly, only another retrospective myth).

If critical thinkers hope to intervene in the current social order and its modes of (cultural) production, the first order of business is to construct an adequate theoretical and descriptive representation thereof, even if it requires a thoroughgoing reconstrual of the very categories that ground the aspirations of transformation—including history. Such an activity is not the private domain of social leaders, but instead is a part of widespread critical citizenship. For, as Andrew Ross has pointed out, in an age of expert rule, the world of popular culture is perhaps the one field in which intellectuals are least likely to be experts.[29] This does not mean accepting things "the way they are," but starting out with an adequate perspective on the discursive strategies that comprise our "world" and relations of knowledge within it. Television's production of history and subjectivity, constituted simultaneously as past and present, old and new, here and there, live and preserved, ended and open-ended, is precisely one of the areas that allows the initiation of such a reassessment, rewriting itself even as we attempt to pin it down.

In his book *Ronald Reagan: The Movie,* Michael Rogin has demonstrated the tendencies of Ronald Reagan to conflate his cinematic roles with his everyday past, seemingly shifting with ease from his fictional past to his personal past and back again, creating a past persona for public memory that is also difficult to precisely pin down.[30] Television's relationship to—or as this chapters has shown, its many relationships—with history can produce similar results for a shared popular memory of postwar American society and culture. Students and teachers need to be aware of this phenomena and consider "the historic" on television from a variety of critical stances and approaches. A part of this consideration must recognize there is in fact some value to the way television produces history, including the opportunity to view audiovisual representations of an array of twentieth century events and experiences.

One of the reasons that television can produce this phenomena is in the fact that history, especially the history of everyday life, is so accessible; a walk down the street, a glance out the window can show buildings and cars of different ages and eras; a trip to the library can show books and magazines of different generations stacked next to each other on the shelves; if the local community has a folklore festival, historical society, or even something as simple as a weekend farmer's market, we are presented with a kaleidoscopic melange of past and present iconography; our language, habits, manners, food, and dress all contain elements of the past as well as elements of the present. This ease of accessibility is one of the joys of history. However, the infatuation of television may someday threaten to take away that joy and exercise a monopoly power over it without society's realization of its loss. Unlike the mythic losses promulgated by a televisual past, society's loss of understanding, experiencing, and writing its own everyday history would indeed be painful. Hopefully, the empowerment of students and teachers with both the critical awareness of television's infatuation with history and the appreciation of the accessibility of history in everyday surroundings will prove a powerful preventative against such future loss.

At the same time media history—however commodified and mediated—is "real" history, it is part and parcel of the cultural and social forces with which we have grown up. Moreover, the fragmentary and dispersed nature of the historical field produced by television may allow for more room for individuals to find their own voice apart from the master's history which is presumably more clear cut than television's pastiche. Television's production of history as a category of knowledge, once broken loose from self-absorption, may hold the potential to empower teachers and students to tell their own histories in new ways which include popular culture.

CHAPTER TWO

TELEVISION ADVERTISING, TELECOMMUNICATIONS DISCOURSE, AND CONTEMPORARY AMERICAN CULTURE

A critical knowledge of media culture—in this case, television—cannot be developed without endeavors toward examination of the advertisements and commercials which abound on American television. At first glance, these short messages seem simple and straightforward, coming and going in a matter of a minute or two, and often ignored or unwatched as viewers wait for the return of their programs of choice. Yet such an assessment of television advertising is uninformed. Although many commercials are ignored during a typical round of viewing, many others are retained at various levels of awareness. This retainment moves beyond the practical purpose of television advertising—the selling of goods and services—and enters American culture in myriad ways. The images and discursive formations of television advertising enter and exit our visual and verbal vocabularies with ease (for example, the shift of the phrase "where's the beef?" from television advertising for a hamburger chain into the 1984 Presidential primaries and election). As such, television advertising is a site for the reception and formation of everyday knowledge and therefore a site of ideological formation. From this perspective, analysis of television advertising has several facets, ranging from effectiveness as a vehicle to sell goods and services to harbinger of cultural changes and expressions.

Although effectiveness studies are important, this chapter will largely examine television advertising as a locus for ideological formation. Such an examination is necessary for a readership who has made the commitment to develop a critical knowledge concerning media culture. To expedite such an examination, the specific focus of this chapter is television advertising for telecommunications and information corporations. The choice is intentional. Through such a case study, readers will be empowered with a dual knowledge: greater awareness of the ideological formations of television advertising, and greater understanding of the discursive formations surrounding the rise of information technology in our everyday lives.

Contemporary American television advertising campaigns for large corporations—especially those centered on the production and consumption of telecommunications, information, and computer services—present to viewers through their visual and verbal discourses the faith and beliefs that underlie what might be called the "corporate soul." Through the dual epistles of technological utopianism and consumer culture, the inhabitants of these television commercials search out (and sometimes find) meaning and significance for their professional and personal identities as well as indicators of the way toward the future. The television advertising campaigns during the 1980s of such corporations as American Telephone and Telegraph, Apple Computers, International Business Machines, BASF, and others on the surface present the image of the new, the bold, the innovative, and the future.[1] On the one hand, such a reading has an accuracy—yet a reading which centers only on the future visions of these ads fails to recognize the process of ideological reification, because the broad concepts and themes, visual cliches and icons, and construction of the body, time and space, and discourse offered in these ad campaigns are all linked to a century of discursive construction, meaning, and empowerment offered through American corporate advertising.

This chapter explores the links between the present and the past in corporate advertising by way of examining corporate television advertising in the 1980s and its lessons of consumer culture and technological utopia. This includes an exploration of the broad concepts and themes offered by corporations in their current advertising and the links between current and past themes.[2] These themes and concepts, these concerns of advertising, utilize a "history" or "mass archival memory" of social tableaux, parables, and visual cliches and icons of corporate advertising throughout twentieth century American culture.[3]

> The change had been long forseen...the popular sentiment toward the great corporations and those identified with them had ceased to be one of bitterness, as they came to realize their necessity as a link, a transition phase, in the evolution of the true industrial system. The most violent foes

of the great private monopolies were now forced to see how invaluable and indispensable had been their office in educating the people...by a series of object lessons, the great corporations had taught the people an entirely new set of ideas.... It had come to be recognized as an axiom that the larger the business the simpler the principles that can be applied to it; that, as the machine is truer than the hand, so the system, which in a great concern does the work of a master's eye in a small business, turns out more accurate results.[4]

—*Looking Backward,* 1888

How great is the power in the control of mass communications, especially when helped by modern inventions, has been made clear recently in countries that have had social revolutions, and which have promptly, in a very short period, brought extraordinary changes in the expressed beliefs and actions of vast populations. These have been led to accept whole ideologies contrary to their former beliefs, and to accept as the new gospel what many outsiders would think as ridiculous. The most powerful means of communication, especially for rapid action in the case of revolution, are the electric forms like radio and television, which spread most skillfully presented ideas to every corner of the land with the speed of light and a minimum of propaganda labor.[5]

—National Resources Council, 1937

The information age that futurists have long predicted has arrived, bringing with it the promise of dramatic change in the way people live and work, perhaps even in the way they think.... More than half of all Americans now earn their living not by producing things but as `knowledge workers', exchanging various kinds of information, and the personal computer stands ready to change how all of them do their jobs.[6]

—*Time,* 1983

My God, what a fantastic time to be alive![7]

—*Megatrends,* 1982

These four passages represent a century of ideological construction for American society built around the promise and perils of the large corporation, global expansionism, the growth of modern consumer culture as a new and better ideal for the common man, and of course a utopian future grounded in the perfection and subsequent distribution of technology as the instrumentation of social equality. The first speaker, Dr. Leete (the narrator of the future for Julian West in Edward Bellamy's *Looking Backward*) could well have told Julian West it is a fantastic time to be alive in the fictional future of Bellamy's Boston,

Massachusetts, 2000 A.D. Yet the last quote is not from Leete or West but instead from the world of present-day nonfiction. "My God, what a fantastic time to be alive!" is the very last sentence in John Naisbitt's *Megatrends*, one of the best-selling books of the 1980s and indeed of the twentieth century. *Looking Backward* was among the most widely read novels of its time, translated into over twenty languages and serving many as a "blueprint" for a perfect future. John Dewey and Charles Beard were two of many who hailed *Looking Backward* as one of the most influential books in American history. Like its ancestor, *Megatrends* has its horde of present-day advocates; two recent Presidential candidates (Gary Hart and Richard Gephardt) as well as many other social leaders offer praise to *Megatrends* in its introduction.

If examinations of these themes of technological utopia and consumer culture were extended to include more of the many treatises in this area, we would find some grounded in "fiction," others in "nonfiction" publications. At times it seems difficult to place a particular text exclusively into one of these two categories of literature. In any event, we would discover a century's worth of projected utopian futures—all with the "transition" to such a society explained in only the vaguest and general of terms—all futures where, as Howard Segal points out, society has reached the end of history. Change, the bedrock of history, has finally ceased because perfection, the goal of history, has finally been achieved. While this century of visions may seem diverse, Segal is correct in that they all share a common earnestness and didactism.[8]

Another century-old ideology has existed concurrently with an ideology of technological utopianism in American culture: the ideology of a culture of consumption.[9] These two ideologies are related, but not the same; some of their principles and tenets are actually in opposition. For example, the widespread encouragement of conspicuous and spurious everyday consumption seems at odds with the rational, efficient, precise management of all commodities so typical of Bellamy and other technological utopianists. These tensions between coexistent ideologies even surfaced in *Looking Backward;* in one instance, Dr. Leete's daughter Edith is an "indefatigable shopper" yet she shops in a system where everyone only purchases the goods their family needs, and where all the stores in Boston and all America stock precisely the same merchandise. Exactly how someone could be an indefatigable shopper in such a closed system of consumption goes by unexplained. Yet such tensions and contradictions of ideological messages should not be surprising. As David Nye argues in his analysis of the visual iconography of General Electric, a proliferation of images and contexts cannot simply be regarded as a conspiracy or a self-conscious attempt at domination. Corporate images, advertising, and public relations have historically spoken not a single ideology but a group of ideologies, each suited to specific audiences and therefore a part of the corporation's discourse, even if certain philosophies and messages were inconsistent with each other. Corporations cannot constantly fulfill all their self-professed multiple roles of research wizards, social benefactors, educators, and profitmakers—yet they can and do consistently present all of these identities to their audiences.[10] The result is akin to a famous spectacle of painting and also of the silent cinema, the triptych with three simultaneous screens of action, a group of images which can be contradictory but still serve a metanarrative. So in turning to an examination of corporate television advertising, analysis should reasonably expect to find not a single, all-powerful media master imposing corporate will upon a monolithic populace, but instead the present-day equivalent of Bellamy's series of object lessons that create among themselves a degree of contradiction but as a whole fall short of challenging or threatening an established history of corporate image creation upholding technological utopia and consumer culture. Instead, these object lessons perpetuate that history.

Given the provision of dual and distinct ideologies, how do the inhabitants of modern American society negotiate between, yet sustain both visions? Further, what public discourses have emerged to address these dual ideologies, and how are these discourses shaped and promoted by American corporations and social leaders? Some of the answers to these questions lie in the history of popular adoption of technologies such as electricity and telephony, and in corporate advertising and public relations to educate and inform the public on the new ways of living electric power and the telephone might bring to society. The technologies of electricity and telephony provided to consumers a gateway to better living, and the corporate pedagogy surrounding the increased utilization of these technologies serves as an infinite road map for those consumers travelling the byways of consumer culture and technological utopia.[11]

The modern American telephone system and the central corporation responsible for its development—American Telephone and Telegraph—have understandably been the topic of many books and articles, approaching the telephone from social, cultural, technological, economic, and historical perspectives.[12] Although Alexander Graham Bell lost financial control of his invention by 1878 to a group of Boston bankers (who themselves would lose control to New York City finance capitalists in the early 1900s), Bell continued to serve American Telephone and Telegraph (ATT) and American telephony as a future forecaster of the uses of the telephone. Along with the usual predictions of spanning distances, issuing commands (not for nothing has "Come here Watson, I need you" been historicized), communicating with loved ones and friends, responding to emergencies, and increasing productivity, came a goal from Bell and others of universal service. While we might now take the notion of telephones for everyone as a given, the concept of a communications technology in as many locations as possible—including all American homes—has its genesis in the expansion of the telephone system in the late 1800s. Interestingly, Edward Bellamy heavily incorporated the notion of universal telephone service into his future Boston, as the protagonists of *Looking Backward* rely on a telephone-like public address system within their homes and shops to deliver music, lectures, religious services, and other aspects of public discourse. But telephones for everyone was not a concept confined only to visionary inventors and technological utopianists; financial and industrial leaders interested in the development of new communications technologies saw universal service as an important avenue for the advancement of a modern consumer culture.

Concomitant with the goal of universal service came the beginnings of an ongoing advertising campaign by ATT that would strive to make increased use of the "last mile"—that least-used section of the public telephone system, the lines between the local central switching office and the various homes and businesses.[13] From the start telephone executives realized that the price to be paid for universal service was massive underutilization of the last mile; suggestions for increased use continue today and are in fact a major component of current telecommunications policy and information age planning. For example, recent telecommunications research has argued that the average telephone residential line—the line from the home to the central office—is in use only twenty to thirty minutes per day (yes, only twenty to thirty minutes a day, as incredible as that may seem to a family with teenagers), and that future management of utility consumption and information databases into the home by telephone companies could utilize the last mile beyond twenty minutes per day and therefore make better and more efficient use of this "underdeveloped" infrastructure.[14] The increased use of pay telephones to call within local switching areas is also recognized as another way to increase use of the last mile, and local operating companies such as Illinois Bell and Wisconsin Bell have recently launched advertising campaigns urging consumers to "call in often" on pay telephones. However, these are only a few of the latest manifestations of an old concern.

The beginnings of increasing utilization of the last mile and expansion of universal service obviously had to center on giving the people something to say. Toward this end, a number of newspaper and magazine articles regularly appeared between 1880 and 1910 on how to use the telephone as a means of communication. This included proper manners, useful phrases, the need for occasional repetition, and how to talk with telephone operators.[15] Of course, as the telephone system changes and expands, this training has been continuous; it has also been largely discreet and unrecognized by consumers as an ongoing site of pedagogy. Advertising encouraging us to use the phone in new ways has been a staple of ATT since its corporate inception.

One of the most interesting re-education tasks was a switch from the male to the female voice. With the continued expansion of the system and the coming of reliable long-distance telephony in 1915, ATT began early in the twentieth century to turn over their work force in operators, moving from males to females, in part to lower their labor costs. This coincided with the rise of the seven-digit number. The first three digits came to signify the local switching centers (the central offices) which, until the advent of nationwide direct dialing in the early 1960s, were often signified by geography or a street name such as Park, Uptown, Davis, Lakeside, University, Oliver, and so on. The remaining four digits owe their existence to ergonomic studies of the female body conducted by ATT in the 1910s. Scientists at Bell Labs found that the typical arm span of an American female could reach a switchboard of telephone plugs that was 100 by 100 rows of plugs. There are 10,000 total number combinations on a switchboard of 100 by 100 plugs, which gives us all possible numbers between 0000 and 9999. We need look no further than the gendered, ergonomic human body—analyzed in terms of productive capacity—for part of our understanding of the American telephone system. However, ATT did not prefer to construct an ideology for the telephone system that reminded the American public of its geographical and physical links to new technology, and our physical and spatial relationship to the telephone system remains largely unknown. An ideology which holds up the telephone as something with which Americans have no shared physical attributes is ultimately a much more effective ideology for promoting dependency and desire, because we are led to believe we must have something we do not have, cannot create on our own, and cannot live without.

During the 1920s and 1930s the telephone began to change from a utilitarian necessity to an object with the possibilities of increased consumption and also an object that might provide a gateway to a better future. In the sphere of domestic events, ATT in 1928 began to reexamine its advertising strategies for promotion of telephones and telephone service. ATT Vice President Arthur Page argued the company should continue to push the telephone as a necessity but also push the multiple installation of telephones as an everyday luxury: "normal families must seek all the telephone facilities they can conveniently use, rather than the smallest amount they can get along with."[16] Page developed a "comfort and convenience" campaign for ATT that suggested the average American home needed two to three phones to be "in style" and the affluent home could use as many as fifteen. A typical ATT display ad suggested

> Enough telephones are an essential of the well-ordered home. They prevent the little annoyances that destroy pleasant moods...no more bustling confusion, no shouting from room to room, no scurrying to and fro.[17]

Concurrent with this incursion of the telephone into the modern American consumption ethic was the continued promotion of the telephone as an increasingly indispensable business tool essential for both an efficient day-to-day bureaucracy and also for a vision of the future. The consumer culture and the business mentality surrounding the promotion of the telephone shared a common ground in the utility of the telephone as a harbinger of a future technological utopia. The ad agency N.W. Ayer and Son retitled the modern American housewife as "The Little Woman, G.P.A" (General Purchasing Agent) in 1930 and in their artwork placed her at the controls of a domestic communications center.[18] Ayer believed their clients could encourage housewives to adopt a business/management ideology but at the same time give up any notions of careerism that involved leaving the home. Again, the telephone was a key to this better way of life and higher ground of the future. The Little Woman GPA had three telephones at her side along with a blueprint of the home and graphs showing consumption of products in the categories of food and shelter. The Little Woman GPA operated a modern factory—the American home—through increased consumption of telephone service and through an ideology of technological utopia in part realized through control and maximization of telephone discourse.

In turning from the *mise-en-scene* of American domesticity to American industry, advertisers again promoted the telephone as the key to a successful present and also a visionary future. A 1934 ATT magazine display ad featured the banner line "Broader Horizons" with a businessman gazing out the picture window of a skyscraper, viewing both city and country at his feet—and with a telephone in reach, the only object visible in the entire office.[19] The linking of the businessman, the telephone, and the picture window became a common advertising refrain for ATT and a number of American industries. ATT exhorted that the telephone symbolized control, the ability to "multiply" one's personality, and the power to issue commands from a distance. In addition, telephoners were up-to-date, an equal in the new socioeconomic network that was beginning to be built around the notion of information. As early as 1928 businessmen were appearing in ads for telephones and other products in wall-to-wall glass offices with panoramic views of their urban locales. Gradually, the scenes in the picture windows shifted from a balance between the city and the factory in the 1920s to the country and a sky-scrapered city of the future in the 1930s. In 1934 Gulf Oil Company posed its vision of the executive in a lavish color display in *Fortune* with the caption "Men Who Live For Tomorrow" and an executive gazing out a window, watching the hustle and bustle of a factory, the activity of a busy port, the sun gleaming off a new city in the distance, and an airplane flying above all.[20] As he watches the future, he holds the telephone at the ready, picking up the receiver to make yet another call that will usher in a brighter, better future for America. His vision is a world built upon but nevertheless above a culture of consumption, a world linked by the realization of utopian visions of the ultimate power and beneficence of technology.

ATT was not the only information company of the era teaching people "how" to communicate. After Charles Lindbergh completed his transatlantic solo flight in 1927, Western Union encouraged Americans to send congratulatory telegrams to Lindbergh, and also offered a number of scripted or "canned" messages from which to choose.[21] When criticized for offering to write messages for its customers (who would then purchase and send the message written for them), Western Union replied they did so only after its many clerks had noted the incompetence and embarrassment of the average citizen when it came to writing a telegram. Western Union had finally taken pity

> on the honest folk to whom the task of writing even the simplest messages is as terrifying as the facing of machine-gun fire.... we could scarcely maintain service or the integrity of our dividend record if we confined our

> employment to the nimble-witted minority...instead of extending patient hands to the inarticulate and ungrammatical majority.[22]

After this explanation, Western Union was hailed for allowing the people to speak to their hero; then, as now, the question of whether the humble recipients of such advice and assistance had gained any permanent competence in grammatical ability was never raised.

The efforts of Western Union in allowing the people to speak to their hero are in a way one of the links to the present of current television advertisements for long-distance telephony, particularly international long-distance telephony. In these ads American citizens become a myriad of everyday heroes—Lindberghs to the world—as friends and relatives scattered across the globe thrill to the sound of our voices and the tales of our everyday lives. It is our voice, the touch of America, that signifies the specialness of an Irish schoolgirl's role in the school play, our voice that brings back the heroics of an amateur German soccer team, our voice that reminds the rest of the world of the joy of contemporary American society. It is the sharing of our everyday lives—lives in large part depicted, shaped and defined through contemporary realizations of modern American consumer culture—that bring meaning, significance, and importance to the everyday lives of our foreign friends.

The education of consumers in the uses and wonders of electricity has a similar history of material abundance, relaxed living, and utopian futures.[23] General Electric advanced the words "science" and "progress" as signifiers of the company name in the early 1900s, and conducted a number of lavish educational displays, shows and lectures in conjunction with their regular advertising campaigns. An exhibit hall for the 1933 World's Fair christened the "GE House of Magic" was dismantled after the fair and taken on a nationwide tour during the 1930s; over three million Americans visited the display. Such campaigns played an important part in educating consumers to the uses of electricity, and in forming public opinion against public ownership of utilities and in favor of the application of private enterprise and private ownership in the field of electrical power generation and distribution.

Like the telephone, proponents and promoters of electricity capitalized on the widespread American fascination and admiration of inventors and inventing, of science and technology, that emerged during this era—a core attribute of modern American society sometimes expressed as "Yankee Ingenuity."[24] This fascination was romanticized in several ways. Some GE ads for light bulbs recreated the poses of figures in classical artwork. GE also sent Charles Ripley, a well-known advocate of beneficial capitalism, on a massive speaking tour in the 1920s. His lecture "The Romance of Power" utilized a carefully prepared script and over 100 slides. He spoke in a darkened room while the audience watched the slide show. GE considered the lecture so powerful they printed up fifty extra sets of slides and sent trained surrogates across the country to replicate Ripley's feat.[25]

The paragraphs above represent only a few of the tracks, the tracings, the residue of the past as it leads up to a present world of television advertising. Current American television advertising for telephones and telecommunications is an important source for providing and understanding the coming future, the next section of the road map, the next leg of the route past the gateways of electricity and telephony. By now, after a century of navigation, it has become clear that the travellers in this marvelous world have devoted their consciousness and their faith to reaching the promised land of this journey; their Trinity is the satellite above, the database among us, the personal computer within. The heroes and models of success depicted in these advertisements, through their special knowledge, awareness, and discourse of information and telecommunications, reify Bellamy's past future and echo Naisbitt's present exclamation: "My God, what a fantastic time to be alive!"

When taken as a whole—instead of as discrete and discreet units interspersed throughout the scope of television viewing—current corporate advertising for information and telecommunications makes for compelling viewing and contains many areas worthy of discussion and analysis. The analysis that follows is confined to the construction of ideology via these advertisements in three areas: the construction of the body; the construction of time and space; and the construction of discourse. Hopefully, readers will have a basic familiarity with some of these advertisements (see note 1) upon which they might draw while reading the analysis which follows. On occasion, brief descriptions of certain ads are offered to begin certain points of analysis when such descriptions are necessary.

CONSTRUCTION OF THE BODY

A number of corporations offer up suggestions for the type of body needed to advance in the coming future, and some ads offer up ways of using our present bodies to better reach that future. The Hewlett-Packard ads center on the body alone at physical exercise—in one case, rowing on a river, in another, swimming laps in a pool—with a mind constantly centered on the question "What if?" as applied to problems and opportunities in the world of information and telecommunications. A fundamental yet unaddressed paradox exists in that the purpose of the exercise is release and isolation from the pressures of the modern world and current careers, yet the exercise is halted when the constant question is finally answered; it seems that this is one area—telecommunications, computers, information—where the exercise of the body is not ultimately a method of escapism but instead a method for reaching and achieving a better world.

We also see the value of a body that is capable of "living inside" telecommunications or somehow inhabiting the inside as well as the outside of a computer. In several ads we see individuals who are just as comfortable with the projection or simulation of their voices, and by implication their identities, through telephones and computers as they are with interpersonal relationships. In one IBM ad, Gary Burghoff (Radar O'Reilly from M*A*S*H*) plays a character who is alone at work when several important calls come in from customers. Using the computer and the telephone, Burghoff easily answers a number of important questions, saving the accounts and pleasing the clients. For each question, Burghoff changes his voice to present the illusion of a large corporation with many different departments and employees. He demonstrates he is capable of reaching a state of multiple personalities through the use of the computer and the telephone and thereby achieves greater efficiency and all-important customer satisfaction.[26] One ATT ad discusses sending an image to a doctor in London for further consultation. Later the same ad shows a future of computer image conferences, where computer-generated images simulate globally-dispersed conferees, yet the participants seem so at ease with the computerization of these bodies they smile and thank each other for their graciousness.

CONSTRUCTION OF TIME AND SPACE

The categories of analysis used herein are of course not completely exclusive; the ads for insurance companies such as Prudential or New York Life are caught up in construction of the body as well as construction of time and space. The New York Life ads offer a preservation of the body—in one case, an actual freezing—which allows consumers to simply sit and wait out a period of transition during which "your future is coming." In one situation, a frozen skier is thawed out in thirty years to discover the daughter of his old insurance agent is waiting with the dividends of his investments. Another case has a female astronaut returning from a mission in which she has been in suspended animation. Among the first calls she receives is her New York Life agent, reporting on the financial abundance to which she has returned. Indeed, the ads are presented as if they are an actual transmission from the future that we are fortunate enough to glimpse. In other insurance ads (Prudential) time, space, and the body all inhabit a computer-generated world which constructs the nuclear family and depicts spectacular fantasies of consumption: the boat, the sports car, money from the sky, the home on the shore.

The computer-generated world—specifically, the variations on fractal imagery seen in this and in other ads, such as for BASF—holds up the space inside the computer as the promised land of a future age of information. In some ads, we as viewers seem able to get inside the fractal space; in other ads, fractal space is generated and launched outside of the computer and sent as a stream into the everyday world. For example, one BASF ad shows a stream of fractal images coming out of a human eye. This stream of imagery travels through the board room and the laboratory, providing significance, meaning, context, and shared discourse to events that would otherwise seem disparate and disconnected.

The image of a stream of information is also common in ads that are less directly related to construction of the body. Contel and Nynex are two of many examples where a stream of information that fluctuates in its decipherability—usually unreadable—but occasionally certain words such as "software" or "telecommunications" become clear. These streams of information conquer both space and time, as well as visually reminding viewers of the concept of information networks. These information networks are presented as having an autonomy, even a life, of their own. Cliff Robertson, in one of a series of ATT ads for which he is spokesperson, reminds us that the ATT long-distance system is a "remarkably intelligent" system that on a daily basis routes over thirty million calls worldwide, "all in less time than it takes to dial" and that ATT networks are the "masterminds" of communication.

Further, the time and space constructed within these ads is even better and more remarkable than the time and space of everyday life.

In the time and space of ATT, we need not even fear catastrophe; disaster has already been constructed, tested, and avoided. ATT takes us behind the scenes to show us how they test their equipment to be prepared for all manner of accidents and emergencies. One scientist at Bell Labs serves the ATT network by happily destroying it; we might fear and marvel at this genius who tells us "I love wrecking things!" But fear not, for the labs of ATT have already constructed the forces of nature which might destroy the space and time of information and telecommunications; the random tendency for destruction that threatens all natural systems is overcome by constant research and development in new communications technology. The result in this ad is that the long distance system of ATT survives the electrical storm so that a daughter can immediately inform her mother by telephone that she is fine and the storm is over. Only the well-being of the human is called into question; the well-being of the communications system is of course taken for granted.

Another area of spatial construction is the corporate environment. A world of glass-walled offices reminiscent of the picture window is augmented with telecommunications equipment and computer screens. The screens are a new type of window, gazing on future space, while glass walls and picture windows reaffirm the present-day achievements which are visualized in modern urban locales. The glass-walled office, the picture window, and the multitude of computer screens are common visual icons. The humans within this environment, especially the decisionmakers such as CEOs (Chief Executive Officers), are often edge-lit; this literally adds to their aura. Edge-lighting and rim-lighting give tangible evidence of the corporate soul, indication of the residue remaining on the body that travels through the space and time of telecommunications and information.

While decisions regarding the best telecommunications and information systems for the time and space of the business world often cause confusion for its inhabitants, to do without telecommunications services is to live in a world of chaos. Whether the choice for inhabitants is between confusion or chaos, the ultimate and continuing desire of the inhabitants is to find the friendly space and time of telecommunications and information and thereby seek respite from paranoia. Those characters failing to find respite in the proper space and time find their worlds at risk. For MCI, the risk is financial loss, as characters repeatedly show us how telecommunications and telephones are the keys to profitability. Those in the time and space of Apple computers who make the right choice find Apple products are the key to peer status and envy; to turn a pun, their judicious use will make you the envy of your coworkers and the apple of your superior's eye. Finally, ATT shows us the all powerful CEOs, appearing almost as if a wrathful Old Testament deity, with confusion over telecommunications decisions earning the poor junior executive a lifetime of corporate plagues.

In addition, one must not just choose any telecommunications time and space, but the right telecommunications time and space. Those who choose, but choose wrongly (for example, the poor fellow still buying IBM stand-alones instead of ATT computers) are exposed as suffering from poor vision; while they believe themselves to hold foresight, we can see they actually have a case of Marshall McLuhan's "rear-view mirrorism" when it comes to perceiving the horizon of the space and time of telecommunications. The danger of rear-view mirrorism in telecommunications foresight is constant for the inhabitants of these ads. The constantly changing nature of technological research and development can, for example, render last year's equipment purchases inefficient or even obsolete. This image of the mirror is inherent within the actual physical surroundings; all glass surfaces, including the glass-walled offices and the computer screens, have the potential to reflect images when viewed from certain angles or under certain lighting conditions. Thus the spatial construction of telecommunications as seen in television advertising can become as disorienting to its inhabitants as a hall of mirrors,[27] or as disorienting as the *Zerrspiegel* of circuses and carnivals.[28] Yet the mirror potential is contradictory, for mirrors can also create an illusion of increased space and greater open areas. Therefore the mirror-like nature of glass-walled offices and computer screens can also provide comfort to its inhabitants. The trick is to draw comfort from the illusion without succumbing to its powers.

CONSTRUCTION OF DISCOURSE

The world of telecommunications is filled with jargon—its own nouns, verbs, and adjectives. The inhabitants of this new frontier have to learn a language to describe a technology, as well as a language to use that technology. Thus we hear of frustration in the 1980s expressed as "all our computers are down" or "that weird fast busy signal again," of relief as "glad I got through" and of wisdom as "its not just long distance—its your business on the line." We also hear of a world of tie lines, data transmission, WATS, digital switching, voice, voice and data, stand-alones, fiber optics, peripherals, and multiple long-distance hookups. In one ATT ad, the frustration of talking to the night watchman while trying to get the latest sales figures suggests that nonvocal discourse might be even better than speaking to another human being.

There is yet another discourse; a discourse of the future. New York Life reminds us "your future is coming"; other ads remind us that we can rely on a future of reliable telecommunications. But it is one ad in particular, for ATT and its history of bringing the future to us, that is particularly fascinating. In this ad, the song "Somewhere Over the Rainbow" is heard as a title slide tells viewers they are seeing 1927 and the invention of color television. A scientist comments that the world is not black and white, and neither can television be merely black and white; research must press on and do better. The scene changes to the present day, where doctors, unsure of a diagnosis, use telecommunications systems to transmit an image of the patient's problem to London so they might get a second opinion. The ad and music continue to show a future of global computer image conferences. Spokesperson Cliff Robertson reminds viewers that the history of ATT is in fact the history of the accomplishments, the successes, and the journey to technological utopia. He mentions all the times in the past the wonder and genius of ATT has advanced our lives and concludes with the comment "Funny—how the future seems to repeat itself."

The work of ATT is presented as a history of constantly bringing a future to the viewer that is a better consumer culture and a new technological utopia, whether it be television in the 1920s, teleconferencing today, computer image conferences tomorrow. At the end of it all, after new technology, new body, new time and space, and new discourse, we find that the end of history is history itself, a history constructed and promoted by ATT beginning with "Come here Watson, I need you" and a history that has historically achieved perfection. The corporate soul can rest assured, because it can know the end of history, for history has ended before; each new telecommunications advance ushers in a new technological utopia. According to ATT and the other architects of our modern ideologies, the consumption of new technology becomes the constant representation of a better way of life. The true utopia of technology is the historical reaffirmation, the reification of new technology as the continuing determinant force in social, political, and cultural decisionmaking. John Naisbitt spoke not just for Edward Bellamy but for a century of true believers when he exclaimed "My God, what a fantastic time to be alive!" Funny—how the future seems to repeat itself.

CHAPTER THREE

TELEVISION NEWS

A major function of American television news is the reinforcement of a set of ideas about the role of information in a democratic capitalist society, and the role of the journalists who provide the information so that citizens can exercise their economic, social, personal, religious, and political responsibilities. One of the most pervasive ideas supporting this function is the value of journalistic objectivity. Both Michael Shudson and Dan Schiller have written persuasively about the development of this concept of objectivity.[1] According to Shudson, objectivity is the belief that a journalist can and should separate facts from values. Facts are considered assertions about events open to independent validation. Values are considered an individuals' conscious or unconscious preferences. Objectivity is preferable to subjectivity because presumably verifiable facts can be trusted, and subjective values cannot. In the American context, the rise in the influence and practice of journalistic objectivity coincided with the acceptance of the scientific method by the academic community and subsequent trust in empiricism as the most reasonable means to reach the truth. In this viewpoint, objective facts are perceived as an improvement over the partisanship of the 1800s or the muckraking of the early 1900s, and as a guard against the ploys of present day high powered public relations campaigns. However, if all information must be able to be validated before it is fit for mass consumption, then whole classes of subjective information must be devalued and ignored. This practice becomes increasingly questionable and difficult to sustain in the face of experiences of the world based on gender, class, and race, as people and disciplines agree that knowledge about these divergent subjective experiences has genuine social value.

Further, to ignore the effect of organizational constraints on the presentation of facts is problematic. Under typical conditions, an event can only be reported if an assignment editor considers it sufficiently significant and is willing to dispatch a crew to its location. Although network news operations occasionally accept footage shot by individuals other than their own personnel, such instances—especially over the course of a long period of time, such as a year—are exceptions to the norm. One of the most important factors influencing editor's decisions and assignments is the economic demands of commercial television. In other words, editorial decisions are influenced by the internal economics of news division budgets, ease (or difficulties) of assigning personnel to stories, and the fact that the initial assignment of a reporter to a specific location results in the bulk of significant expenditures for that particular story. This latter factor tends to produce situations whereby network news broadcasts continue to prominently report a story after their initial arrival on location, regardless of the relative "newsworthiness" of that given day. External economic factors can also influence decisions. Throughout the 1980s, the editorial content of both national and local news broadcasts have increasingly been subject to decisions based on the results of ratings and other audience research rather than questions of newsworthiness. Thus economic constraints and pressures can discreetly push the decisionmaking process away from objectivity and toward productivity.[2]

When the decisionmaking processes of editors and news crews are taken into consideration, objectivity can begin to be viewed as a way of validating dominant privileged views of what is significant and ignoring less privileged views. People without institutionalized resources that provide regular access to mass audiences remain marginalized, and groups with goals that have minority-perspective value judgements at their core may not be considered appropriately objective fare for regular inclusion in national news stories. Although it is true that marginalized points of view do in fact receive network news coverage, the issue in question is the relative frequency of such coverage.

Another common and rarely questioned assumption about information dissemination in this country is that there is an open competitive marketplace of ideas. One of the main functions of the Federal Communications Commission (FCC) is to ensure that (through the licensing of broadcast stations in such a manner that viewers and listeners always have a choice of outlets for reception) there are diverse and contrasting sources of information available so that citizens can determine the "truth" through an open competition of ideas. In his *Aeropagetica* Milton suggests that if a man is exposed to both good and evil, he will pick good over evil—a view of humanity suggesting a substantial break from puritanism. But there are limits to Milton's view, especially in his assumption that the reader is white, male, and Christian. Similarly, the FCC's assurance of open competition assumes that the competing ideas must be marketable and therefore appealing to large numbers of viewers. This implicitly imposes clear limits on the range of acceptable information in broadcast journalism (that is, all radio and television news broadcasts in the U.S. taken as a whole) and on network television news. It might be countered that the majority should not have to consider ideas that are unacceptable or alien to them. But of course, how can someone determine whether ideas are unacceptable if new ideas are only encountered with difficulty, and outside the context of mainstream broadcast journalism?

In *News From Nowhere* Edward Jay Epstein suggests some mythic beliefs and tensions that operate in the production and reception of television news reporting.[3] The first is the myth that television is a mirror on reality because of the involvement of the camera. Such a metaphor is problematic because it suggests an all inclusive, immediate, accurate reflection of reality and ignores the organizational and technical constraints placed on workers in the news business, as well as the representational capacity of the video camera. Newscasts are planned in advance, and only a few stories are selected from the number covered. About half the news stories report events that occur on the day the stories are broadcast, and the other half cover events that took place from two days to two weeks earlier. The ability to cover stories depends on the availability of camera crews in certain locations. The overwhelming majority of national television network news is produced by a few dozen film crews based in half a dozen major cities. The assignment editor makes choices, the correspondent makes choices, the cameraperson and sound technician make choices, and the writer and editor make choices. The results are nothing like the reflection of a mirror. We do not see reality; instead we see a highly edited "slice of reality" that is much closer to definitions of narrative construction than unmediated experiences or conceptions of real life.

Epstein also examines the competing values of the journalist as a "professional" and as an "outsider." In the first view, the professional journalist is held to high standards by others in the profession, just as doctors and lawyers are. The standards are supposed to assure the quality of journalistic effort. However, unlike doctors and lawyers, journalists have no particular required training, no examinations, no licenses, and no legally binding oaths of allegiance to written codes of ethics or standards of practice. Such requirements are considered restrictions and, therefore, violations of First Amendment rights. Most journalists work their way up through the ranks just like other workers in medium-sized and large corporations. In many cases, no particular prior knowledge of any field is required in order to report on it, although a few journalists do develop a reporting speciality demanding a level of expertise, such as sciences. The idea of journalism as a profession with standards like medicine or law runs contrary to the position of the journalist as outsider, a person with allegiance to no profession, organization, or political party, and therefore, able to respond dispassionately to anything or anyone. The outsider represents "everyman," but "everyman" is not a professional. Further, most journalists—and especially network television journalists—are employees of large corporations. Despite occasional individual idiosyncrasies, as a group they do have allegiance to the goals of corporate America and to the economic and political system that maintains it. This shared allegiance, whether conscious or unconscious in any given individual, raises questions as to the ability of that group to fully articulate a broad range of questions and views on any given issue.

An examination of students' common knowledge of American broadcast journalism brings these contrasting myths to light. Some students can describe how the experience of their cultural subgroup is routinely under-represented or even left out of the news. Others can relate experiences when their group's points of view were changed to fit a preconceived idea held by a journalist. Still others will swear that everything their family's favorite anchorman says is absolutely so. Some students will only object or call into question the occasional story, while others will have doubts about the entire "system" of network news—doubts that, unfortunately, often lead to disinterest or cynicism. If students are to be part of a critical citizenry, open and informed discussions of the values that underlie American broadcast journalism must occur. The values of subjectivity and objectivity must be reexamined. The meaning and values of the First Amendment must be examined in the light of the people's everyday experiences. Students must assess the kinds of information available to them in this society and determine if it is sufficient. If it is not, they must be encouraged to seek more information from different sources. Students must come to grips with the limitations of American broadcast journalism so that they do not complacently believe that they are watching all possible information on the news or that the information they see is the only truth about events in their nation or in the world. Perhaps most important of all, students need to discuss the concept that the airwaves belong to the people, not the individual station owners or networks—and why the broadcasters sometimes seem so loath to acknowledge this concept and report the news in a manner keeping with the principle of public ownership of the airwaves. Ultimately, the networks are nothing more than temporary holders of broadcast licenses subject to regular renewal—yet that is nowhere near their self-representation. The networks instead promote an image that suggests their permanence and unquestioned status as both foundation and pinnacle of American broadcasting.

In *Deciding What's News*, Herbert Gans suggests some myths that reinforce and justify economic, political and social values in contemporary American culture and are repeated over and over in nightly news stories. The first myth involves ethnocentrism. Americans are assumed to value their nation above all others and to consider America the best country in the world—the freest, the richest, the most principled, the most astute in business, etc. Therefore, Gans suggests, in nightly news, other countries are judged to be good or bad based on the degree to which they imitate or reproduce American practices and values. Degrees of similarity and difference are used as justification for continued friendship or hostility. The unacceptable differences too often are presented as only cultural traits rather than policies created by leaders acting in specific political contexts. After the hostility ends the irreconcilable differences fade from the news and positive similarities appear. Changing conceptions of Germany and Japan for the positive, Iran for the negative, and more recently, China for both the positive and the negative, exemplify how this phenomenon operates. Citizens of many countries are ethnocentric, but in this culture where there are so many people whose roots are in foreign soil, the movement in and out of favor of so many different countries can be a threatening or alienating experience for many American citizens and residents. As an historical example, during the Second World War the Japanese were popularly considered a bloodthirsty, cruel, and fanatical people. The war propaganda film *My Japan*[4] depicts all of these disagreeable cultural traits. That portrayal of the Japanese people was seen in newsreels in movie houses all over the nation during the war. *My Japan* was joined by a host of less overt but nevertheless similar portrayals of Japanese in American feature films and cartoons. Such portrayals most likely helped make the acceptance of Japanese-American internment in this country palatable. Now, of course, the Japanese are often seen as the ultimate capitalists; as industrious, intelligent, essentially friendly if a little bit mysterious, and devoted to their families and jobs just like Americans. At times, these values take on negative aspects, particularly in light of international trade and business competition.

In the representation of politics, broadcast news reinforces the idea that politicians should be public servants. The myth of altruistic democracy[5] suggests that politicians have the responsibility to be honest, efficient, and dedicated to acting in the public interest regardless of institutional pressures. When corruption or abuses of power are discovered, personal failure is blamed rather than flaws in the system of government or business. Scandals in the Nixon and Reagan administrations were repeatedly pinned to the idiosyncratic behavior of flawed individuals rather than the consequences of agreed upon policies. This schism is maintained because the exercise of altruistic democracy by politicians and the exercise of economic or military policy are considered mutually exclusive. The figure of Oliver North is interesting in this regard. During the Iran-Contra hearings the news media began the search for the flawed individual responsible for breaking the law. It appeared that Oliver North might be that individual. He seemingly broke the law repeatedly in order to pursue activities he felt were in the best interests of the nation. But segments of the media audience considered his behavior heroic (or at least were represented in news coverage as holding that consideration.) In response, the news media then focused on North as a possible hero. Ignored in the attention to the goodness or badness of an individual was any serious consideration of the long-term U.S. policy of involvement and intervention in Latin American affairs, a policy running through the entire history of our nation that can be traced back to the early 1800s.[6]

The view of American business maintained on television news is that the success of the American economic system is the result of responsible capitalism.[7] Individual capitalists within this system compete in order to create increased prosperity for all—lower prices and better quality goods. American capitalism not only creates a high standard of living, it maintains the arts and contributes to charity. American capitalists should not exploit workers or consumers in order to make unreasonable profits either here or abroad. However, economic growth is necessary and the astute businessperson must find a way to maximize profit. The problematic side of capitalism is not regularly presented as regular news. Even when stories such as the pollution of Love Canal in New York are investigated, the centrality of a system of capitalism in fostering such problems are downplayed.

Gans also discusses myths of the small American town, and of rugged individualism. News stories frequently reinforce the myth of a small town pastoralism. The small town is depicted as a place where the good life is led, where traditions are protected and where nature is appreciated. Additionally, small towns are represented as having a closer connection to a past when things were simpler and therefore, supposedly, better. The rugged individual as represented in American news is responsible to no one, able to do whatever he/she wants, and able to buck authority. The rugged individual who pushes others around, rather than be pushed around, has been a popular dramatic hero in American popular culture for many years. The Hollywood portrayal of the cowboy who is forced to take the law into his own hands, the sympathetic gangster of the 1930s, the policeman fighting the mob as well as police corruption in any way he can, and recently, the revenge-seeking, avenging Vietnam veteran, have great appeal to American audiences. Representations of the rugged individual in broadcast news carry with them this representational legacy from American popular culture.

The positive representation of the rugged individual contrasts with the representation of law and order. Not only are citizens who abide by the law valued, but extremism is considered dangerous. Social disorder, even revolution, is presented as the result of extremism. Moderation maintains the social order and upholds the law. The initial response of television news to social movements such as the civil rights or antiwar movements was to invalidate them by portraying them as the work of extremists. But when the protesters became part of the mainstream, the movement was represented in television news as the result of democracy in action.[8]

The final myth Gans discusses involves national leadership. Frequently, stories on nightly news depict the quest for a strong national leader. Individual leadership is presented as preferable to shared leadership. A single individual is sought to be in charge. That person must be able to give orders that others must carry out. A president should represent national will. He should be male, white, middle-aged, wealthy, physically attractive, healthy, intelligent, forceful, moderately religious, heterosexual, and monogamous. As of yet the image of leadership does not fully embrace anyone who does not fit those criteria.[9] For a party to support a candidate who falls outside those boundaries is considered political suicide.

Not all viewers respond identically to the common myths and stereotypes they see in news stories. In *Processing the News* Doris Graber argues that the selection process which allows individual viewers to resonate with the values found in certain myths and ignore others is governed by schemas that an individual develops in childhood through social learning, operant conditioning, and imitation.[10] The schemas individuals develop incorporate overarching values of national, racial, ethnic, sexual, or religious groups. Schemas influence views of good and evil, suggest ways to cope with life, support ideas about the purpose of life, and provide norms of behavior for individuals within larger groups. Schemas can incorporate compatible aspects of several groups' values and beliefs and, therefore, account for intergroup consensus about some myths supported by television news. Information that doesn't fit within an individual's schema cannot be absorbed. If certain information is ignored it cannot become part of an individual's common sense knowledge. Graber does suggest that new schemas can be created later in life because of the influence of powerful experiences or as the result of abstract reasoning.

One of the valuable results of the growth of women's and minority studies as legitimate avenues of academic pursuit is the growing acceptance of the view that there is not one universal way of constructing history, art, and/or culture; instead there are a number of comparative approaches with some shared meanings. The myths marshalled together on television news tend to reaffirm values that protect the dominant ideology of the culture. Of course, not all of the values contained in the dominant ideology are worthless. However, the unexamined acceptance that the myths portrayed on television news as accurate representations of all citizens' experiences of these values should be challenged rather than unquestionably accepted. Stuart Hall contends that there is an inherent tension between the structure of a television text which contains the dominant ideology and the social position of viewers which may put them at odds with that dominant ideology.[11] These tensions can be made explicit, leading to the critical reconstruction of the myths that are part of the nightly news. If cultural myths are interpreted differently by subgroups with different schemas, the different interpretations of the myths in television news can be brought to the surface and validated. Paulo Freire argues that a major function of pedagogy is to empower people to understand and improve their own lives.[12] Thus critical reconstruction is an important contribution toward Friere's pedagogical function.

Television news is a unique subject of study because it is ubiquitous. Because the medium as a whole is generally disavowed by the cultural elite, it is not "owned" by the educational establishment as literature is. Therefore, it is not automatically associated with the domain of the educator, and television news can be more easily perceived as neutral ground for the comparison of responses of students and teachers alike. Comparing subcultural interpretations of national myths can function as an approach to demystifying the process of representation and myth. Dominant groups tend to lose sight of the fact that other groups' common knowledge differs from their own. Conflict can occur when assumptions are made about the universal acceptance of the meaning of certain values as they apply to certain cultural experiences. The experience of the myth of small town pastoralism can be radically different for the oriental family in a small town than for a white suburban family or for the native American family on a reservation or an urban black family.

Exploration of the development of schemas that lead to differing versions of common knowledge also acts to further our understanding of how experiences are mediated. The contrasting consequences of rugged individualism with its insistence on personal freedom, and of placing the smooth functioning of the community above all else, as found in some Oriental and African cultures, can lead to new understanding of the minority ethnic experiences some have had in this country. Expectations of what journalists "can do" versus what journalists "should do" can help to control unreasonable expectations and the cynicism that follows repeated failures to live up to such expectations. It also leads to the realization that each individual must assume responsibility for seeking out and interpreting the news rather than accepting it without qualification.

Another function of examining multiple interpretations of national myths is to encourage a less passive response to the actions of those in power. Friere's experience indicates that having a voice increases one's sense of power. Curtis Gens, director of the Washington-based Committee for the Study of the American Electorate, reports that the U.S. has the lowest rate of voter participation of any democracy in the world.[13] Gens in part attributes this to television news turning citizens into spectators, more interested in being entertained by political activity than participating in it. Perhaps viewers are reassured by news stories that everything is working as well as can be expected and jump to the conclusion that their vote is unnecessary. On the other hand, perhaps that acquiescence continues partly because the voices that could challenge the reassuring myths are not heard.

The comparison of diverse views of national myths by critical viewers leads to a desire for more information that breaks the boundaries set by dominant political or business institutions. Interest in subjective views of experience may lead to an active attempt to search for alternative sources of information in international magazines, or in the publications of particular ethnic groups or genders. The goal of helping people to understand and improve their own lives can be furthered, not by agreeing with a single dominant interpretation of national myths, but by holding those myths up to scrutiny, along with considering the reasons why we continue to encourage their existence. Teachers and students must accept the challenge to examine their own schema and mutually search for the generative themes that describe group relations in this culture.

American television journalism not only deals with national stories and myths; it also reports on a significant amount of international news, and is the major source of information about the rest of the world for most Americans. Critical viewership has to also recognize this facet of television news and approach coverage of international affairs with a similarly informed stance. Here again, a wide and diverse range of views is often subsumed to a single issue or a supposedly clear-cut, black-and-white stance, thereby disregarding the common knowledges of different nations, regions, and cultures. This journalistic involvement with international affairs has its roots in the history of American foreign relations.

In the 1800s when the "penny press" became the vanguard of the advertising-supported mass information industries, international news was not usually an important item on the menu of interesting information made available to the American consumer. Events occurring in cities and on the western borderlands tended to dominate the newspapers.[14] The Spanish American War in 1898, and especially the coming of the First World War in 1914, obviously increased interest in receiving updated international news. However, for various reasons the war limited the availability and reliability of information, including British control and censorship of many of the transatlantic undersea cable systems, and, with American entry into the war in 1917, American government control of information dissemination through the Creel Committee on Public Information. The Creel Committee functioned as a middleman or gatekeeper for dissemination of all war-related information to American magazines and newspapers, as well as functioning as an international propaganda outlet for dissemination of American views to the world at large. By the time of the Second World War, American government attitudes toward war coverage had progressed considerably. Although the government did control news dissemination through the Office of War Information, in general international war correspondents and reporters were allowed to use their own judgement as to what to report far more often than had been the case in the earlier world war. Furthermore, during World War II the government did not take over radio, telegraph, and telephone communications as had previously been the case.[15]

After the First World War, and especially after the Second World War, as the U.S. assumed an increasingly significant internationalist position in global affairs, the need for more and more accurate international information became necessary. There has been a steady increase in the amount of time devoted to international information on broadcast network (first radio, then television) nightly newscasts since the 1940s, although the number of international correspondents employed by the networks has steadily decreased. By the 1980s, roughly forty percent of a typical evening broadcast was related to international issues.[16] That figure is heavily influenced, of course, by American involvement in various international crises. A disproportionately large amount of coverage may be given to some parts of the world and relatively little coverage given to others. The increase in international news coverage is in part due to postwar geopolitical conditions and in part due to the tremendous expansion in information gathering, dissemination ability, and new audio/visual technologies ranging from the satellites in geostationary orbits to handheld video cameras.

It is ironic that the increasing technical ability to rapidly communicate across borders from one nation to another coincides with the increasing ability of more and more nations to rapidly destroy each other with atomic, biological, and chemical weapons, because since the end of the First World War more and more government diplomats have perceived rapid and reliable international communications as a key to lasting world peace.[17] This irony can be interpreted in a dialectical manner—for example the Cuban Missile Crisis of 1962 breeding in 1963 the USA-USSR "hotline" telephone system between those nation's leaders as a protector of peace. This need for communication and information (not only between superpowers but between all nations) extends from national leaders to national populations. How and what Americans learn about foreigners has become a vitally important area of critical inquiry.

Few viewers can compare a television news story about an international event with their own experiences of the event, or with the direct results of the event.[18] They can only trust that the major evening news programs provide them with a reasonable understanding of foreign government positions, social events, and economic trends that eventually influence lives in the U.S. American domestic news is often characterized by a set of charges, threats, official pronouncements, and demands made by major national figures that are followed by reactions provided by representatives of the groups challenged or affected by the initial assertions.[19] In international news the assertions are made by American journalists and attributed to foreign heads of state or political and social movements, and there is often no reaction provided. There are no international news reporting standards and practices that assure all major positions of controversial issues are aired. In the absence of international libel laws, there are no legal consequences if willful misrepresentation occurs. Attempts made by some countries to create codes of ethics requiring rights of correction to false or misleading international news stories have not met with support from the U.S., where such measures on the part of other nations are considered to be threats to the American rights of free speech.[20] Suggestions to license or otherwise certify international journalists—suggestions which usually emanate from the underdeveloped nations of the world, long victims of misleading coverage—are usually met with scorn by American and other Western journalists.[21] In general, then, the public is forced to accept American network coverage of international affairs largely on faith (an acceptance to which most of the audience seemingly consents). The result is an audience highly vulnerable to misrepresentation.

The form that has evolved for reporting news on electronic media does not always lend itself well to the coverage of international affairs. The news values of American broadcast journalism—including timeliness, uniqueness, and controversy—influence news gathering at the international level. Stories are selected for their perceived ability to attract large audiences. A prevalent assumption among broadcast producers is that the majority of Americans are not very interested in international news unless it directly affects the U.S., an attitude they claim is verified in their own audience research.[22] Consequently, news stories are chosen by producers because they involve American government officials, American business interests, or American citizens. However, some foreign stories that do not immediately involve Americans—and therefore are likely to go underreported—have great significance in shaping future events that will affect the nation (one example might be the return of Ayatollah Khomeni to Iran from exile before the taking of American hostages in 1979).

An emphasis on timeliness leads to covering easily attainable stories in accessible places. The long-term importance of stories can become secondary to their timeliness when it comes to criteria for coverage. Moreover, stories that need to be developed quickly can rarely be researched carefully.[23] At the same time, the need to find stories that are unique and controversial creates the tendency to hop randomly around the globe, presenting the audience with a series of contextless stories connected with convenient segues. Paradoxically, the search for uniqueness (and attempts to deny competitors a scoop) also encourages a sort of "herd mentality" where all the networks suddenly show up reporting the same story that seemingly did not exist the day before. These practices can make international affairs appear ephemeral, fragmented, and discontinuous.[24] As a result, the public is prevented from being able to readily follow the evolution of international events, even when they may lead to American involvement in crisis situations. Often when an international crisis does arise, the American television viewer feels as though the crisis has materialized overnight, or in a matter of a few days. This can lead to the mistaken assumption that many foreign governments and citizens are erratic and irrational rather than responsible and reasoned.

The need to produce a story that will be interesting and understandable to an enormous general audience, and the need to fit that story into a tightly controlled time period (controlled literally to the second) leads to the employment of several techniques that can be counterproductive to the understanding of international affairs. For example, language and content must be simplified so that concepts can be understood quickly because (unlike a reading audience) the broadcast audience will not have a chance to review them.[25] This leads to the oversimplification of complex stories, especially those concerning international economics or social issues. Without context an international monetary problem cannot be explained meaningfully in the few seconds available. The technique of mirror imaging or explaining foreign events in terms of situations familiar to Americans can also be misleading, or simply inaccurate.[26] This is frequently done with foreign elections. But the political process and the issues at stake in foreign countries are usually dissimilar to the election processes and issues here at home.

The technique of personalizing stories to increase audience interest can cause distortion of the events portrayed. Stories are frequently written about an individual's involvement in a complex political situation as a way of personalizing the story. If the person chosen has an unsophisticated understanding of the event they are being used to represent, attempts to create human interest can result in a highly stereotyped caricature of both the individual and the situation.

Another form of personalization is the development of the personality of a news anchor or reporter. The networks present news programs featuring a highly credible anchorperson. It is assumed that viewers will be more likely to remain loyal to a news program if they feel some sort of relationship exists between themselves and the anchor.[27] Allegiance to an anchor helps to influence many viewers' responses to the importance of news stories that anchor delivers. News that a trusted authority reports may even be considered the only significant news in the world. There is no clear attempt by any of the networks to suggest that material presented in a thirty minute news program is a very small, highly selected portion of all the newsworthy events that have occurred around the globe that day.

In addition to the words offered by anchors and reporters, images are also an essential of television reporting. The arrangement and pacing of images is important in a television news story to maintain viewer interest. In a thirty-second story on network news many cuts from image to image (and also from sound to sound) are employed to increase the tempo of delivery, and hopefully prevent viewer boredom. Events that are not visually interesting or inaccessible to cameras are often left out, and stories with interesting visuals may be used in place of other stories that are perhaps more deserving of audience attention. As might be expected, visual information usually plays a determinant role in whether an international story will make it on to an evening news broadcast. This places clear limits on the dimensions of an international event. Usually, a visual story centers around one idea that is supported by the visual material. The journalist must focus on a fragment of a more complicated event and depend on the anchor to set up the story.[28] Television journalists sometimes imply that the camera tells an objective story; however, the pointing of the camera (and setting the lens focal length anywhere from close-up through long shot, or zooming in or out), the selection and juxtaposition of shots in editing, and even the soundtrack decisions are components of narrative development.

Often if pictures are not available, a story simply is not aired. If a story is of such importance that it warrants airing without visuals, the alternative to visual information of the event is often an interview with an eyewitness or an expert. Interviews, although potentially interesting from an audio and visual perspective, can allow misrepresentations to occur without contradiction. The American public in 1978 and 1979 could hardly have guessed the dissatisfaction of Iranian citizens with the Shah if their only source of information was American television interviews.[29] Journalists may end up serving ideological interests by default, if they take for granted the objectivity of official sources or individual first hand accounts of international events.[30]

A desire for action and emotionality in news reporting can influence the construction of an international story. Competition between correspondents for network airtime may result in beefing up the drama of the moment in the hope that a producer will respond to potential audience interest and be less concerned with the significance of the information.[31] The necessity to supply a good narrative with a beginning, middle, and end can convey closure on an issue when closure has not in fact been reached.[32] And a regular emphasis on visually interesting negative occurrences, such as coups or natural disasters, can reinforce stereotypes that the developing world in particular is constantly plagued with misfortune, catastrophe, and social unrest when that "crisis journalism" is not balanced with information on positive achievements and progressive social developments.[33]

The profitable operation of the news business also influences how much and what kind of international news is reported. Day-to-day economics of operation limit the effectiveness of international reporting by reducing the number of permanently stationed foreign correspondents. Cost effectiveness is more easily reached by flying journalists abroad on a case-by-case basis to cover fast breaking stories rather than to pay the living expenses of a correspondent assigned to a foreign location for an extended period of time. The tradeoff is a loss in the education of the correspondents themselves in terms of deeply absorbing the political, social, and cultural particularities of a given nation or region—the kind of knowledge that can only be gained by living in a locale for an extended period of time. Without such an understanding, the journalist is at greater risk to misinterpret events and misunderstand the historical, social, political, and cultural preconditions that have led to a particular newsworthy moment in a given nation. The risk of misinterpretation is exacerbated when the journalist, at a loss to thoroughly understand the "national mindset" of another nation, instead resorts to American stereotypes to assure that the story will be easily understood by an American audience.[34] Some producers judge international stories from unfamiliar countries by the rule of "uncertainty absorption." If the story contains information that is contrary to popular expectation and verification is difficult, the story is passed over, because it is assumed that the audience will only respond to plausible stories in the first place.[35]

Daily decisions are made by producers concerning which stories will be transmitted via satellite. Satellite transmission is costly and in order to meet budget constraints editors must exercise restraint. Although budgets can be stretched and additional stories can be flown in on videocassette rather than transmitted via satellite feed, the demand for up-to-the-minute coverage not only necessitates satellite transmission, but also means that a story sent in on videocassette has less chance to air because it is perceived to have lost some of its timeliness. As a result, the majority of international television network nightly news comes from countries with ample facilities for satellite transmission and frequent air links with the U.S., while nations and regions with minimal satellite links and infrequent air connections go underreported. The most cost efficient method of all is to turn to sources in the U.S. federal government and write the story largely from the perspective of those sources. This is a common practice which essentially reinforces government positions on international issues while doing little to provide a broader perspective. Recently, American news programs have entered into arrangements with foreign production crews to provide additional footage. Voiceover narration will be added at the network, thus reducing the number of trips abroad for American network news production crews. With editorial control and final cutting at the hands of the networks, however, the impact of foreign crews on changing American news reporting is probably minimal.

One of the most difficult analytic questions regarding American television network news coverage of international events is in the textual material conveyed in broadcasts. For example, analysis that examines the vocabulary or discourse of network news broadcasts reveals that words like leftist, procommunist, unstable, war-torn, disorder, irrational, barbarism, and corruption consistently find their way into the coverage of events in underdeveloped countries. Motifs of social disorder, flawed development, and primitivism regularly emerge in reporting about these regions.[36] During the 1980s American news coverage about Central America tended to link the term "rebel" to anticapitalist military forces and the term "freedom fighter" to procapitalist military forces regardless of the political leanings in the national governments those forces opposed.[37] Although this examination of discursive practices is admittedly difficult for anyone studying the news (because such an examination in part involves inspection of our own discursive habits), students and teachers must meet the challenge and take up the questions surrounding discursive formations in their overall examination of the reception of television news and the structures of knowledge in their everyday lives.

Another important question centers around identifying and understanding the personalities and individuals who have control in determining the structure, operation, and discourse of international news coverage. The impetus for determining the importance of international stories on American network television news comes from public leaders such as the President, his executive office, the American military, foreign policy makers in Washington, and officials at the United Nations headquarters in New York, as well as from private leaders such as influential American businesspeople (from Armand Hammer through the Rockefellers to Robert Vesco) and the major American newspapers (such as the *New York Times, Washington Post, Los Angeles Times,* and *Chicago Tribune*) and wire services such as Associated Press (AP) and United Press International (UPI).[38] Government officials are heavily relied upon; it is not an exaggeration to say that many "international" news stories begin and end in Washington. Unlike the situation in domestic news coverage, American government officials regularly enjoy unchallenged access to the media in coverage of international affairs. It is possible that this unchallenged access assists the government in mobilizing public opinion behind the goals and policies of an administration under the guise of journalistic objectivity.[39] Because international news is tied to American foreign policy, governments that agree with American economic and political positions generally bask in a favorable light, regardless of internal public opinion in their own countries. This can lead to misunderstanding on the part of the American public, and even moments of embarrassment for American government officials, when internal conditions in such nations finally result in broad social and political changes—Ferdinand Marcos and the Philippines being a recent example. Governments that are critical of American actions are usually cast in a negative light, if the spotlight shines their way at all. Because of their dependence on American government sources for international news reporting (a dependence fostered from economic and ideological needs), broadcast journalists are often quick to accept official designations of which nations are friends and which nations are enemies and to interpret global events accordingly. Such an interpretation can be problematic.

Because the American press utilizes extremely advanced communications technologies that allow information to be quickly transferred over great distances, Americans often value finding out immediately about an international event over being well-informed on that event. But the constraints of the American press system lead to a relatively simplified view of international events no matter how quickly they are "discovered." The following critical analysis of press coverage of the Iran hostage crisis from 1979 to 1981 demonstrates the results of eschewing the complexity of an international event in favor of a simple dramatic story. It also reveals the extent to which American audiences were mobilized by the supposedly objective news media against citizens of another nation on the basis of very little information. This analysis illustrates the need for a closer reading of international news stories. It also presents the need for the availability of comparative sources of international news from foreign capitals so that audiences in the U.S. can contrast approaches to the same news events.

On November 4, 1979 the U.S. embassy in Teheran was occupied by Iranian revolutionaries and American hostages were taken. The revolutionaries demanded that their deposed ruler, Mohammed Reza Shah Pahlavi, who had recently received asylum in the U.S., be returned to Iran for trial. The hostages were to be exchanged for the Shah. For over a year the hostages were held in Iran while negotiations stopped and started between the two nations. During that period the American press—both print and broadcast journalism—created and fueled a national obsession about the hostage's release.

Regular reporting by the American press on the Iranian revolution began in January 1978.[40] The general journalistic interpretation of events confirmed by State Department officials, interviewed on television and in print, was that religious extremists opposed the Shah's attempts to modernize Iran.[41] The inability of the American press to articulate the reasons for opposition to the Shah's modernization process was instrumental in creating an oversimplified view of events surrounding the embassy takeover.

For the most part, American journalists are generalists who move from story to story around the world. Because timeliness is an important American news value, little background research can be done on a story before it is released. Instead, journalists attempt to fit present-day events into an easily understandable narrative. In Western Europe journalists that cover international news are often assigned to a region of the world for many years and are expected to know a great deal about its history as well as speak its language. These standards are not commonly practiced in contemporary American journalism.

Unfamiliar with the intricacies of Iranian history, unable to speak Farsi, and without reliable sources cultivated by years of living and travelling in the region, most American journalists assigned to the hostage crisis story knew little about Iran in particular and little about

Moslem societies and Islamic culture. If they had travelled to Iran before the revolution, most spoke primarily to Americans working there and were referred to members of the English-speaking Iranian elite who were often part of the Shah's coterie.[42] Gifts and lavish entertainment were rewards given to those who wrote favorably about the Shah.[43] The view of the Shah that emerged was that of a benevolent but strict patriarch leading his backward children into the enlightenment of Westernization. Unable to communicate with intellectuals and religious leaders who were part of the opposition, journalists were unable or unwilling to clearly see or communicate the view that the Shah was a pawn of the U.S. government, and a brutal dictator who was replacing Islamic culture with Western materialism. Even after the Shah was deposed, the positive view remained largely unchallenged in the U.S. press. The history of American involvement with Iranian politics—particularly after the Second World War—was ignored by most journalists and certainly never became part of the common knowledge of the situation for most of the American audience. The strategic nature of Iran's 1,600 mile border with the USSR as a motivation for years of American intervention was scarcely mentioned. The fact that the U.S. government played a leading role in putting the Shah's father in power and keeping him there in the face of opposition during the 1950s and 1960s rarely entered most reports.[44] The fact that the Shah's modernization was in the areas of military and technology rather than health and social services was also largely ignored, as were the restrictions on freedom of speech, the press, and lawful assembly. Instead the immediate interpretation of the embassy takeover was that it was the irrational, illegal act of religious fanatics and that the U.S. could not give in to "blackmail" by scoundrels. Further, the U.S. had to protect its ally, the Shah—whom U.S. diplomats had already forgiven for any possible excesses and errors of judgment—rendering a trial unnecessary from an American point of view.[45] Instead of trying to explain the complexity of the situation that had precipitated the crisis, the U.S. press opted to create unity among citizens around the U.S. government position that the hostages must be released without turning over the Shah. Of course, given the sources of information and the reporting habits of the American press, such a development in reportage was hardly surprising. In order to promote this reductive view of the hostage crisis American journalists portrayed a fight between good and evil pitting modern American secular beliefs and customs against primitive Islamic beliefs and customs. The point here is not that taking hostages was legitimate or should be condoned in any way, but that such a simplistic view of a complex historical problem did not help the American audience to understand why the Iranian revolutionaries acted as they did.

The American audience responded with shock and surprise to what seemed an irrational attack on the U.S. embassy and readily accepted the view that revolutionary Iranians were Marxist-inspired religious zealots who opposed modernization and wished to return to an ancient repressive Islamic past.[46] Paradoxically, few questioned the emergent modernist politics of Marxism in relation to Islamic beliefs and customs. Hence, the anti-American sentiments apparent in 1979 seemed irrational and mean-spirited to the American audience.

Critical theorists Miles Breen and Farrell Corocran explain the mythic dimensions given to the hostage crisis by the American press during the year the hostages were held. "The ethnocentric view of the American news media is fundamentally dualistic, resting on a series of mythic polarities which oppose the pure 'we' to the evil 'they'."[47] Edward Said's analysis is pertinent here. "While 'we' were 'normal', 'they' displayed 'neurotic' moral fervor and writhed in 'self-provoked frenzy, longing for martyrdom.' Iran was reduced to the 'rage of thwarted religious passion' and 'Islam amok.' While 'we' were democratic and fair, 'they' were militant, dangerous, and anti-American."[48] Reducing a complex problem to a simple morality play made for easy reading and listening, but after 444 days of news coverage the audience still did not know much about what was going on.

One of the most ironic elements of the ordeal was the attempt by the Iranian revolutionaries holding the hostages to use the U.S. media's news values for their own ends. Many Iranian students were familiar with the structure and performance of American journalism. More Iranians attended U.S. universities than universities in Iran.[49] Sending students to school in the West was a way to promote westernization in Iran. The student revolutionaries treated American journalists as customers for newsworthy items and traded these items for time on U.S. national television to present their view of the Iranian revolution directly to the American viewer.[50] The student revolutionaries did not anticipate the American patriotic fervor that framed their halting attempts to be instructive. Reading English translations of prepared messages, dressed in traditional Iranian clothing, the students usually became perceived as threatening examples of the "other." The American audience proved largely unreceptive to the Iranian student's presentations of the revolution. National loyalty swept away the notion of hearing the other side—at least when it was presented by the other side rather than by American journalists.[51]

The intense mobilization of public opinion by the news media may have actually limited the government's ability to negotiate for the hostage's release. News reports accompanied by images of crowds chanting and unfamiliar religious rites heightened feelings of separateness. The more threateningly the enemy was portrayed the less able the audience was to settle for anything less than their total capitulation. Appeals by the Carter administration to downplay coverage of the event were interpreted as infringements of journalist's first amendment rights.[52] It certainly appears in retrospect that the U.S. press' reduction of the events in Iran to a good-evil dichotomy narrowed the range of debate not only in the public sphere but in Congress as well. It was not until late in the first full year of the crisis that Congress began to realize that the Iranian revolution was not communist-inspired and that Iranians had compelling historical reasons to distrust Soviets almost as much as they distrusted Americans.[53]

When Iran finally capitulated and released the hostages without the return of the Shah in January 1981, the press declared, during the coverage of the ticker tape parade marking their triumphant return home, that "the national nightmare was finally over." Certainly 444 days of captivity was a personal nightmare for each American hostage and their families back home. But the "national nightmare" was created by the press itself.

How can people guard against being swept away by sensational stories about occurrences in places of which they have little knowledge about or understanding of? How can readers or listeners verify international news stories and achieve a balanced view of world events? First of all people must insist on access to international news that is not solely driven by a competitive market place. It would be in the best interests of the nation for citizens, including politicians, to have access to news broadcasts from foreign capitals, either translated, dubbed or subtitled. Both the Public Broadcasting Service (PBS) and National Public Radio (NPR) news programs should continue to expand their attention to international news (admittedly difficult in the face of budget constraints) and should include more interpretations of international events by foreign journalists. Cable News Network (CNN) is now proving that in-depth, extensive news coverage far beyond the scope and practices of the broadcast networks is both popular and profitable. Schools should encourage students to listen to foreign news broadcasts on shortwave radio. Even listening to a potentially strident broadcast such as Radio Beijing can inform students as to the vast array of decisionmaking and points of view that the rest of the world, for better or worse, brings to journalism. The point is not to listen or view foreign broadcasts in order to become indoctrinated, but in order to become informed as to how others—including journalists—interpret the world. Such an understanding has an indirect effect on the understanding of the American press; by hearing how the rest of the world does journalism, students become aware that the journalistic process, no matter the nation of its origin, is rife with decisions, ideologies, tastes, and nuances as well as "truth."

Americans operate under the illusion that they are the most well-informed citizenry on earth, because of the wealth of channels of information. But there is a great deal of similarity among the various channels of print and broadcast journalism, and there is little opportunity to hear the channels of other nations regarding international events. This is the inverse of most other nations and regions of the world, where the proximity of nations and their smaller size make the flow of broadcast signals and print across borders a commonplace occurrence. The fact that the U.S. is a media self-sufficient nation serves citizens well at the national level. The monolingualism (which may be changing) of American culture promotes national understanding. But internationally, our self-sufficiency and monolingualism are limiting.

In 1840 Alex DeTocqueville published *Democracy in America*. DeTocqueville observed "An American should never be allowed to speak of Europe, for he will then probably display a vast deal of presumption and very foolish pride. He will be content with those crude and vague notions which are so useful to the ignorant all over the world. But if you question him about his own country, the cloud which dimmed his intelligence will immediately disperse; his language will become clear and as precise as his thoughts."[54] Over a century later DeTocqueville's words still ring true, not only for perceptions of Europe but also for the rest of the world.

Although a critical examination of American network news and international affairs can sometimes leave an individual with the lingering question "what is to be done?" there are in fact a number of measures that can be accomplished in gathering a critical knowledge about the reception of international news. The proliferation of cable television in the U.S. has led to incredible increases in the demand for programming, and news is no exception. This demand is opening new channels for viewers to see news coverage from other nations. For example, CNN offers compilation programs of various news stories gathered from around the world. The Soviet news program *Vremya* was broadcast briefly in January 1990 on the Chicago public (PBS) television station WTTW. For the first time, a significant portion of the American public has access—through cable, public television, and the video recorder—to see and hear how the rest of the world tells the story.

Further use of the video recorder can be made on American news broadcasts. One interesting and revealing exercise can be to videotape the coverage of a story over several weeks, then compile that coverage and watch it unfold. Although it is true that to pull a single story out of the broadcast for close examination is to break from the typical viewing experience, such a break holds the potential to understand more about the story itself as well as offer a glimpse into the structure of news operations. Yet another enlightening exercise is to tape all three networks on a typical newsday (the same can be done with local news), then compare story selection and order of presentation—and this can be taken one step further by comparing those presentations with a newspaper published the same day.

Students and teachers would do well to consider these and other exercises that allow for dissection and analysis of the newsmaking process. In taking apart the news, we expose its seams and become better aware that, despite appearances, television news is not an effortless operation but is rather a highly crafted and sophisticated product. Just as the auto mechanics class gains a greater knowledge by taking apart the engine to demystify the process of internal combustion, or the biology class learns from dissecting a frog, so too can English, humanities, and media classes take apart the evening news and thereby gain greater knowledge.

CHAPTER FOUR

DRUG ABUSE, RACE RELATIONS, AND THE PRIME TIME NEWS PROGRAM

co-authored with Ronald B. Scott

While television news routinely plays upon dominant cultural values, and asks viewers to continue adjusting and accepting representations of an ongoing worldview, the network news special reports and in-depth analyses offered during evening prime time hours shift the relationships between viewers and television journalism. In the presentation of prime time specials as well as in regular prime time network news shows such as *60 Minutes, 20/20, Saturday Night With Connie Chung,* or *48 Hours,* viewers by and large consent to the implicit assertion that the airing of such programs in prime time viewing periods denotes a comprehensive, objective, fully-documented presentation of an important issue. What is all too often lost to critics and viewers in this process of validation through scheduling is the ongoing process of reification in news reporting—the resubstantiation of views and opinions believed by program creators to be representative of a majority of public opinion.

Although the prime time news special is nearly as old as network television itself (for example, the early work of Edward R. Murrow and Fred Friendly at CBS), the past ten years have witnessed a steady growth in this format for presenting television journalism. It is probably safe to assume that this approach is here to stay. A number of factors have contributed to the increased appearance of this program form, including such phenomena as the ongoing reporting of the Iran hostage crisis from 1979 to 1981 (which also helped create the ABC late-night news program *Nightline*); the viability of all-news cable services such as CNN; the overall growth of network news departments (despite occasional and well-publicized cutbacks); a growing tendency for local news services (as well as national networks) to devote more time to election coverage, including primaries and non-Presidential election years; and the increasing sophistication and availability of electronic news-gathering (ENG) equipment such as the minicam and the satellite, offering an ease of both news gathering and news dissemination from any point on the globe.

Furthermore, the overall scope of television programming during the 1980s saw rapid growth in a wide variety of "nonfiction" programming—an admittedly ambiguous term, but used here to include an array of supposedly nondramatic programming including daytime shows such as *Divorce Court, The Judge,* and *People's Court;* a multitude of cable networks, from the aforementioned CNN to networks such as Discovery, The Learning Channel, or the Weather Channel; the mercurial televangelists; the talk show phenomenon; and the recent surfacing in prime time network television and prime time syndication of such programs as *Hard Copy, A Current Affair, Rescue 911, D.E.A., Cops, Inside Edition, H.E.L.P., Unsolved Mysteries,* and *America's Most Wanted.* This is not to suggest that these aforementioned programs strictly adhere to the popular or professional conception of "news": it is instead to point out that in the past ten to fifteen years American viewers have been presented with an ever-increasing range of non-fiction programming outside of the realm of the regular evening network news broadcast. The increasing presence of the prime time network news special is also part of a wide-ranging change in the general scope of television programming.

When the familiar faces and personnel of the evening network news broadcasts appear in the less familiar ground of the prime time viewing hours, they carry with them their implicit role as commentators and validators of public opinion and urgent social problems. It is with these journalists, above all others (at least in commercial American television programming), that the values of objectivity, fairness, and truth are most convincingly projected to audiences. Although most members of the viewing audience have achieved the sophistication to recognize that the nonfiction or documentary form often has a persuasive dimension, this recognition is too often forgotten or ignored by audiences viewing prime time news specials. In other words, while audiences are capable of recognizing the potential persuasive nature of the nonfiction and supposedly objective program form, the actual engaging of that recognition during any particular moment of the viewing process remains largely indeterminable. Therefore, the recognition factor for most viewers is probably not a constant act but a shifting awareness, akin to a flickering candle. Once an event is placed within the context of a nightly news program, and subsequently appears in a prime time news special, the very magnitude of the problem and its terms of definition are affirmed. A particular social issue can be elevated to a level of consciousness that not only makes it appear worthy of serious attention, but legitimizes the public need and right to immediately respond and perhaps remove a blight on an otherwise tranquil national horizon.

As a way of demonstrating this process, this chapter focuses on a specific issue—drug abuse—as it works its way through regular evening news broadcasts and into a special prime time news report. One prime time report by ABC, *The Koppel Report—D.C./Divided City*, is discussed and analyzed in detail. After analyzing this program, the chapter concludes by discussing the implications of this process of prime time news reporting for critical viewers.

Drug abuse is continuously presented as the latest blight on the American horizon, both in news and special reports. Due to a lack of historical context, reporting on the drug story often seems to give the impression that the plague of drugs has reached such epic proportions that at any moment the entire country will either be forced to live in a violent society created by dealers and addicts or become the subjects of an amoral foreign drug cartel that is uncontrollably forcing its products upon an innocent American citizenry. Drug abuse has bridged the gap between American domestic problems and American foreign policy, most recently in the invasion of Panama by American troops ostensibly to remove a major international figure in the world of drug abuse (Manuel Noriega) from a position of power. The reportage surrounding the drug abuse story has taken on the trappings of an ever-widening narrative encompassing nightly gang wars, million dollar transactions, manhunts, glamorous lifestyles, and zombie-like users. Such narrative elements within the reportage increasingly lead to conclusions that mandatory testing, profile stops on interstate highways, embargoes and invasions of other nations, segregation and isolation of users and pushers, and "zero-tolerance" seizures of property might be the most reasonable—indeed, the only—options for controlling the drug problem. Viewers are presented with the dilemma of trading constitutional rights for the promise of security. The trade value of the proposed exchange is potentially skewed by the presentations of the drug problem, presentations that often favor drama over comprehensiveness and strictly defined, immediate law-enforcement solutions in favor of evolving, long-term social and cultural solutions.

A complicating factor in the drug abuse story has been the intertwining of race with the drug story. Specifically, the urban black male has become a leading character in the drug narrative. Serving simultaneously as both villain and victim, the urban black male is often represented as the predator of domestic drug abuse, the go-between for the foreign supplier and the user, adding drugs to his criminal litany and/or gang activities. Yet the urban black male is also represented as the prey, the target, metaphorically trapped in an environment where confrontation and eventual submission to his criminal counterpart/ blood brother is narratively inevitable. Adding to the tragedy is the fact that the narrative dichotomy begins at a very early age, in grammar school and on the playgrounds, working its way up through the rest of inner city life.

In fact, the image of the black male as drug abuser has its roots in the years just after the American Civil War. David Musto contends in *The American Disease* that postwar violence against recently freed blacks escalated in the South coinciding with the advancement of an argument by whites that access to narcotics by blacks might embolden blacks and escalate racial confrontations by giving blacks the courage to "fight back." The unfounded speculation about a drug-induced black rebellion served as a rationale for suppression of blacks by whites. Cocaine became the tonic most often feared as having the potential to set off a black revolt. One contemporary myth even suggested cocaine gave black men the power to stop bullets. Thus the notion of the drug abuser became tied to the black community as a way of enforcing racial hierarchies and promoting separation.[1] Troy Duster suggests that in the latter half of the 1800s drug addiction was approximately eight times more prevalent among urban populations (and primarily an activity of middle and upper class whites) than was the case in the 1960s. Addiction was not considered the social anathema it is today, and narcotics often made up some of the ingredients in a variety of over-the-counter medications, soft drinks, and other consumer products. In the early 1900s this relaxed moral attitude toward drugs began to shift toward prohibition.[2]

The recurring conflation of the drug abuse narrative with the mediated image of the black urban male is particularly alarming in that it tends to cast the domestic causes of the drug problem at the feet of racial minorities. This negative aspect of media portrayal—that racial minorities are largely to blame for their own problems—can be traced in television journalism back to the reporting surrounding the American civil rights movement of the 1960s, particularly when the black consciousness movement migrated out of the rural south into the urban areas of the entire nation. The wholesale laying of responsibilities upon racial minorities for the current-day drug problem leads to a melding of issues, a kind of social fusion where the drug problem is only the latest manifestation of the race problem, the "uncontrollable" blacks.[3]

It is supremely ironic and paradoxical that the civil rights movement of the 1960s now receives a new kind of historical respect and validation through such respected PBS documentary series as *Eyes on the Prize* while television evening news reports and specials repeatedly construct a narrative surrounding the contemporary drug problem that portrays the urban black male as a major perpetrator of the drug plague. The drug problem in the life of the contemporary urban black male—and it is indeed a problem—is not reported as the latest of obstacles tied to a rich history of black achievement over seemingly insurmountable problems. Instead, the problem remains ahistoricized, a rationale for mistrust and the loss of personal rights and freedoms. These tensions, interactions, and contradictions are visible in an analysis of *The Koppel Report—D.C./Divided City.*

On the night of April 27, 1989, ABC aired a prime time news documentary titled *D.C./Divided City.* The host of this one hour program was veteran television journalist Ted Koppel. *D.C./Divided City* was later followed by a special town meeting on the late evening ABC news show *Nightline.* As the title of the show implied, the show would focus on the nation's capital, Washington D.C., and an array of problems that have divided the city into two discrete populations along racial lines. The report began by suggesting that the entire nation experienced similar problems to those found in the nation's capital, and that Washington D.C. was an effective microcosm for understanding the various problems of drugs and racism that confront the nation. The rationale of the capital as microcosm was narratively compelling. If the problems of drugs cannot effectively be addressed in the nation's seat of power, then by extension what element of American society could lay claim to be effectively dealing with the problems? As the national center for such federal drug enforcement organizations as the Federal Bureau of Investigation, the Drug Enforcement Agency, and the Bureau of Alcohol, Tobacco, and Firearms, as well as the headquarters for the newly appointed drug czar William Bennett, the program's geographic location carried significant weight for national viewers. The major narrative motivating force, set up early in the program, was that the one element dividing the city, and by implication dividing the nation, was the widespread use, abuse, and sale of drugs.[4]

While drugs alone may be enough to divide any community, *D.C.: Divided City* went one step further by introducing the issue of racism as another major dividing factor in the capital district. The choice of Washington as a typical example of the problems confronting the U.S., and especially its black population, appeared well-reasoned. If, despite the resources and talent in the district and its place as the heart of the nation's government and judicial systems, problems of race could still not be transcended, could any other city or region in the nation hope to transcend its own particular manifestations of problematic race relations? Yet the result of introducing the race issue is an implicit bonding of the problems of drug abuse and the problem of race relations. An examination of the program reveals that the linking of these two issues in some ways leads to an implicit conclusion that argues for the continued, if not enhanced, division of the nation—a conclusion markedly at odds with the ostensible aims and goals of the program.

In the program's opening scenes, shots of a black tour guide pointing out the sites to a busload of white tourists are intercut with shots of a black police officer. This police officer symbolically serves as Koppel's—and by extension the audience's—tour guide. The officer directs attention to various drug havens and discusses the influx of drugs into his own patrol beat. After a sequence of cutaways and narrative bits that depict this drug-infested area, Koppel returns to the screen, shown standing on a street corner, to deliver this message:

> Only blocks from the Capitol eleven-year old boys stand watch for fifteen-year old drug dealers who are guarded by seventeen-year old enforcers who kill on behalf of a twenty-four year old drug king pin. The year is not yet four months old and already more than 150 people have died in drug-related violence. Almost all of them were black. This is *D.C.: Divided City.*

With this narration, the notion of drug abuse being a problem in which all of us participate begins to shift. Now it is a problem which "concerns" us all—but at least in the visual imagery of this program —a problem in which blacks and blacks alone are the overwhelming participants. To add to the impression that the active participation in drug abuse activity is confined to one segment of the population, additional images of the black community and a series of sound bites that all relate to drugs, violence, or police intervention follow Koppel's opening narration. Koppel then suggests that if one were to place a grid over the district, most of the violence would be confined to the predominantly black neighborhoods. Koppel returns onscreen to conclude this opening sequence with:

> Good evening. Much of what you'll see has to do with drugs, violence, money, and young people...threads lead back to the Kerner Commission Report twenty-one years ago that...white society is deeply implicated in the ghetto. White institutions created it. White institutions maintain it and white society condones it.... What we are about to see may appear to be just a black problem: it is not.

On the one hand, the script does hint that racism is a factor leading to division of the district and by extension the nation, and suggests that the implication of white institutions in the living conditions of urban blacks means that the drug problem is at least indirectly tied to the white community. However, the images of this opening sequence tend to suggest to viewers that the violence, the crime, and the deepest tragedies of drug abuse are contained within the black community, thereby raising the specter of de facto segregation as a sort of picket fence containing the spread of the drug problem. This may undercut the initial idea that "dividedness" is itself a problem. Instead it may lead to the conclusion that dividedness may be socially undesirable but nevertheless serves a practical function of containment and safety for the (white) majority in the face of the (black) drug issue. One is left to wonder whether Koppel's verbal insistence that the program is not only about black problems is sufficient to counter the visual imagery of this opening sequence.

The contradiction of the opening sequence contains the problems that pervade the entire program and, by extension, the failure of the drug abuse story across the landscape of television news. It fails to clearly demonstrate that the relation of the drug problem to the African-American community is in many ways only a symptom, only the latest manifestation, of the larger historical problem of race relations. The drug problem is not presented as one of the most recent of a legacy of seemingly insurmountable obstacles that blacks have faced in the history of American social relations. Instead, drugs *are* the isolated, decontextualized problem and if they could only be eliminated from the ghetto, somehow the district and the nation would automatically become a more unified place. The relative absence of white victims, users, and pushers on the screen tends to identify the drug problem as a black problem. By extension, intentionally or not, it also suggests that white avoidance of the black community is tantamount to protecting whites from drug abuse.[5] The result is a new sense of dividedness, an unspoken assumption that the district is divided between black users, pushers, and victims against white nonusers whose larger social system is threatened by this racially marked drug problem.

Following this introduction, *D.C./Divided City* consists of two sections. The first half focuses on the effects of drug-related violence and drug addiction on a black neighborhood. This section also includes attempts by local residents to cope with the drug problem. During the second half of the program, the topic shifts more directly to issues of race relations.

Through three vignettes, the first half explores drug problems in the Anacostia neighborhood of Washington. The first vignette opens with a scene of a young man lying dead on the street while his mother, restrained by the police, cries hysterically. Certain shots of this scene had been previously shown in the opening sequence. In a voiceover Koppel tells the audience that similar scenes of death and despair are being acted out all over the nation. As the young man's story unfolds, Koppel interviews his mother. Koppel talks of her son's involvement in the drug business and identifies the murderer as an employee of the Edmunds family. The mother appears not to know what he is talking about. Whether she is simply naive or unwilling to acknowledge the depth of her son's activities remains unclear.

The Edmunds family is described as a successful drug organization headed by another young black man. Each member of the family is identified for viewers through a wedding photograph. As each person's role in the organization is described, cutaways show the results of their enterprise—more young black men either dead on the street or under arrest. It is revealed that the Edmunds family paid for luxury autos, houses, vacations, and other desirable commodities with drug profits and provided these items as perks for faithful employees. Koppel mentions that some members of the Georgetown University basketball team socialized with Edmunds. As another cutaway shows young blacks dancing at a nightclub, a voiceover describes the club as a frequent gathering spot for black college students, basketball players, and drug dealers. Georgetown basketball coach John Thompson is also interviewed. Thompson explains that upon learning of his players' association with a supposed drug dealer, the coach arranged a meeting with Edmunds to voice his concern for the safety of his players. The vignette concludes with a scene of the arrest of the Edmunds family in a recent drug bust carried out by Washington district police, the FBI, and the DEA.

The second vignette explores the worlds of two young black women who are drug addicts. The first woman is interviewed as she leaves her children with her sister and enters a drug treatment program. As she describes her foray into prostitution as a way to get money for drugs, her sister comments how the children had been left to wander the streets alone at night. The doctor in the treatment program identifies her as a second generation drug user, a multiple substance abuser, a high school dropout, and an unwed mother. The second woman, whose whereabouts are unknown, has left her children with her mother who now cares for them. The youngest child has tested HIV positive, increasing the likelihood that the child will eventually contract AIDS. First Lady Barbara Bush is shown holding this child at the special home where he must be kept, and the grandmother praises the efforts of Mrs. Bush in dealing with this problem.

The last vignette is about two community volunteers, middle-aged black men nicknamed Uncle Skeezy and Peter Bug. These men are shown talking with elementary school children, trying to convince them to avoid drugs, get a good education, and become gainfully employed. The men and Koppel agree about the need to reach children and instill good values before "it's too late." They express concern that children may become addicted to making money and that may, in their own minds, justify their becoming involved in the drug business.

During the second half of the program, the focus shifts more centrally to race relations. Black churchgoers hear a sermon about "American-style apartheid" as an opening to this segment. In a voiceover, Koppel discusses the high infant mortality rates among black children and high homicide rates among black adults while viewers see shots of hospitalized children and the bodies of murdered young black males. A series of interviews with successful black professionals and businesspeople reveals their concern about de facto segregation in housing, the corporate world, and recreational facilities in Washington. They speak of an unfulfilled American Dream. The white chairman of a large bank struggles to explain why his firm has no black vice presidents. This segment eventually returns to the streets of Anacostia, where a resident explains that the drug business is one of the few ways for young blacks to become entrepreneurs and assume controlling interest in their own enterprises.

Finally, Koppel introduces a videotape produced by three black high school students. The students have tried to demonstrate how whites are fearful of young black men. In the video, the students stop whites on the street and ask for directions to the Corcoran Museum. Typical reactions of avoidance or inattention are shown. The students report on a sense of fear in many whites whenever they approached. *D.C./Divided City* concludes with Ralph Ellison's poem *The Invisible Man*—a poem also included in the student videotape.

The ways of reading *D.C./Divided City* are somewhat contradictory. On the one hand, viewers see how racial divisions are partially to blame for the current social condition of the community. Yet at the same time, not so much in its soundtrack but in its visual images, many of the shots and scenes seem to reinforce the perception of danger that surrounds blacks and their communities and the perception of safety through white avoidance. The introduction of a typology of familiar black media representational schemas—the dysfunctional black family, dangerous and irresponsible young black men, immoral young black women, enduring black mothers, and good-hearted but simplistic black uncles—becomes a weird kind of mediated historical legacy, reappearing as the contemporary reincarnations of ghosts from media culture past.[6]

Anacostia is represented as a neighborhood of chaos and confusion rather than stability and order. A mother is unaware of her murdered son's involvement in the drug business. A "fixture" of the community is a ruthless criminal family. The chaos reaches out beyond Anacostia, touching a basketball team and a nightclub. Despite the fact that black employment in Washington surpasses eighty percent of the adult male population (a figure that nevertheless could certainly stand improvement), the drug business is presented as the major substitute for business achievement by black males. Conversely, the fact that less than twenty percent of drug users nationwide are black goes by with scarcely a mention, and the equivalent visual representation of drug use in white neighborhoods and the suburbs is remarkable only through its structured absence.[7]

In the latter half of *D.C./Divided City,* as the focus shifts more squarely to race relations, the implicit message behind the interviews with successful blacks is that white society is desirable because it is—compared with Anacostia—drug and crime free. Anacostia, and by extension any urban black neighborhood, fails to become a challenge for all, white and black, to enter and transform. The finale with the student videotape brings the guilt and blame for a divided city to all community citizens regardless of color. Yet an effective argument for an end to racism cannot and should not primarily be based on white guilt and a plea to middle and upper class citizens for magnaminity. Like so much of the contemporary reportage of drug abuse and race relations, *D.C./Divided City* ultimately fails to show any significant positive value to be gained from an integrated culture or show compelling positive aspects of the current and historical American black experience.

ABC followed *D.C./Divided City* that evening with a special edition of its late-night news show *Nightline,* billed as a live town meeting of the air. The town meeting expanded the local examination of drug abuse and race relations in Washington to urban areas across the nation, including stories from Los Angeles, Denver, Chicago, Atlanta, and New York. Reports from these cities underlie the national, even international, scope of the drug problem. However, the reports had little, if anything, to say about race relations, further isolating the Anacostia experience and implicitly denying any national or international scope to problems of drug abuse, or race relations. The strongest link made in this opening segment was an implication that any large black urban population exacerbates our national drug problem.

The expanded coverage of the drug story began with local angles from Los Angeles, Denver, Atlanta, and New York. The first clip was from Los Angeles, where correspondent Ken Kashiwahara informed viewers that Los Angeles is "a city that has become the major distribution center for more than half the nation's cocaine." James Walker, reporting from Denver, added that the drug problem in Denver was largely attributable to imports of crack by drug gangs from Los Angeles. Having established the West Coast distribution center, the focus shifted to Atlanta, which Jackie Judd described as "a major stopping point along the cocaine corridor...vast supplies come up from Miami." Jeff Greenfield reported that in New York the major problem was the "sheer size" of demand for illicit drugs. These segments work toward reinforcing the national nature of the drug problem, with Koppel later adding that the town meeting is held not only "to talk only about drugs and violence in Washington.... The problem is a national one, Washington has merely become the symbol."

Paradoxically, questions of race relations are left out of these various correspondent reports, despite their foregrounding in the Washington-based examination. Nothing in the four news reports reminded viewers of the evening's expressed dual purpose of exploring issues along with drug abuse that divide cities. Implicit, however, is the linkage between the urban inner city and the core of the national drug problem, again sidestepping suburban and rural drug abuse and suggesting the bonds between illegal drug behavior and urban black society. A bit later in this segment, Chicago correspondent Judd Rose, in response to a question by Koppel, goes so far as to assert that the Chicago drug problem has whites only tangentially involved in drug trafficking, with blacks and Hispanics controlling most of the trade. The overall impact is to suggest to the viewer that drugs are exclusively in the control of blacks and other minorities, and therefore it is those minorities who are responsible for the spread of drugs and accompanying violence. Blacks become the veiled yet real "threat" to the security of American whites.

The national town meeting segment, done live from Washington, immediately followed this series of reports from urban centers around the nation. The location of the town meeting was a church in the Anacostia neighborhood with several hundred people in attendance, ranging from local neighborhood residents to a number of representatives of the Washington black community—educators, police personnel, corrections officials, DEA agents, members of the Nation of Islam, National Guard officers, members of Alcoholics Anonymous, directors of various drug treatment programs, community organizers, and local as well as national politicians. Ted Koppel, serving as host and moderator, occupied a central location on an elevated platform with guests and the audience around him. Koppel proved to be less a facilitator of open discussion than a motivator for rapid action and immediate, brief dialogue. For example, in discussion with Washington Mayor Marion Barry, Koppel asks "Who is to blame for the drug problem?" When Barry responds theoretically that all of us are to blame, Koppel replies there is no "time for generalities," asking the mayor to "point to one, two, three segments of society that are to blame."

This tendency to direct rather than facilitate dialogue was evident in a number of instances. When audience criticism turned to *D.C./Divided City*, with a high school principal expressing concern over the visual imagery of young black people destroying the neighborhood and by implication the entire district, Koppel replies she has "got it backward" in reference to her interpretation of the program. Koppel also exhorted the audience to strictly adhere to the demands of commercial television, reminding speakers to "make it quick, we have about forty-five seconds before the commercial break."

After a thirty minute pause for local news broadcasts by ABC owned-and-operated stations and ABC affiliates, Koppel and *Night-*

line returned with Secretary of Housing and Urban Affairs Jack Kemp and drug czar William Bennett as town meeting guests. After instructing the church attenders to use the half-hour with Kemp and Bennett productively, he then turned to Kemp and Bennett for opening comments by both men. When Bennett criticized *D.C./Divided City* for its somewhat negative portrayal of the black community, reminding Koppel that the majority of black people in Anacostia and Washington are law abiding citizens who work hard for a living, Koppel told Bennett he "missed the point...(we are) not representing a profile of the city of Washington (but) a profile of drug violence in the city of Washington." In his role as active interventionist and moderator, Koppel also pushed for a passive viewer with a singular, narrow, "correct" reading of *D.C./Divided City* rather than an active and critical viewer with broad, multiple readings—even when that viewer might be William Bennett.

When Kemp and Bennett finished, Koppel selected audience members to stand up and speak. If a person raised their voice and began to speak in a cadence familiarly associated with black religious rhetoric, Koppel interrupted and insisted that they be brief and ask a question of Bennett or Kemp. During the course of this segment, Koppel controlled the discussion with phrases like:

> Sir, if everyone gets up and gives a speech here, maybe five people will have a chance to speak...you're not asking a question...forgive me, but I want to take advantage of the time these gentlemen are giving us.... I think there's a question mark at the end of that...we are going to have chaos here if we don't establish some kind of order.... I'm going to give you a chance to raise your questions, if possible, but we still have to take commercial breaks. That's one of the imperatives of television.... If it's just going to be the people with the loudest lungs, then I've got the mike, OK?... Folks, don't be naive about it, that's how commercial television works.

Ostensibly, Koppel is being a tough but fair moderator, controlling a potentially unpredictable and unruly audience and forcing them to abide by the structure of commercial television. But the subtext presumes that the audience will be unruly and that only a certain kind of rhetorical behavior is appropriate. The insistence on questions to Kemp and Bennett tends to effectively force speakers to constantly yield the floor in favor of government officials who correct the audiences's supposed misconceptions and refocus attention on official government policy. Statements of personal belief or attempts by others to move beyond questions into statements and positions of their own rhetorical strategies are repeatedly construed as bad manners, a lack of respect to authority, or a feeble understanding of the inviolability of the paradigms of commercial television programming. Despite the location of the town meeting in a black neighborhood, in a black church, in the midst of black citizens and community workers, the rules of rhetoric are brought in from the outside.

Here, at the town meeting, the representational system is the inverse of sound and image in *D.C./Divided City*. Formerly, the image track depicted the violence and despair of the black urban experience while the soundtrack suggested this was a problem in part fostered by the white community. Yet in the town meeting, the visual track shows the earnestness, the sincerity, the urgency sensed by the black community as they truly attempt to engage this problem in a sensible manner based on their own rhetorical culture and experiences, while the soundtrack, in part through the interventionism of Koppel, presents the meeting as teetering on the edge of chaos. The strict preservation of order and the efficient management of time take precedence over the emancipation of black voices to national audiences.

Throughout the rest of the evening, voices grew in emotion and questions concerning race, class, and even genocide became more common. Koppel and ABC news producers continued to rein in the action in favor of order and time management. This was done through Koppel himself (when asked why ABC showed one hour of blacks killing blacks, Koppel replied "you must have been watching another program"), commercial breaks, cutaways to correspondent reports in other cities, and finally a rerun of the student video from *D.C./Divided City*. At the end of the town meeting, a woman is called on who identifies herself as a former drug addict and ex-convict. She says her oldest son was recently killed in a drug-related incident. Declaring the problem is "on the inside, not the outside," she goes on to describe her attempts to be a productive member of society, saying she does not need welfare, just to believe in herself. Allowed to go beyond the usual thirty to forty-five seconds of most other speakers, she speaks emotionally on the power of self-improvement as cutaways to women in the audience show several of them wiping tears from their eyes and cheeks. As she finished her soliloquy, Koppel concluded the town meeting with:

> Folks, do me a favor and sit down. There is one thing I've learned in twenty-six years in the business. Every once in a while somebody says it like it is. There is not much point in saying any more. This lady has wrapped it up.

With this wrap-up, Koppel wipes away the earlier accusations of genocide and race/class struggle, as well as the implication of government and social institutions in maintaining racial inequities. The victim is left to assume the blame for the drug problem and the victim's self-therapeutic ability is offered as the only solution. This may have been a convenient, entertaining, even compelling, exit for a television program. The audience was left to wonder if it was a fitting conclusion to the examination of a significant social problem.

Our analysis of *D.C./Divided City* and subsequent programming by ABC is not some attempt on our part to denigrate the news division at ABC, Ted Koppel, or other participants in program creation. Indeed, ABC deserves support for tackling this thorny issue. However, our analysis does reveal in detail how the ideological biases and exigencies of American commercial television operate to produce a representation of reality that tends to reinforce and reestablish existing social and political structures of inequality, even in cases when the ostensible intentions of program creators and news personnel are to question and perhaps even undermine those unequal structures. In the case of *D.C./Divided City*, viewers are presented with an intellectual argument to end racism but simultaneously with an emotional argument that justifies the safety of separation. The viewer can hold an intellectual affinity to the elimination of racial oppression and injustice while simultaneously reinforcing, in large part through visual imagery, perceptions of the security derived from racial separation.[8] The end result is stasis.

Understanding and analyzing how television news reinforces and reestablishes existing social and political structures of inequality can lead to pessimistic judgments of the social value of television news. However, a critical citizenship and active engagement with media culture and the viewing process implies a lifelong process of active questioning as a vital component of social change. Critical citizenship at its best does not end with pessimistic judgments, but rather moves beyond those judgments in hopes of stimulating the process of change. In the area of television news, critical citizenship on the part of viewers must be centrally occupied with the kind of active engagement and questioning demonstrated throughout the chapters on television journalism and in the above analysis of *D.C./Divided City*.

A part of critical citizenship in relation to media culture also means a viewership that regularly includes alternatives to network television news. As an example that can serve as an alternative to *D.C./Divided City*, early in 1990 the cable network Black Entertainment Television

(BET) aired a two-hour prime time special titled *Black Agenda 2000*. Structured with a moderator, a number of panelists, and a participatory audience, *Black Agenda 2000* opened with an exploration of the representation of blacks in the media, from news and non-dramatic programming to sitcoms and feature films. This initial premise instigated over two hours of discussion that often wandered from the original topic, yet returned to the question of black representation over and over again after rhetorical forays into questions concerning education, parenthood, economics, and the drug problem. At times the discussion grew somewhat chaotic; at times one or two commercial breaks were ignored; at times voices were raised as debates became heated; yet overall, this program showed a workable commercial alternative to the tight structure considered sacrosanct in ABC's town meeting.

Other such programs, often found on the cable rather than broadcast networks, also give evidence of alternatives to the network news structure for the critical viewer. An increasing utilization of toll-free "800" telephone numbers are allowing more viewers to call in and voice opinions on topics or to ask social and government leaders questions of concern. Cable channels such as C-SPAN are not only showing Congressional activities but also the proceedings of a number of conferences and meetings, providing access to in-depth discussions on a wide range of topics, with opinions of participants covering the political spectrum. Just as a critical readership in twentieth century American culture has often meant reading beyond the large daily newspapers and into the contents of a number of books and magazines of divergent political and social opinion, so too the critical viewer at the end of the twentieth century will probably move beyond the networks more and more regularly in search of alternative and partisan news and nondramatic programming.

Finally, a future of critical viewership for the first generations of the twenty-first century may include a more active role from the viewers themselves in contributing to both the sound and image tracks of television news. The ownership of video camcorders in the U.S. is, as of 1990, over ten percent of the population, and this figure will undoubtedly grow. Consumer equipment is already influencing newsgathering; many stations and networks have provisions for individuals to send in newsworthy material, such as CNN's "Newshound" service paying $125 for material used on the air. Of course, this participation by viewers in the program creation process is not limited to news. The most obvious instance of this practice is the remarkable popularity of *America's Funniest Home Videos*, an ABC show where people send in home tapes for potential national screening, and a program that following its premiere reached the top of national ratings in a matter of weeks. The success of this show has already spawned several inevitable spinoffs.

Granted, the banal and trivializing material screened on *America's Funniest Home Videos* is not the stuff of an active, critical viewership concerned with broad social change. Rather, we believe the program represents the tip of an iceberg in terms of the future potential for critical viewership evolving from an active engagement with the viewing process towards an equally active engagement with the production process. The rise of the camcorder and the surprising ease of entry for camcorder material into broadcast and cable television—from entertainment programming through news and including various cable access channels—presents an unexpected opportunity for a critical citizenry to engage a community dialogue through very powerful instruments of media culture. Cable access channels providing for public access are showing a steady rise in use across the country, and in a few instances (New York City) all available access time is filled.

Therefore, an active, engaging viewing process that is capable of multiple readings of television news (and other forms of television programming) is of great urgency, because it may well lead to the viewer as program creator. For students, a fluent grammar of media literacy holds the potential to empower themselves in the theory and practice of both the word and the image. This empowerment comes at a crucial time in the history of modern communications, at a time when established institutions of ideology and power—such as the television networks—are facing eroding audiences, increasing competition, and an increasing number of viewer alternatives. In light of all this, the future of American media culture remains more indeterminate than ever before. The empowerment of a young critical citizenry, fluent in the language of media, holds the potential to shift society away from the overdetermination of a dominant ideology in favor of the healthy indetermination of multiple points of view.

CHAPTER FIVE

POPULAR CULTURE AND THE PEDAGOGY OF FEMINISM

In the past decade, work in feminist media theory and criticism has been concerned with the representation of gender roles in a range of cultural artifacts—literature, film, television, magazines, recorded music, and advertising. These representations are seen to play a central role in structuring social subjectivity, not only in the range of roles they depict but also through their particular modes of rhetoric. In this regard, material aimed at predominantly female audiences has provided an area of major interest for feminist theorists. Women's pictures, melodrama (in film and television), and popular literary forms are privileged because they afford insight into the channelling of women's fantasies, potential avenues and strategies of protest, and the nature of women's voice within the confines of an otherwise male-oriented culture.[1]

As it emerges from the context of film studies, such work enacts, at a minimum, a double-edged intervention in the field. On the one hand, it has forced a shift in theory, insisting on the importance of sexual difference as it is figured in systems of representation, the construction/interpellation of the viewing subject, and formations of pleasure. Concomitantly, attention has focused on a range of previously ignored or disparaged works. This includes women directors (both within and outside the Hollywood studio system), and specific genres, most notably the melodrama, the women's picture, and television soap opera. The results of such inquiry has exposed the limits of previous modes and models of inquiry, and changed and augmented the objects that formerly were sanctioned as "valid" for scrutiny.

While the impetus for such work began in feminist film scholarship during the 1970s, scholars no longer limit themselves to film *per se.* Grounded in the broader perspective of feminism as cultural analysis, scholars have now also embraced other areas of mass culture as important avenues for elaborating the concerns originally raised in feminist film theory. This newer work has shared a concern for elucidating how television, popular literature, video art, and other artifacts of mass culture may negotiate the conflicts at stake in the construction, confirmation, and/or containment of women in patriarchal society. Such studies acknowledge that these artifacts, especially in genres such as the soap opera, carry the conservative, recuperative weight of patriarchy. But they also suggest that in addressing female audiences, these narratives must enact tensions specific to women and their experiences.[2] The works may be complicit, but in demonstrating the contradictory forces that position women and delimit their social roles, the texts can also express a critique of the very (conservative) system they ultimately serve.

A number of Hollywood films from the mid-1980s feature women as central characters in variations on the romance-adventure genre. In different ways these films engage recognized fantasy scenarios—women's fantasy scenarios—as a crucial agency of romantic adventure. This relationship is figured through the narrative prominence of a textual model serving as the basis for, and measure of, the fictional trajectory assumed by each film. The most obvious films in this respect are *Romancing the Stone* (1984), its sequel *Jewel of the Nile* (1985), and *American Dreamer* (1984). But this impulse also includes *Thief of Hearts* (1984), and *Desperately Seeking Susan* (1985). These films can be seen as the contemporary cinematic expression of mass-produced fantasies for women, reworking the classical Hollywood woman's picture refracted through the "new" woman's picture of the 1970s and the romance novel.[3]

To some extent these films can be construed as the popular expression of issues explored in recent feminist theory and criticism, particularly with regard to questions of fantasy, pleasure, and spectatorship. While the films in question do not decisively disrupt received forms of women's fantasy, romance, and pleasure within patriarchal culture, they do offer a markedly problematic version of these forms. On the one hand they attempt to construct, address, or fulfill the socially perceived and circumscribed demands of an audience with an increasingly feminist consciousness, as female protagonists are afforded narrative agency within fictions that engage strategies of self-conscious fictionality. At the same time the films can be seen in terms of postfeminist and neoconservative pressures, as the weight of narrative development hinges on and concludes in the formation of a traditionally conceived couple.

The films express contradictory tensions, as they emphasize the positivity of the heterosexual romantic couple which is at once an avowedly fictional model and the goal of the filmic fiction. Within the narrative, true love is proposed as the fulfilling choice of an independent heroine; but from a narrational perspective, true love functions as the structural/social constraint on her independence. The films thus negotiate a range of discrepant, multiple ideological positions. Insofar as they might be claimed, with relative ease, by both conservative and progressive interpretive positions, they exemplify the constitutive ambivalence of a cultural-representational system stretched to the limits. And in this they are not necessarily "unique," but are perhaps exemplary of the radical ambiguity of contemporary spectacle. A closer look at these films thus provides a case study in feminist analysis, exposing the tensions and contradictions generated in the context of a contemporary example of a mass-produced culture that is concerned with women's subjectivity. At the same time the analysis aims to describe the specificity of these films as products of recent American culture.

The emphasis on adventure and romance, along with the tendency to generate fictions based on preconstituted fictional models, marks a distance from the "new" women's picture of the 1970s, which encompasses such films as *Alice Doesn't Live Here Anymore* (1975), *An Unmarried Woman* (1978), *Girlfriends* (1978), and *It's My Turn* (1980). The 1970s films were embraced for offering ostensibly more "realistic" portrayals of women than that afforded by conventionally conceived Hollywood stereotypes. As Charlotte Brunsdon notes, "'70s heroines were, *at some level*, offered as representative of 'real'—natural as opposed to Hollywood—women."[4] While the terms of distinction here between "natural" and "Hollywood" women can only be taken as extremely relative, these films represent one effort to portray the concerns of an emergent popular feminism within commercial narrative cinema, however equivocal the results. Indeed, in her article, Brunsdon focuses on the problematic aspects of the films' construction of "appropriate modes of femininity in contemporary Western culture":

> The existence, and construction of [a] "new" female audience can only be properly understood in relation to a whole range of extra cinematic social, political, and economic patterns (for example, changing patterns of women's employment and education; increasingly effective and available contraception; the fall in the birthrate, with changing patterns of marriage and divorce; the impact of the Women's Liberation Movement itself) whose interplay is too complex to be investigated here. The cinematic history of these films lies partly with the "woman's pictures" of the '30s, '40s,

> and '50s, and, later, with the television soap-opera. Crucially, all these texts can be read to be concerned with the conflicting demands on, and contradictory and fragmented nature of, femininities construed within masculine hegemony (which is not to suggest that these texts are all reducible to the same concerns, or can be compared with "non-patriarchal" femininities).[5]

For example, Brunsdon argues that in *An Unmarried Woman* conflicting demands emerge in the film's negotiation of gender roles and their attendant social expression. Thus "the film is extremely ambiguous in its sexual politics—criticising the 'institution of marriage and taking the 'impossibility' of romance seriously, yet constructing an unmarried woman who signally fails to do anything but find another man."[6]

By contrast, films such as *Romancing the Stone, American Dreamer,* and *Thief of Hearts* reintroduce romance with a vengeance. However, romance here is inextricably bound up with the free choice exercised by a female protagonist and with preconstituted fictional texts. The question is whether free choice is construed as an effect of self-determination and individual discretion, or as a constraint of broader social and ideological forces; and whether the preconstructed fictional models are seen as an agency of social constraint, as an acknowledgment of women's pleasures and anxieties, or precisely as the singular site for representing the passivity of romance. Insofar as the films are able to sustain an equivocal position in relation to these questions—a constitutive undecideability, so to speak—they can neither be seen as a simple return to an oppressively monolithic "ideology of true love," nor be immediately interpreted as a liberating advance.

If the films of the 1980s are, like those of the 1970s, supremely ambiguous, there is a significant shift in the nature of the ambiguity at stake. In Brunsdon's terms the earlier films might be seen as operating according to a neither/nor logic: neither the ease of falling back on the institution of marriage or the eternal romantic couple, nor a reconceptualized reconstruction of conventional gender roles. In the more recent romance adventures, ambiguity is rewritten in terms of an all-inclusive both/and logic. Romance and marriage are represented as available and satisfying choices for a female protagonist who is able, nonetheless, to break out of conventional roles and exercise independence no matter what her initial status seems to be. Indeed, independence usually emerges in proportion to the ability and willingness to function in unusual ways in unforeseen circumstances.

Joan Wilder, the romance novelist in *Romancing the Stone,* is at first represented as timid, sentimental, and unenterprising. But in the jungles of Colombia she quickly learns to keep up with Jack Colton, the adventurer-hero, and demonstrates aggressive self-confidence dealing with hostile environments and strangers. She literally blossoms in the unfamiliar, tropical terrain. In the end she triumphs in a solo confrontation with the villain Zolo, forcing him to fall to his demise in an alligator pit. Meanwhile her "hero" struggles to hold the alligator, which has swallowed a precious emerald, then scales a wall to come to her rescue, only to arrive on the scene after Zolo has been overcome.

Cathy Palmer, the protagonist of *American Dreamer,* is introduced as a conventional middle-class housewife who dreams of visiting Paris. After she assumes the identity of Rebecca Ryan—the fictional adventuress-heroine of a series of popular novels—she proves to be a competent spy. The suspects and spy rings she generates in her amnesiac fantasy in fact turn out to be criminals and they expose their guilt under the pressure of her relentless accusations. Even after she regains consciousness of her identity as Cathy Palmer, she retains the adventuress' cunning, and is instrumental in conceiving a plan—borrowed from a Rebecca Ryan novel—that enables her and Alan McMann to escape from a drug dealer who is holding them captive and is planning to kill them.

In *Desperately Seeking Susan* Roberta Glass is an equally conventional, if somewhat dissatisfied, New Jersey housewife whose fantasies are vicariously sustained through personal classified ads and old movies on television. But when she is mistaken for the street-wise Susan, she successfully eludes a man who is trying to kill her (as Susan), even though she is hampered by a ridiculous costume and a bird cage and has to negotiate the unfamiliar terrain of lower Manhattan. Later, Roberta is instrumental in helping Susan finally capture the villain, while Susan's boyfriend, attempting to save Susan, shows up too late to be of any help.

These descriptions, however, are partially and significantly incomplete. Joan Wilder is stuck in the jungle in the first place because, upon her arrival in Colombia, she is too flustered to find the bus to Cartagena. Instead she follows misleading instructions offered by Zolo in the form of helpful advice. Hours later when she realizes she is on the wrong bus, she panics and confronts the driver. With this distraction he wrecks the bus and the natives all promptly disappear, leaving her in the middle of the jungle to face Zolo. It is at this juncture that Jack Colton first appears, to provisionally rescue her. Later she is persuaded by Jack to follow the treasure map rather than turning it over directly to her sister's kidnappers, even though Jack has already contrived to steal and photocopy the map for his own use in case she is unwilling to pursue the treasure with him. This occurs after she has been "feminized"/glamorized by Jack when they get to a village where they can bathe and relax, and he buys her a new outfit (and, of course, after they have slept together). In these instances she is subject to, and manipulated by, men in proportion to her "weakness" as a woman.

The female characters in *American Dreamer, Thief of Hearts,* and *Desperately Seeking Susan* are similarly constructed in ambivalent or alternating terms. Although they never simply submit to male domination within the narrative or to display for the camera, they are never decisively extricated from familiar mechanisms of narrative and representational control. As Cathy Palmer acts out the role of Rebecca Ryan, her detection successes are often comedically accidental. Dancing with the Spanish Ambassador, she discusses her fluency in a variety of languages, and offers a Nietzsche quote she previously heard at home on a language lesson tape: "What doesn't destroy me makes me stronger." The Ambassador, visibly shaken, retires to the bathroom in order to consult his code book and discovers that this particular quote is an order to terminate himself immediately. He injects himself with a drug, but is saved by Alan McMann in time to confess to his crimes. Indeed, the protagonists of *American Dreamer* and *Desperately Seeking Susan* are freed to act out unusual roles through the agency of decisive memory loss; a blow to the head that triggers amnesia. The suburban housewife must literally lose consciousness and assume a fictional persona so that when she regains consciousness of her proper self she will retrospectively reject the dissatisfactions of middle-class American life.

A schematic plot summary of the films results in familiar romance formulas. In *American Dreamer* and *Desperately Seeking Susan,* a suburban housewife undergoes a series of urban adventures and ends up leaving her husband for another man. The wife in *Thief of Hearts* has an adventurous affair only to rediscover the romance and value of her marriage. The heroine in *Romancing the Stone* finds true love with an adventurer-hero in an exotic locale. The sequel, *Jewel of the Nile,* extends this formula as Joan and Jack decide to provisionally separate to pursue individual interests, but are reunited for further adventures culminating in marriage.

However familiar these stories may be, the prominence of female subjects acting and choosing according to both/and logic offers an image of women who can have it all; an ideal female subject of postindustrial consumer society. In this the films not only revise the neither/nor ambiguity of the 1970s woman's film, but also offer a rewriting of the classical Hollywood woman's picture with its emphases on women who are punished for exhibiting strength and independence, or who are forced to make choices which require sacrificing their own interests in favor of their children, their husbands, or conventional stability.[7] The new heroine is not forced to submit to conflicting or restrictive choices, nor is she confined by conventional middle-class morality. On the contrary, she is rewarded for seeking something more, and the choice of an exciting male partner is represented as a class/lifestyle image which includes a decisive anti-middle-class bias. The demand for exciting, mutual romantic relationships is thus linked to a desire to escape the mundane routine of middle-class concerns with earning a living, maintaining a budget, and so forth.

In *Romancing the Stone*, Joan Wilder exhibits a distinct lack of interest in the men at a New York singles bar she goes to with her publisher, though earlier she toasts the shadowy figure of a western hero in a promotional poster for one of her own romance novels. The suited businessmen initially may seem more real than the fantasy poster hero, but they retrospectively pale in comparison to Jack Colton, the boyish adventurer who lives in the South American jungle scheming to get rich quickly so that he can buy a ship and spend his life sailing leisurely around the world. At the start of *Jewel of the Nile*, Joan's publisher warns her that Jack is not the marrying kind, and vocally disapproves of his behavior at a promotional affair for Joan's work. But if Jack and Joan aspire to something more than the routine of conventional domestic life, they are ultimately united in an exotic marriage ceremony after surviving yet another series of life-threatening adventures.

In *American Dreamer*, Cathy Palmer leaves her businessman husband for Alan McMann, the purported business manager for, but actually author of, the Rebecca Ryan novels, with whom she shares her fantasy spy adventures. In the process she exchanges domesticity in a suburban Ohio house for domesticity in a remodeled farmhouse near Paris. In *Desperately Seeking Susan*, Roberta leaves her middle-class husband and house (a house, incidentally, that her fantasy idol finds very agreeable) for Dez, who initially mistook her for Susan. As a projectionist he may make less money than husband Gary Glass, but he seems to live comfortably enough in a large loft space in trendy, punky lower Manhattan. Mickey Davis in *Thief of Hearts* ultimately chooses her husband over fantasy lover Scott, but only after she realizes Scott is a thief, and after her affair forces her husband to pay more attention to her, resparking their mutual affection. Moreover, the Davises are not middle-class suburbanites, but upscale, stylish urbanites. (He is a successful author of children's books, and she is a high fashion interior designer.) Thus in terms of the trendy, upscale lifestyle bias exhibited in these films, it is appropriate in this case that narrative resolution entails Mickey's electing to stay with her husband. In every case, narrative resolutions of romantic fulfillment are represented as a choice in favor of an unconventional, trendy or leisure standard of living.

The both/and structure of choice in these films pervades the terms of narrative construction and offers the possibility of interpretation from a series of positions within contemporary social and cultural ideology. This is in turn a function of the films' positioning of their fantasy-generated adventure plots as the reconstruction of fictional-textual models. Narrative is generated through remodeling texts which are themselves forms of writing familiarly associated with women readers and writers. The fictional trajectories to which the heroines are subject—their "real" lives in terms of the filmic fiction—are inextricably associated with the texts they produce and/or consume within the fiction. In the process, as the films play out their fictional hands, they insist on a logic of identity and difference as a measure of events with the terms of the comparative paradigm fully laid out.

Not only do we know that Joan Wilder writes romance adventure novels in general, but we also see a filmic dramatization from one of her books at the very start of *Romancing the Stone*. Joan, a successful author, ultimately functions equally well as the heroine of her own romantic adventure, albeit with a few twists. When Joan tries some of the tricks used by her novelistic heroine in the film's opening sequence, they do not always play by the book; but she nonetheless succeeds in finding the coveted emerald and in rescuing her sister from kidnappers. Cathy Palmer is a suburban housewife and is not Rebecca Ryan, who is only a fictional character. But she is (mis)recognized as Rebecca Ryan by an array of strangers, and successfully exposes spies and drug dealers. *American Dreamer* also opens with a filmic "dramatization" of a scene from a Rebecca Ryan thriller—Cathy's excerpt-in-progress for the contest that wins her a trip to Paris. Ironically, Cathy's most decisive and embarrassing failure as Rebecca Ryan comes from her attempt to reenact the episode she wrote for the contest. In *Thief of Hearts* we hear specific passages from Mickey Davis's journals as they are read by

Scott. While he really does act out the semi-steamy fantasies contained in them, he is also after all a thief who can finally only pose as, but not be, the man of her fantasy texts.

The repetitions and discrepancies between textual models and their subsequent reenactments construct a relational space affording a range of potential interpretive positions for a viewer depending on, (1) how one understands the fictional model, and (2) how one understands the interplay of identity and difference between the fictional model and its renarrativisation. The status of the model texts is equivocal because romance genres have variously been seen as feminized soft-core pornography; as a trivial and derided form of popular culture; and as a crucial channel for expressing women's anxiety and women's pleasure within dominant popular culture.[8] Building on this, one might then see the films, with their remodelings, as simply reproducing the tendencies of the reference genres (however they are construed); as offering a parodic rewriting to position the reference texts as inferior; as a critical-but-progressive or critical-but-conservative rewriting; or as acknowledging the patent fictionality at the core of all contemporary romance-adventure stories, including the films themselves. These are at least some of the permutations made available through the course of the films.

The narratives are generated through strategies of staging and restaging of scenes, in a play of mirror construction and regressive derivation. Motivated by the readings and writings of the heroine, this mode of textual generation evokes the structure of fantasy described by Elizabeth Cowie.[9] Cowie stresses that fantasy is a process involving the staging or arranging of desire, and does not depend on particular objects or forms of resolution. In both daydreams and fiction, pleasure lies in the way the story is set in place:

> For though we all want the couple to be united, and the obstacles heroically overcome, we don't want the story to end. And marriage is one of the most definitive endings. The pleasure is in how to bring about the consummation.... This can extend into producing endings which remain murky, ill-defined, uncertain even. It is thus not modesty which veils the endings of romantic fictions but wise caution.... Fantasy as a *mise-en-scene* of desire is more a setting out of lack of what is absent, than a presentation of having, a being present.[10]

While fantasy is thus understood as a setting or a process of staging, and not as an object, the films I have been discussing may seem to end by putting things in place all too clearly, filling the space of lack in response to, and beyond the wildest dreams of, the protagonists' desires. Susan and Jim, Roberta and Dez, Cathy and Alan, Mickey and Ray, Joan and Jack: all of these characters are happily and finally ensconced in unambiguous coupledom. Yet even this fixity is equivocal, figured hyperbolically as if to signal that this fulfillment is itself only a remodeled fiction and therefore doubly absent.

Toward the end of *American Dreamer,* Cathy Palmer, having regained consciousness, is on her way back to the United States with her husband. At the airport immigration control desk she rather abruptly decides to leave him to return to Alan McMann. Their reunion, however, is not the end of the film, but initiates another series of adventures when they are abducted by a drug dealer who thinks that Cathy knows too much about his operations, based on her prior behavior in the persona of Rebecca Ryan. After successfully escaping from this, yet another, life-threatening situation, they are finally seen settled into the McMann's French farmhouse with Cathy's sons, reading an extract from the newest Rebecca Ryan novel—based of course on their adventures—as a bedtime story. (Earlier in the film Cathy was seen reading her Rebecca Ryan contest story entry to her sons at bedtime.)

The finally idyllic representation of a reconstituted nuclear family bears the hyperbolic weight of the films' both/and logic. Cathy Palmer can have a lover/husband surrogate as well as her sons, and contribute to the writing of the novels she has read for so long. Insofar as this final image is simply a displaced duplication of Cathy's previous suburban life, complete with Rebecca Ryan excerpts as bedtime reading, one might wonder if her new life will prove any different or better than before. By the same token one can argue that the problem from the start was the person of the husband (decidedly unsympathetic, and overly paternalistic), so that with that change, the situation is ideal. These varying potential responses, and probably more, converge on this scene because it depicts domestic union in such extreme terms on the heels of a narrative generated as a highly self-conscious fiction.

Romancing the Stone similarly concludes in the constitutive ambiguity of both/and logic stretched to the limits. In the final scene, Joan Wilder, back in New York, presents her publisher with her latest novel, modeled on her adventures in Colombia. In her rewriting, the heroine and hero end up together. When the publisher accuses her of being a hopeless romantic, Joan explains that she is in fact a hopeful romantic, rewriting the popular phrase to stress the positivity of her position. Joan is then seen returning home with an armload of groceries and a bouquet of flowers. Rounding the corner she confronts a huge boat parked in front of her building and is greeted by Jack, who is sporting alligator boots.

This is a temporally displaced realization of Joan's adventures, fulfilling the conventions of the romance-adventure plot on which they were originally modeled in the very terms in which Joan has already rewritten them for publication. In this sense it is avowedly artificial, a self-declared gesture to the fictional intertext. At the same time it is the conventionalized narrative response to, and fulfillment of, the filmic story of Joan and Jack. It is at once "really" artificial and "really" satisfying, patently fake closure and real closure. This ambivalence is underscored by the hyperbolic terms of its representation, in particular the presence of a sailboat on the streets of Manhattan. (A more conventionally credible happy ending might have Jack appear to invite Joan on his sea travels but omit the boat; or have her receive a phone call or cable requesting that she meet him at some pier. In the model of the 1970s woman's picture, Jack probably would not appear at all, leaving Joan suspended in the ambivalence of hopeful, romantic singledom.)

The conclusion of *Jewel of the Nile* is, in its own way, equally extreme. Jack and Joan are married by a mystic Arab leader, surrounded by the Arab and Nubian tribes they encountered during their adventures in Africa. Joan's publisher is the only other Westerner present, and Joan is dressed in a white designer bridal gown. The incongruity of this traditional garb in the midst of the more primitive tribal wedding party underscores the relationship between the culminating ritual of the romantic adventure and the fictional locales that are its support.

In these films the terms of closure offered in the happy ending restate the problematic of staging and restaging, the very motive of the fictions, as the ending is so patently *put in place* as a fiction. In *American Dreamer* and *Romancing the Stone* in particular, the films could conclude at a number of points prior to "The End." According to the conventions of dominant cinema, *American Dreamer* might reasonably end with Cathy's return to the United States with her husband, retrospectively positioning her Parisian adventure as a bittersweet memory, a hopelessly frivolous fantasy. The reunion with Alan McMann, a romantic embrace in front of his hotel, is an obvious moment for another conventional conclusion. Instead they are once more thrown into danger, until they are finally seen as a reconstituted family. Through these deferments the viewer is referred back to the prior narrative trajectories of self-conscious fictionality that determine the film, and the concomitant construction of subjectivities which are always multiple, provisional, and in movement.

One might further note that if marriage or coupling is one version of a definitive end, and one at issue in these films, it is also a definitive beginning. With the exception of *Romancing the Stone,* all of these films open with the protagonists in established monogamous relationships that are represented as being inadequate to a sense of fulfillment and excitement. Mickey and Ray, Roberta and Gary, and Cathy and Kevin are all married at the start; and Joan and Jack are a steady couple at the opening of *Jewel of the Nile.* All of these couples separate, through the initiative of the female who most strongly feels something is lacking, in order to be reunited or recoupled with another male partner. Thus in contemporary cinematic formulations, marriage by no means precludes the sense of loss or absence that initiates fantasy as the *mise-en-scene* of desire.

In elaborating on the functioning of fantasy in film Cowie explains:

> What is necessary for any public form of fantasy, for their collective consumption, is not universal objects of desire, but a setting of desiring in which we can find our place(s). And these places will devolve, as in the original fantasies, on positions of desire: active or passive, feminine or masculine, mother or son, father or daughter.

She proceeds to analyze *Now Voyager* and *The Reckless Moment,* two classic women's pictures from the 1940s.[11] She argues that in original or primary fantasy the staging of desire encompasses multiple points of entry, "where the subject is both present *in* the scene and interchangeable with any other character." [12] In relation to primary fantasy, narrative serves to organize material, much like secondary elaboration in dreams:

> What is interesting in the analysis of *Now Voyager* and *The Reckless Moment* is that in each film the subject positions shift across the boundary of sexual difference. Thus while subject positions are variable the terms of sexual difference are fixed. It is the form of tension and play between the fixing of narrative—the secondary elaboration—and the lack of fixity of the subject in the original fantasies which would seem to be important, and not any already-given privileging of one over the other.[13]

Subject positionality in contemporary romance adventure films can also be seen as shifting across, and as unstable in relation to, boundaries of sexual and social difference. As previously noted, female characters frequently assume positions of narrative control and are instrumental in the discovery and resolution of adventure-crime situations within the fictions. They also demonstrate a readiness to discard the terms of social and class decorum that initially define or confine them (even if it is only to return to a state of social or class equilibrium by the end). More crucially, through the staging of desire as the restaging of prior models, the narrative that works to hold things in place also serves to disturb its own relative coherence and continuity. From this perspective it is possible to see these films as fantasies of fantasy, as the representation of the secondary fantasy-adventure rewrites and restages texts that have, as always/already, offered their own *mise-en-scene* of desire. It is useful to recall, in this regard, that the romance novel, rather like the television soap opera, is a highly repetitive genre with respect to both narrative conventions and patterns of reception. Not only do the same sorts of things occur in the same order, but readers also rarely read just one.[14]

American Dreamer, Romancing the Stone, and *Jewel of the Nile* all open with scenes that are revealed to be romance-adventure texts written by the protagonists, who themselves proceed to experience events according to the conventions of the fictions they write. Not only the female protagonists, but also secondary characters are revealed to be caught up in the interplay of model texts and their restaging in the course of the filmic fictions. Ray Davis, the husband in *Thief of Hearts,* is the author of children's books. In one of his confrontations with Mickey he declares that she is the only "real thing" in his life; but from her perspective, his success as a writer has led to an all-consuming preoccupation with his fiction, leaving her unsatisfied.

In *Desperately Seeking Susan,* Gary's sister is at first sympathetic to the idea that Roberta's disappearance is linked to a presumed affair. She questions her brother as to whether he has satisfied Roberta sexually, according to the terms of popular sex literature, and rebukes him for his affair with another woman. Later, as the search for Roberta continues, the sister promotes the idea that Roberta has probably been working as a prostitute. As evidence she cites an article about suburban housewives who lead secret lives as prostitutes while their husbands are at work. Her reconstruals of what Roberta may be up to—which the audience recognizes as inappropriate, given their awareness of her more accidental masquerade—refer to other texts, all offering versions of an illicit excitement that is absent from her suburban existence. In this context, Cathy Palmer's choice of Alan McMann, author of her favorite novels, over her businessman husband in *American Dreamer* also assumes added significance.

To promote further the filmic narratives as fantasies of fantasy, and to complicate further the ideological valence one might ascribe to the various positions made possible through the films, it is crucial that the female protagonists are represented as authors, and not merely readers, of the fictional models which (in)form their narrative fates. Joan Wilder is the only professional writer, but Cathy Palmer gets to Paris in the first place by writing an excerpt of an imaginary Rebecca Ryan novel in a publisher's contest; Mickey Davis writes her private journals on the model of popular romance fiction; and Roberta Glass writes the tabloid classified ad that involves her with Susan by imitating the classified ad that originally sparked her fascination with Susan as an abstract persona. The staging of fantasy, and its restaging in redoubled fantasy, is thus not simply a function of fictional reconstruction as the motive strategy of these films. Rather, it is more fully promoted in the expressed linking of reading to writing, or of consumption to production. In the process, the films offer a reconstrual of the common association of reading-as-consumption with women, which is in turn opposed to writing-as-production with men.[15]

Instead, reading and writing are represented in a reciprocal process of exchange, as are consumption and production. Joan Wilder and her female publisher do not only produce, but also consume romance novels, and both of them even cry at the end. Here, involvement in the process of production does not necessarily extricate one from being affectively subject to the finished product. Joan's subsequent adventures in Colombia provide the material for yet another novel. Thus her active role in finding the treasure, rescuing her sister, and writing, combine to provide yet another occasion for her to read.[16] In *American Dreamer*, as already noted, the reading of Rebecca Ryan's novels and the simulated writing of part of one furnishes the context for Cathy Palmer's active involvement in international crime, which in turn leads to more writing and more reading. In *Desperately Seeking Susan*, Roberta and Susan not only read and write classified ads, but are thereby brought together and end up as front page heroines for capturing an international murderer and thief.

Moreover, women are not represented as the only consumers or producers of the material conventionally identified in terms of sexual difference. In *Thief of Hearts* the thief, Scott, reads Mickey's journals and adopts the fantasy they express as his own as he makes himself over in their image. Even more than Mickey, Scott pushes for their realization as he urges her to run off with him. Mickey's rejection suggests that for her the value of the journals lies in nonfulfillment; or, she recognizes their value as staging, and is less interested in achieving the object of desire. That he so eagerly adopts what is conventionally perceived as woman's fantasy suggests the reversibility of the gender determination of the fantasy scenarios set in place by the film. However, one cannot forget that this particular woman's fantasy not only requires him being a spectacle for Mickey, but also functions for him as an upwardly-mobile class fantasy.

This reversibility is not unique to *Thief of Hearts*. In *Romancing the Stone*, Joan and Jack, in search of a car, end up in a village notorious as a center of drug trafficking. They are followed by a small armed group, and as Jack prepares for a confrontation, Joan turns and graciously explains what they are looking for. They are referred to the "bell maker" and followed to his house. There, the bell maker refuses to help them, pulls a gun, and tells them to "hit the road." When they turn to leave, they are confronted by the guns of the toughs who have been trailing them. Jack says, "Okay, Joan Wilder, write us out of this one." Suddenly the bell maker gets extremely excited and asks if she is Joan Wilder, the novelist. He introduces her to the rest of the village, and they respond with reverential delight. It turns out that the so-called bell maker, Juan, is a long-standing fan of her work and reads Spanish translations of her novels aloud to the other villagers. Her Western romances are extremely popular with the drug traffickers in this Colombian village. With Juan's assistance (including a souped-up truck and a hidden mechanical bridge, both designed to help him in the drug trade) Joan and Jack proceed to escape from Zolo, who is hot on their trail, and continue on their route to Joan's sister.

In *American Dreamer* it is apparent that the audience for Rebecca Ryan novels cuts across gender lines. As Cathy Palmer storms through Paris, couturier designers, hotel bellhops, and even government spies recognize the name of Rebecca Ryan as that of the famous international adventuress. Moreover, the reversibility of gender associations provides grounds for one of the major revelations, and jokes, of the film. Throughout her adventures the audience, and later Cathy, assumes that Alan McMann is simply the business manager for his mother, the author of the Rebecca Ryan novels. When Cathy and Alan are attempting to escape from the drug dealer Victor Marchand, they argue over which novel Cathy's plan come from. In the course of their dispute Alan confesses that he is in fact the author of the novels, but used his mother's name and public persona because he did not want anyone to know he wrote "that cheap pulp." Moreover, his explanation assumes the form of linguistic transvestism as he proclaims, "I am Rebecca Ryan." Indeed the difficulty of enunciating a proper gender identity opens the film as a whole, in the dramatized scenes of Cathy's excerpt for the contest. Rebecca Ryan apprehends a (male) villain disguised as a woman, triumphantly revealing the man beneath the woman by removing his wig. As an author, Cathy struggles with the appropriate line to accompany this gesture, finally settling on, "You know I always get my man, even when he's a woman."

Males not only consume these texts, but are also subject to the productive activity they generate. Juan, a reader of the Wilder novels, becomes an active participant in Joan's adventures. Jack's ostentatiously romantic appearance at the end of *Romancing the Stone* occurs after Joan has already written a version of their exploits with a happy ending. His appearance can thus be taken as an effect of her text or as an effect of his having succumbed in a more general way to the dins of romance adventures that Joan writes. In *American Dreamer,* Alan McMann is pulled squarely into the intrigue stirred up by Cathy Palmer as Rebecca Ryan even though he is simply trying to keep her in line to preserve the reputation and name of the character he has created. In *Desperately Seeking Susan,* Susan, Roberta, and Susan's boyfriend Jim all read and write the personal classifieds that link them in the plot, and none of them is exempt from generating potent intrigues on this basis. It is Jim who initially declares that he is "Desperately seeking Susan" in print. Later, when he reads Roberta's ad with the same tag line signed "A Stranger," he is convinced that Susan must be involved with another man. The fact that she is represented from the start as involved with other men is irrelevant; it is precisely the derivative newspaper text that carries effectivity in sparking his jealousy.

Thus the shifting of subject positions in these films is cut across and accompanied (redoubled) by shifts in the positionality of the producers and consumers of the texts that generate the film's fictional trajectories. Crucially, the strategies and genres of fantasy represented in the films are not rigidly differentiated by gender. In this the films challenge conventional affiliations of specific genres with specifically gendered audiences even as they engage the problematics of genres commonly defined as "woman's" possession to address an audience that is not narrowly confined to women. In the course of restaging these fantasies, the films not only disrupt the fixity of subject positions within the narratives, but also challenge or undermine the very notion of gendered texts.

In almost all of the films this mobility of identification is facilitated by deployments of point of view. As noted earlier, while the heroines in these films never merely submit to the male gaze, they are not decisively extricated from conventional structures of looking affiliated with the dominant narrative cinema. *Desperately Seeking Susan* is the most obvious film in this regard. Roberta Glass's fascination with the "Desperately sought" Susan assumes the form of an investigation, and her look frames Susan's meeting with Jim and subsequent walk through Manhattan. Susan flouts convention, presenting herself as a self-conscious spectacle, especially in her sexual costuming, and brazenly stares back at the men whose looks she attracts.[17] And yet these female gazes are only directed to characters in the fiction, while both Susan and Roberta are presented as objects of the film's gaze in more than one (dis)guise.

To further complicate the issue, narration is explicitly articulated with questions of the gaze and filmic enunciation in these films, as characters assume the roles of spectacle and holder of the gaze within narratives which are scripted by female characters. In *Thief of Hearts* we hear a long section from Mickey's journal involving a fantasy of water, and of an imaginary boating excursion with the mysterious man who rescues her from her boring, safe life. This includes her watching him as he covers himself with suntan oil. While we see the thief, Scott, reading the journal, we hear Mickey's voice reciting the text from her journal. Later, when Scott (re)enacts this scene, Mickey is placed in the position of the one who looks, in a scenario of her own writing. However, it is also clear that Scott is manipulating her by returning her fantasy to her as a real life event, as the film's viewer watches Mickey watching Scott with obvious unease and discomfort. Thus Scott's assumption of the position of spectacle for Mickey's gaze confirms the control of her fantasy over him, but does not give her the power usually associated with the male gaze. Indeed, in all these films, slippages and reversals in points of view do not definitively destabilize conventional regimes of looking and power in the cinema, though they do offer sufficient disruption to call them into question, if only provisionally.[18]

This is not to argue that these films are singularly or particularly "radical." Rather, they represent popular fantasy—in all its possibilities and limitations—as an arena for expressing contradictory positions, allowing a range of ideological responses. One might argue that like commercial television, one approach to the production of successful films (or, of films which will prove to be successful in the marketplace) involves heterogeneous strategies of address to appeal to a variety of demographic influences. That these films initiate strategies of dispersed positionality with reference to so-called women's genres remains important, as the initial major figures of narrative identification are the film's women characters. (In this they perhaps represent a reversal of, and counter to, the glamorization of male stars such as Christopher Reeve, Richard Gere, Mel Gibson, and Tom Selleck.) If the films do not offer a thoroughgoing rewrite of sexual difference, they begin to displace the narrative functions that have been traditionally associated with the representation of men and women in the cinema, and do so by starting out from a perspective that privileges women.

But even as the films offer restagings of prestaged fictions and fantasies of fantasy, they also offer the romantic couple as the product of romantic triangles, misrecognitions, and chance encounters. And even as reading/consumption is inevitably transformed into writing/production and back again, we are held in the organization and coherence of narrative. If it is all simulation, it is also all too closely bound up in the reality of consumer lifestyle images, as plain old middle-class life takes a beating at the hands of lifestyles represented as offering more leisure time.

The both/and logic unleashed by these films ultimately exercises discursive and ideological constraints. In their inclusiveness they begin to trace the limits of dominant representational practice. At one end of this spectrum they incorporate/embody the most narrowly conceived traditional romance plot with fixed, conventional gender identities. At the other end they offer a delirium of simulation in narratives whose coherence and logic lies in an infinitely regressive reference to other narratives, signaling the absence of any reality or referent beyond the spectacle of the simulacrum itself, including sexual difference.[19] In between these two extremes the films encompass multiple explanatory and interpretive positions. They can be read in relation to models of extended triangulated desire, or in terms of variations on and reversal of the Oedipal plot.[20] They can be construed as liberal tales of women's self-realization or less progressively, more moderately, as narratives that hold women—and men—in mediated balance between independence and romantic dependence.

What is significant is that the films express and hold all of these positions within their boundaries in a very immediate way. With their strategy of multiple restaging they represent a broadly conceived model—incorporating a history of narrative genres and a cacophony of theoretical positions—of a free market place of ideas, for and in a social formation which is itself structured by an elaborate apparatus of mediation and consumption. The danger in rejecting these representational models out of hand is that we will find ourselves trapped by, and subject to, a singular, potentially repressive reading from the panoply of interpretations they make available; or that we will mistake a single, perhaps one progressive perspective for the whole story. But the danger of embracing the multiplicity of positions, in all its inclusivity, as good in and for itself, is that in a delirium of apparent freedom and mobility we will too readily buy into a system that sustains itself precisely through extended reproduction and consumption.

CHAPTER SIX

LEARNING THE ELECTRONIC LIFE

A typical morning (circa December 1989) begins for our family when our son wakes up and we hear him moving about over the radio monitor that links his bedroom to ours via the electromagnetic spectrum. We change a diaper and stumble downstairs together, pop his rice cereal in the microwave oven, pull it out after two minutes, thirty seconds of wave-based heat-producing molecular vibrations, and commence the feeding. Plop into the playpen while mom and dad squeeze in some morning exercise, usually in front of the television with remote control handy. Then showers, get dressed, and adults eat breakfast.

Out of the house and, if not a walk-to-work day, into the car, lowering the garage door with the automatic opener as we drive away on errands. Stop at the bank—or rather, the nearest automatic teller machine to get some cash for groceries and shopping (done with cash, checks, and credit cards, with access to the first electronically verified by local computer network, the latter two verified at the point of purchase by national computer network)—and upon returning home, check the phone machine before going off to the office or upstairs to the study to work on the computer. A typical work day can include not only personally interacting with students and colleagues, but also interfacing with long distance telephone calls, photocopies, printouts, hard drives, programs, modems, electronic mail, floppies, audio and video tape, and once in a while a fax. If we do not work into the evening, a typical night may well include (along with returning phone calls) radio listening, recorded music (albums, tapes, or compact discs), broadcast television, cable television, or videocassettes. The most probable result, of course, is some combination of the above choices, with too many TV nights degenerating into an uninspired channel-hopping via remote from the comfort of the couch. In the background the baby monitor provides the sound of sleeping baby, a sound that accompanies us into bed each evening. The cycle, with a slight degree of variation, begins anew the next day.

All in all, an unremarkable series of events—not at all unpleasant, but not adventurous either. Certainly millions and millions of adult Americans can easily recount a similar daily diary. But how did we all learn so easily to behave this way, particularly our interaction with electronic devices of information, communication, and media culture? It is not the actions that are so remarkable as the ease of learning and pace of assimilation, for much of the learning of the electronic life has taken place only in the last decade, the 1980s. And while many quite rightfully marvel at the nonstop array of technological wonders purported to improve everyday life in the twentieth century, few stop to marvel at how quickly and unthinkingly certain aspects of technology—in the case of this chapter, telecommunications services based on the electromagnetic spectrum and various wire-based telecommunications networks such as the telephone—become part of our everyday experiences. Yet the process of assimilation—including the discreet pedagogy that encourages and familiarizes the adoption of these technologies—that surrounds the electronic life is an important topic for analysis. Learning the electronic life is a type of learning that does not come from schools but from the discreet sites of pedagogy that pervade modern American life, and in particular from media culture.

That our habits and daily activities surrounding the electronic life go largely unnoticed is not justification for ignoring those activities. Indeed, the discreet nature of the pedagogical process encouraging the adoption of new communication technologies warrants close analysis, because this pedagogy is the latest manifestation of a modern social ideology that promotes technological determinism as a positive social value in contemporary American society. Therefore, an analysis of the pedagogy of technological determinism in American culture must be anchored in the experiences of the everyday and the unremarkable, despite the fact that, on the surface, such an inquiry seems perhaps prosaic. Yet the examination of the everyday is a crucial component of social analysis for societies past and present:

> I began with daily life, with those aspects of life that control us without our ever being aware of them: habit or, better yet, routine—those thousands of acts that flower and reach fruition without anyone's having made a decision, acts of which we are not even fully aware. I think mankind is more than waist-deep in daily routine. Countless inherited acts, accumu-

> lated pell-mell and repeated time after time to this very day, become habits that help us live, imprison us, and make decisions for us throughout our lives...[this] is the life that man throughout the course of his previous history has made a part of his very being, has in some way absorbed into his entrails, turning the experiments and exhilarating experiences of the past into everyday, banal necessities. So no one pays close attention to them any more.[1]

Fernand Braudel was thinking of the fifteenth through eighteenth centuries when he offered the above comment, but his mode of inquiry into the habits of everyday life is germane to this inquiry. Within a remarkably short period of time, the electronic life in American society has shifted from an experiment (if not also an exhilarating experience) to an everyday, banal necessity—one example of which opened this chapter.

However, on the pages that follow, close attention is paid to these everyday habits of telecommunications in pursuit of a number of issues and questions. The pedagogical forces that teach and reinforce such a way of living are one important area of inquiry. Where throughout modern society does the pedagogical process take place? How do advertisements, newspaper and magazine articles, television programs, feature films, and communication with peers function as components of the discreet pedagogy of technological determinism and thereby encourage the adoption of technology in our everyday lives? The earlier chapter in this book about television advertising—chapter two—addressed some facets of this question. In addition, the question of proprietary rights looms large for both individuals and institutions. What are the proprietary values of individuals in regard to the use of telecommunications systems, both wire and wave based? How do the various uses of these communications systems imply a sense of proprietary values by individuals and institutions? How and why do consumers learn and believe these proprietary rights are important and have real value? Finally, the important question of privacy looms large. What sacrifices of privacy—sacrifices largely unknown—do individuals make in exchange for the comfort and convenience of an electronic life, and why do these sacrifices remain so unknown and misunderstood, seemingly out of the stream of pedagogy that promotes the learning experience and knowledge of how to assimilate telecommunications into everyday life? While this chapter may not give complete and detailed answers to all of these questions, these are the major themes and issues guiding this inquiry into learning the electronic life—the everyday pedagogy of technological determinism in American culture.

A realistic assessment of these issues has to recognize that, to paraphrase Braudel, American society already is at least waist-deep in the everyday use of telecommunications and information systems. Therefore, the overwhelming majority of students and teachers concerned with self-empowerment and critical thinking do not have a simple choice of "to use or not to use," but instead are likely to find themselves somewhere on a social continuum ranging from total rejection to total embracement of these electronic goods and services. Compounding the situation is that most individuals are somewhere in the middle, and an individual's position is not fixed or static but instead subject to movement between the poles over time (that movement being influenced by such factors as economic status, political beliefs, employment, and cultural factors, to name a few). The goal is not so much to pronounce a judgment of good or evil—for technology can simultaneously be both and neither—but instead to be aware of the ramifications resulting from one's individual position and the tradeoffs between convenience and privacy such a position implies, as well as the location of the two poles and the "bulges"—that is, the location of large segments of society and the problems and prospects such locations suggest. Through such understanding can come the knowledge of the pedagogical process surrounding the electronic life and the implications of that process for individuals and societies.

Such an understanding begins with a basic grounding on the nature of the systems of everyday telecommunication. The various electronic networks that provide the opportunity for a multitude of linkages can be divided into two general types, based on their method of information distribution: wire-based or wave-based. In other words, does the system largely depend on a system of wires for interconnection (such as local telephone service) or does the system largely make use of the electromagnetic spectrum (such as broadcasting)? Distinctions between wire and wave become important in determining issues of property and privacy; traditionally, a wire is considered to be private property (for example, owned by the telephone company) and considered a better guarantor of privacy, while wave-based information has until recently been subject to interpretations that allow for the reception of wave-based information by any listener, whether they are the intended audience or not.

In practical application, most telecommunication systems in fact make use of both wire and wave based systems of distribution in their overall operations. One of the most obvious locations of this "hybridization" is in the changing nature of the public telephone system, especially with the advent of portable and cellular phones. Similarly, cable television makes extensive use of wave-based satellite communications to distribute programs from the cable network to the local franchise operator, and the local operator then turns to a wire-based system to further distribute the programming to subscriber homes. The everyday reception experiences of telecommunications, utilizing wire and wave based systems interchangeably, is also indicative of the entire vertical structure of telecommunications systems.

Among the most familiar and commonplace American telecommunications experiences is using the telephone system. For the past thirty to forty years, virtually all Americans have learned the rudiments of telephone use at a very early age, earlier than most can even remember such a learning process taking place. Not only is the telephone a site of early-age learning in terms of interpersonal communication, it also represents a location for the initial learning of codes and signifiers, because the automation of the telephone system has replaced the human operator with a series of tones and signals. "Hello Central" and "number please" have become the dial tone; "I'll ring it" has become an electronic bell (or on some new phones, a warble); "I'm sorry, that line is busy" is now a repetitive buzz; and a number of other supervisory and control signals (rather than the operator's eyes and hands on the switchboard) tell the system the call is over, bill the customer who placed the call, and open both phones for use again.

The learning process becomes more complex when one utilizes what Colin Cherry has aptly described as "the biggest machine in the world"—the "machine" that enables long distance telephony.[2] Here, the complexity increases with additional numbers, and, on certain overseas calls, operator assistance. Here too, in the 1970s and 1980s, was the site of the restructuring of the American telephone industry, with the advent of alternative long-distance telephone services such as MCI, various private and corporate long distance systems, the divestiture of ATT, long-distance competition, and the current need for Americans to choose a long-distance carrier for their everyday service.[3]

The various complexities of long-distance calling that became well-known following the divestiture of ATT were coupled with the introduction and growth of a wide array of new telephone options for everyday users. During the 1980s, personal answering machines, portable and cellular telephones, various paging devices and services, three-way and conference calling, speed dialing, portable dialing devices, call forwarding and call waiting, telephone credit cards, fax, cellular phones, cellular fax, and computer hook-ups via modem devices (now including cellular modems) all became more widespread in American society. These changes and additions to the telephone system brought a fundamental pedagogical shift to the everyday reception experience: the telephone has now become a site of lifelong learning, both in terms of its ever-expanding array of options and in its use as a system to gather and disseminate information. For prior generations of telephone users, the telephone represented a fixed, finite location for the application of knowledge. However, the telephone has now become a center of constant education for users who wish to maximize its potentialities through competing long-distance services, call-waiting, conference calls, fax, and so on. The educators range from the manufacturers through the advertisers promoting these products to the salespeople distributing these products to consumers. Here too, word-of-mouth, peer pressure, and the perceived social status of such devices also act as forms of pedagogy encouraging consumption.

Formerly, people "learned" the telephone once; now, they "learn" it anew with each new technological innovation. Advertising campaigns trumpeting the convenience of such new uses and services suggest that such new uses enhance life, thereby implying that new technology is a determinant of improved living conditions. The results are becoming visible in less than a decade, as the knowledge of the American public concerning telephone use can no longer be defined by a very small set of shared habits but has instead become a broad continuum upon which the specific location of individuals and their telephone skills can be discerned. The telephone and its relationship to American culture, something once considered a shared experience of all, has now been transformed into a site of perpetual pedagogy, hierarchy, status, and knowledge-as-power.

If the long-distance telephone system is the biggest machine in the world, then the biggest natural resource in the world is the electromagnetic spectrum. Larger than any nation or continent, any ocean, or the planet itself, the electromagnetic spectrum is even larger than the air we breathe and other various layers of atmosphere which envelop us—for example, we cannot breathe in the emptiness of space, but as the Voyager satellite flyby of distant planets proved, we can receive radio signals from those distances. It is admittedly difficult to conceive of the electromagnetic spectrum as a tangible entity, but its utilization in the everyday experiences of telecommunications is extraordinary, ranging from satellite communications high above us to remote control devices in the palm of one's hand.

In theory, the electromagnetic spectrum has infinite room for all conceivable wave-based applications, but practical circumstances of spectrum use mitigate against such unlimited space. The historical development of specific communications technologies is one circumstance. For example, in retrospect it is clear that certain services (for example, AM radio) do not make nearly as efficient use of the electromagnetic spectrum as they might. In the example of AM radio, stations could be closer together than they are (currently 10 kilohertz spacing in the U.S.) but such a change is economically and socially impractical because it would require consumers to replace many of their sets and broadcasters to revamp their transmitters on a national scale. The historical development of a technology and its widespread adaptation has created other instances where despite the inefficiency, the technology is too socioeconomically entrenched to be reasonably shifted and/or converted to a more efficient use of the spectrum. Interference between signals is another factor that can reduce the efficiency of the spectrum. Obviously, two differing signals at the same spot on a radio dial or television channel cannot be sent out from the same location, because the resultant interference would render both indecipherable to listeners and viewers. Care must therefore be taken in the spacing of signals sharing the same frequency. Interference can be accidental, intentional (such as the jamming of radio signals by nations) or inherent in the use of the spectrum, because the greater use of the spectrum tends to raise the chances of interference and also undermines the reach of a signal by increasing attenuation—the tendency of a signal to get progressively weaker as it travels from its origin.

The greatest danger of interference is a lack of cooperation among users of the spectrum, from local to international levels. This can range from something as mundane as the problems caused when two neighbors have remote control garage door openers on the same frequency (creating a situation where they simultaneously open and close each other's doors as well as their own[4]) to international disagreements between nations over the reception of broadcast signals within each other's borders. An example of the latter is the tension in the 1980s and 1990s between the U.S. and Cuba over Radio Marti and TV Marti, two broadcast propaganda services of the United States Information Agency aimed at Cuban audiences. In opposition to these broadcasts, Cubans have occasionally jammed these signals as well as transmitted other radio signals at such a high wattage that they occasionally interfere with American domestic commercial stations.

With a single, shared global resource that is so highly subject to problems in its use if all users do not cooperate, it is reasonable to expect that governments and nations have an important role in determining the uses of the electromagnetic spectrum and policing the behavior of its users. In fact, this is somewhat true. In the U.S., the Federal Communications Commission (FCC) polices domestic uses of the spectrum to help contain interference and also prevent unauthorized, unlicensed, or other improper uses of the spectrum. The FCC also represents the U.S. in global matters concerning spectrum decisions, and regularly sends several representatives as part of the American delegations to international conferences regarding spectrum decisions. These conferences are convened by the International Telecommunications Union (ITU), now part of the United Nations but an international organization initially formed in the 1860s when nations first needed to deal with international telegraph usage. The ITU provides a regular forum that keeps track of the world's use of the spectrum and brings nations and users together in determination of new allocations of sections of the spectrum for various uses.

However, governments are not the only institutions involved in spectrum decisions. Many of the decisions regarding uses of the spectrum are effectively made by various multinational corporations through their research and development of new uses for the spectrum and new services that can utilize wave-based communications. Since the 1920s, the nations of the world have agreed to a plan of allocation which does not give each nation a section of the spectrum to do with what it pleases but instead sets aside sections of the spectrum for new technologies of wave-based communications. It then becomes incumbent upon nations to prove to the rest of the world their need for a portion of the spectrum that carries that service. This system was designed by American communication corporations and promulgated by American delegations at international radio conferences. Needless to say, the industrialized nations of the world generally have a far easier time proving their needs than the underdeveloped nations of the world—a hierarchy of telecommunications that has existed throughout the twentieth century.[5]

With the coming of communications satellites in the 1960s, this principle has been extended to the communication world's other single shared resource, the geostationary or equatorial orbit. A satellite positioned approximately 22,300 miles above the equator remains fixed in relation to the earth's particular landmass below it; therefore, such a satellite can be used nonstop. The geostationary orbit is the *only* satellite orbit that can provide nonstop use, thereby making such a position of immense value. But despite the fact that the underdeveloped world occupies most of the landmass beneath such an orbit, decisions concerning the geostationary orbit and uses of satellites within it are dominated by the industrialized world, and third world nations experience extreme difficulty in securing a coveted equatorial slot.[6]

Insofar as counting up users of the spectrum, it might well be argued that modern American society—particularly in pursuit of a life of leisure associated with consumer culture—is the biggest user of the spectrum. Certainly the 10,000-plus radio stations, 2,000-plus television stations, preponderance of remote control devices, growth of portable and cellular phones, and other such devices use vast sections of the spectrum. However, in terms of the actual amount of spectrum space utilized, the largest single user in the world is the U.S. government, with the military the largest user of all government branches. In 1985, over fifty different federal branches and agencies used portions of the U.S. government master spectrum file, ranging from small-scale users such as the Architect of the Capitol (who used 0.0024% of the master file) or the Federal Home Bank Loan Board (0.0005%) to mid-size users such as the Department of Energy (3.23%) or Department of Agriculture (5.47%) to the major users such as the Air Force (12.93%), the Army (13.10%), the Federal Aviation Administration (12.85%), and the Navy (14.40%). Nonclassified American military uses of the government master file in 1985 represented over 48% of the entire file.[7] This figure excludes federal marshals and police forces such as the Secret Service or Federal Bureau of Investigation; it also, of course, excludes classified domestic activities as well as the military's extensive uses of the electromagnetic spectrum assignments to other nations, classified work abroad (such as the work of the Central Intelligence Agency or the Naval Intelligence Agency), and the shortwave radio and overseas television broadcasts of the Voice of America.

So the uses of the electromagnetic spectrum in the U.S. are more complex than at first appears. Certainly Americans enjoy, more than any citizenry in the world, a life of convenience brought about by various uses of the electromagnetic spectrum. Yet at the same time, American consumers use a relatively small portion of the spectrum when compared to the American government, particularly the military. The government and military uses of the spectrum in all nations play contradictory roles, from saving lives at sea to spreading dissent and falsehoods and inciting violence through propaganda, from keeping the peace through rapid communications with other nations to waging war against enemies, from gathering and disseminating information that can improve the lives of all the world to spying and gathering classified data about other nations—sometimes, gathering information about other nations that those nations themselves do not even know.

Implicit in the growing use of both wire and wave-based communications systems by modern Americans in their daily lives is a sense of bettering one's life through the exercise of control over and participation in a world beyond the confines of the home. One aspect of this process of betterment is in the growing trend to equate access, control, and participation with personal proprietary rights regarding information. In a sense, this is the 1980s manifestation of a trend that began in American society at the dawn of the twentieth century. Concurrent with the closing of the American frontier and the end of manifest destiny in the 1890s was the rise of new communications technologies such as the radio and cinema. The development and spread of these two communications technologies—along with others to follow—marked the end of an age based largely upon human expansion through exploration and settlement and the beginning of an age based largely on mechanical expansion through technology and information.[8] These communications technologies became surrogates for the industrialized nations, reaffirming their empires but also reconstructing them in economic and cultural manifestations, helping to confirm the proprietary rights the industrialized world believed it held over the poorer regions of the world. Thus technological determinism became inextricably bound up with ideologically charged values such as American manifest destiny and global expansionism.

When examination turns to a social continuum based on access to and control over information, the proprietary advantages of telecommunications usage and reception become clear. Consumers of American telecommunications services increasingly enjoy access to privileged information not readily available—or not available at all—to those who lag behind in their telecommunication skills. The list, which grows daily, can include databases, computer bulletin boards, electronic mail, shopping and information services such as *Prodigy*, banking and financial information, games and entertainment services, and home alarm and security systems. *Prodigy* is a coventure of Sears and IBM that allows subscribers to use their personal computers and a modem to call a videotex information service that offers such features as online shopping, special-interest forums, and stock quotes. Operating on a flat monthly fee (roughly $10.00 as of January 1990),

Prodigy is also user-friendly and equipped with appealing graphic displays, both of which have contributed to its rapid acceptance by users. Most of the various information screens available on *Prodigy* are accompanied by advertisements sharing screen space with information. IBM and Sears expect to be serving 10 million homes with *Prodigy* by 1995.[9]

While services such as *Prodigy* hold the potential for some individuals to open a new world of consumption, other individuals are already being locked out of such worlds due to a lack of basic access equipment, from computers to telephones. Those individuals and families without access to basic touch-tone telephone services—a small but growing segment of the American population, and a segment that contains some of the people most in need of social assistance, such as the homeless—will increasingly find a world closed to them, a world where access is gained only through the telephone and/or computer. The growing use of computerized touch-tone telephone answering services that use the telephone keypad to chart the caller through a large directory (or to register for university courses, reach the proper extension at your bank, and so on) will hasten the development of a new kind of "untouchables" in the U.S. A social and class disparity within the nation divided completely upon the ability or inability to use the telephone seemed unthinkable as recently as twenty years ago. It is a reality today. As has always been the case with the ownership of property, the creation of new proprietary rights and the enfranchisement of individuals with those rights has simultaneously disenfranchised other individuals.[10]

Another factor which compounds the question of propriety is the age of the user. In general, the heavier or more active adult users of telecommunications technologies tend not only to be upscale professionals but also below the age of fifty. The fastest growing segment of users are individuals below the age of twenty-five, many for whom these services have always been a part of adult life. A common and warmly touching motif in advertising has been the youngster demonstrating to the grandparents how to use a new piece of electronic equipment such as a videocassette recorder. While the image of the youngest generation teaching the older generation is pleasurable, on a national scale it is also largely unrealistic. Although it is true that many senior citizens are not excluded because of their socioeconomic status, and some seniors do demonstrate regular use of some aspects of the electronic life (for example, televised shop-at-home services),[11] nevertheless the electronic life has created a new kind of "generation gap" that overall is growing rather than shrinking. The implications are that senior citizens may also find themselves partially disenfranchised from growing sources of information as American society becomes further engulfed by a sea of telecommunications.

Yet it would not be fair to refuse to acknowledge the genuine evidence of social progress the growth of telecommunications has fostered, and it is pessimistic to assume that the problems of unequal access prevent any positive developments at all in the growth of telecommunications. To use the medical field as one of many examples, the uses of telecommunications devices and services are already allowing individuals with injuries and diseases to spend more recuperative time at home rather than in the hospital, through at-home monitoring. The transmission of medical information to specialists at distant locations can provide valuable additional opinions when a doctor is faced with a puzzling case. And the increased use of telecommunications in matching up organ donor transplants has saved lives.[12] This prolonging and extending of life, including enhancing the successful matchup of organ to recipient, represents one of the most positive of proprietary rights, the right to enjoy good health and a long life. Other examples include disaster relief, such as the 1989 San Francisco earthquake and Hurricane Hugo. Here electromagnetic wave-based systems are vitally important to coordinating relief efforts as telephone lines are often down and destroyed following such events.

As stated earlier, the questions concerning the technology of the electronic life carries a complexity far beyond a simple good-evil dichotomy. The rise of the electronic life in American society is forcing more and more American consumers and users of telecommunications services to reconsider some of the basic tenets and beliefs of American society, including the assumptions and definitions of property. Probably the most well-known example of this is the rise over the past twenty to thirty years in the protection of intellectual property. This period has seen a rising concern with the identification and protection of individual and corporate property rights through all possible communicative manifestations of a thought or idea beyond the spoken word. One need go no further than the copyright pages of books, which have changed from the simple and straightforward "all rights reserved" to the more complex and specific "No part of this publication may be produced, stored in a retrieval system, or transmitted, in any form or by any means, electronic, mechanical, photocopying, recording, or otherwise, without prior permission...."[13]

These proprietary rights have recently been extended into questions concerning consumer access to the electromagnetic spectrum. The 1980s saw a wave of encryption from a number of spectrum users in attempts to prevent the "unauthorized" reception of signals that travelled through a spectrum shared equally by all citizens of the planet. The most publicized of these efforts dealt with broadcasters and cable networks encrypting their signals to prevent their reception from owners of backyard satellite dishes (who were not paying the monthly fees that cable subscribers paid for these channels).

In the electronic life, American consumers now find themselves in a proprietary world where the rules of ownership may be rather difficult to understand but nevertheless the drive for proprietary accumulation (and the rules which seem to govern it) is increasing exponentially. News stories, magazine articles, and popular film, television, and novelized fiction all regularly depict, in their own ways, individuals grappling with the process of owning information. Cultural and subcultural reactions to this process are visible everywhere, including a public flouting of this new social order. For example, in 1987 an unauthorized transmission of a Max Headroom look-a-like took place over a television channel in Chicago. This well-publicized prank of video piracy had a certain irony in its choice of fictional television personality, for Max came from a fictional future where the overriding purpose of the legal system is to protect the proprietary flow of information.[14] Probably the most publicized disregard of intellectual property and information ownership rights within American culture is bound up in the figure of the computer hacker. Viewed by the media simultaneously as mischief-makers, recluses, geniuses, and vandals, the ability of hackers to time and time again penetrate the sanctity of private computer and telecommunications databases has both shocked and entertained the public while frustrating the victims of their actions. Yet the actions of hackers point out the ambiguity of defining intellectual property rights, and the difficulty in protecting intellectual property.

The illegal copying and distribution of copyrighted computer software and audio and videocassettes is another activity in this area that publicizes the debate over intellectual property and demonstrates the difficulties of enforcement. Copyright piracy is a global problem, and efforts to fight piracy on a worldwide scale are a major concern of American industries and the U.S. government. Government and industry have launched a concerted effort to stem the tide of infringements on intellectual property rights held by American corporations. In 1985, a new trade association, the International Intellectual Property Alliance, complained that intellectual copyright losses in the ten worst-offender nations cost American industry more than $1 billion annually.[15] American government and industry leaders are now encouraging other nations to begin to promptly protect the intellectual property rights of their own "legitimate" citizens and corporations. They argue that the developing countries of the world need to

> adopt adequate protection before their rapidly advancing economies spawn pirate industries of a magnitude equivalent to those in, for example, South Korea or Taiwan...as one set of economies advances to a point where the economic importance of legitimate businesses based on intellectual property causes the government to strengthen protection, they will be replaced by another group of countries prepared to take advantage of the easy profits to be made through piracy ...improved intellectual property protection can encourage economic development...permitting piracy to continue discourages the development of creative industries...adequate protection practices also help to create the investment climate necessary to attract and/or maintain the foreign direct investment and the attendant technology transfers that developing countries need.[16]

Just as the stakes are increasing at the global level, so do they increase for individual consumers. As more and more individuals come to depend more and more heavily upon telecommunications for their economic livelihood and social well-being, the perceived value of intellectual property tends to increase for more and more consumers. Thus Americans should expect to see slower telecommunications growth in free services (although some services, such as over-the-air broadcasting, will always be free) and more rapid growth in specialized services (with attendant growth in the cost of those services.) The coming competition for ownership of intellectual property rights in telecommunications services are in a distant way akin to the land speculation of the American West during the 1800s. Is it any wonder that Japan, where ownership of land is so difficult to come by, is one of the leaders in ushering in a global age of information?

American consumers utilizing the electronic life will, therefore, face increasing economic costs in exchange for the goods and services available through wire and wave-based communications. These increases in economic costs are probably to be expected, what with increasing demand and also the inflationary spiral that seems an unavoidable component of modern capitalist economies. However, another hidden cost for users receives less publicity and attention: the sacrifices of privacy the users of telecommunications services unknowingly surrender with increased use. More and more often, without their full awareness, American consumers of the electronic life find that their private lives are in the public eye. In his superb book *Privacy in America,* David Linowes investigates the increasing ease of access to supposedly confidential information about individuals and the role telecommunications services and computers play in gaining that access.[17] This invasion of privacy takes place in both professional and personal spheres of data.

In the workplace, telecommunications and the computer allow for new surveillance and employee-monitoring techniques in attempts to increase productivity. From the factory to the grocery store, electronic devices (such as the device that scans bar codes on grocery items) allow employers to track the pace of productivity of their employees (such as grocery checkers) unbeknownst to the employees themselves. The keystrokes of typists and word processing workers are counted and minimum standards are enforced. Telephone operators are monitored for time spent in conversation with customers.[18] And no matter your occupation, the increased recordkeeping duties of personnel departments at large and small corporations, businesses, and institutions (especially those with employee medical and insurance plans) have created a host of confidential information on employees that may—intentionally or inadvertently—be used without the individual's knowledge in ways the individual (and sometimes the employer) never imagined.[19]

The accumulation of data regarding individuals and their habits is not confined to the workplace. Along with being the largest publisher in the world, and the largest user of the electromagnetic spectrum in the world, the U.S. government also holds the largest inventory of computers of any single organization in the world. In 1962, there were slightly over 1,000 computers in use by the federal government; twenty-five years later, the federal government operated over 27,000 mainframe computers, over 100,000 microcomputers, and over 170,000 mainframe computer terminals. In 1982, the government held a total of 3.5 *billion* personal files on people in all its federal agencies, or an average of fifteen files for every American citizen.[20] While the sinister motives for such accumulation may be few (which is not to say they are insignificant), the sheer volume of data collection increases both the risk of mishandling data and the risk that data could intentionally or inadvertently fall into the wrong hands, needlessly violating the right to privacy of American consumers. The government also shows an increasing trend to collect data in areas it previously did not investigate.

> As recently as three decades ago, a person's daily activities—financial and personal—were generally beyond the government's reach, except when crimes were involved. Today, records are, as a matter of course, made available to the government whether such disclosure is required or not...[in most cases] a record keeper may disclose information about an individual to the government voluntarily without the individual being able to intervene.[21]

One of the major problems government agencies face in the handling of their data is unintentional disclosures of supposedly confidential information. Sometimes these disclosures are through carelessness in the handling of data and lack of enforcement regarding access to databases and processing centers. Problems can also arise through the difficulties in developing a comprehensive and fair system that safeguards individual rights of privacy, because the rapid rate of technological change and innovation has created situations where agencies and institutions find it difficult, if not impossible, to enforce confidentiality. The need for rigorous handling of data to ensure confidentiality is paramount, but exceedingly difficult to accomplish. The government is not alone in this problem; it is also faced by corporations in the control of their own data.

In the private sector, the widespread use of credit cards and automatic teller machines is shifting the financial transactions of more and more American consumers away from cash transactions and toward electronically verified transactions. Credit agencies are a major collector and distributor of information and data on the financial habits of individuals, and your credit rating can not only influence your ability to purchase, it can also have a bearing on whether and where you are able to rent or purchase a home, your ability to participate in employee medical and insurance plans, and even your ability to travel. And the goods and services you purchase can lead to the placing of your name on a number of computerized consumer mailing lists that can identify you and your family, your residence, your occupation, your education, your hobbies, your membership in church and/or social organizations, your telephone number, the stores at which you shop, the magazines you read, and the types of goods and services you buy.

This compiling and building of demographic information is extending beyond the economic and consumer sectors and into other areas of society. One of these areas is politics. Telecommunications services are playing an increasingly important role in promoting candidates and identifying potential supporters and voters. During the

1980s, political organizers developed highly sophisticated direct mail campaigns using computerized databases culled from a wide array of demographic analyses of consumers past voting habits, personal purchases, voluntary contributions, magazine subscriptions, travel and vacations, and responses to direct mail inquiries. Telecommunications and demographic skills have become nearly indispensable components of campaigns for national and state-wide offices, especially in primary elections.[22] American consumers—especially those making widespread use of wire and wave-based communications services—are at the same time influencing political decisions and providing information for political organizers without even knowing it.

These encroachments via the electronic life upon personal privacy are not only the result of corporate and government activity. Private individuals can and do invade the private lives of others through telecommunications technology. One commonplace occurrence is eavesdropping on an individual's portable phone, but some eavesdroppers and computer hackers have extended this activity to the nation's long distance telephone networks. These "phone phreaks" obtain phone numbers and access codes to usurp the supervisory and control systems of long distance telephone networks. Phone phreaks communicate with each other and share information via surreptitious telephone bulletin boards that provide information on how to access long distance lines. In an incident that received media attention in January 1990, a male phone phreak who had a falling out with a former girlfriend (also a phreak) tapped the girlfriend's family phone lines and taped all family conversations without their knowledge. Some male phreaks have posited Ally Sheedy, the actress who played the girlfriend of a computer hacker in the film *War Games*, as a sort of underground idol. Sheedy's home telephone has been subjected to unauthorized access by infatuated phreaks intent on becoming closer to her.[23] Unfortunately, such personal invasions are likely to become more routine in the 1990s given the increasing sophistication of electronic equipment and the increasing familiarity and knowledge of such equipment held by a growing number of users.

It is this unawareness of the ramifications of the electronic life that probably presents the greatest danger to the privacy of the modern American consumer. As the twentieth century ends, indications are that this invasion of privacy through telecommunications on a multitude of levels will only increase, touching more and more aspects of our lives. As has been the case so far with the use of credit cards and other modern conveniences, the perceived betterment of living standards supposedly achievable through telecommunications in our everyday lives will also serve as the agent that unknowingly opens the gateway for further invasion of privacy.

Although this process will likely unfold in a number of technologies and social institutions, the increased uses and services of the telephone planned for the 1990s will undoubtedly be a major location of this activity. Planned phone services for this decade (some of which are already available) offer a large array of new features. Call blockers will allow phones to be programmed to only accept certain numbers, or to exclude certain numbers. Centrally located equipment will provide message services for those who do not own answering machines, or are travelling. Distinctive ringing will allow each member of the family to program the phone in such a manner so that each individual has a different ring that announces his or her calls. Auxiliary services on the same line will allow for the reading of gas and electric meters, a security alarm system, and a fax—all on a single telephone line. A call identifier device will allow you to identify (by telephone number) the caller before even answering the phone. While some of these services, such as the call identifier, require rewiring and new technology at the central switching location, the ongoing maintenance and updating of these central switching systems by telephone companies means that significant numbers of consumers will have these services available within the next ten to fifteen years.[24]

While these services may be eagerly anticipated by some consumers, other interests are even more anxious for their arrival. One of the major applications of call identification is in the field of "900" phone numbers. "900" service, a pay-per-call service that began in 1988, is already avidly used by a wide range of advertisers and sponsors as a new conduit to consumers. "900" lines are usually used in conjunction with national television advertising campaigns to attract viewers into calling. A caller can hear information and news, make choices about what to hear next, enter contests, win prizes, get advice, and ask for coupons in the mail.[25] The calls—which can cost up to $50.00 per minute—can generate more than revenue. Within seconds, an advertiser can get automatic number identification and learn the number from which a caller is dialing. Computerized reverse directories then provide addresses for mailing lists. Other information gleaned from callers (when compared to and combined with other mailing lists) can include income and education levels, what car the caller owns, number of children, and brand name preferences. It is highly unlikely that most consumers who use "900" services have any idea of how much information about them is gathered simply because of a supposedly innocuous telephone call. In essence, the "900" number allows market researchers to put the costs of conducting market research upon the consumers, the subjects of that research. The forthcoming telephone services of the 1990s will only make these kinds of information-gathering processes even more discreet, more effective, and more pervasive.

While an entire chapter could be devoted to new telecommunications services forthcoming in the 1990s, one more device deserves brief mention here. Private corporations working in conjunction with the U.S. Defense Department have developed a palm-size device that uses satellite locators and the electromagnetic spectrum to tell the user their exact position anywhere on the globe. These locator beacons are touted as "road maps of the future" for their ability to instantly pinpoint user location within fifty feet of any point in the world. Utilizing twenty-one Defense Department satellites in geostationary orbit (several of which are already launched), the system is not only designed for military applications but also is aimed at consumers, motorists, campers, pilots, hikers, and boaters.[26] Expected to enjoy the same consumer acceptance as the cellular telephone, the locator device is projected to be on the market by the mid-1990s.

One can only wonder at the potential tradeoff between proprietary rights and privacy protection this device will cause. The device has the simultaneous power to give the user the illusion of "ownership" of his or her given location, and the tracker the power to oversee each and every move. The possibilities for market research alone are mind-boggling. Clearly, the implications behind the use of telecommunications services and the everyday electronic life enjoyed by more and more Americans are staggering.

Gaily wrapped in the pedagogy of consumer culture, the electronic life poses serious ramifications for our shared notions of property, causes growing disparities among social sectors, and discreetly threatens to truly expunge one of the most important rights of all—the right to be left alone. Ultimately, the final tradeoff may be a choice of continuing to invest in the perceived social value of technological determinism versus the traditional value of personal privacy. The discreet pedagogical process that fuels embracement of technological determinism threatens this age-old right of aloneness. This chapter has tried to show how the coupling of social status, advertising, perceptions of property, and consumer aspirations centered on technological accumulation all combine to create a pedagogical force of quantum proportions, and a pedagogical force that constantly reaffirms technological determinism as the primary creator of new social progress.

Students and teachers concerned with the pedagogical processes implicit in learning the electronic life have to examine and think critically about a number of issues. One issue of the pedagogical process is centered on the area of technology. The evidence that technological progress is not simply a benign or a utopian solution to social problems exists in the underlying ramifications of our daily lives as citizens interact with telecommunications technologies. The solution for a critical citizenship in the living of the electronic life does not lie in rejection of all telecommunications goods and services but instead in a basic grounding of the implications of use coupled with a judicious self-policing concerning exactly what kinds of goods and services to engage. Students and teachers must also begin to recognize that heretofore simple everyday devices such as the telephone have been transformed into sites of lifelong learning. Finally, all citizens must insist that public dialogue concerning the protection of intellectual property be inextricably coupled to the stringent protection of personal privacy. Telecommunications and the electronic life, despite its many problems, can be a source of potential social progress. It would be a supreme irony if the lack of an informed citizenry someday meant that the pursuit of intellectual property at the expense of personal privacy resulted in our individual self-determination through birthright becoming virtually meaningless. A new understanding of the pedagogical process that promotes the electronic life coupled with the lifelong practice of critical citizenship is our best insurance against preventing such an outcome.

CONCLUSION: Pedagogy, Popular Culture, and Critical Citizenship

Students and teachers in the 1990s who consider incorporating the study of media culture into the classroom also involve themselves, whether they desire to or not, in a growing national debate over the relevance and value of popular culture as a site of serious study. We believe that the careful study of popular culture is not frivolous or escapist but instead timely and important.

Investigations into media texts and artifacts provide the gateways to answering crucial questions, including many questions raised by present-day teachers: What connections do students perceive between their schoolwork and their everyday lives? Can student's everyday cultural experiences be incorporated into the classroom without simply confirming what they have already learned outside the classroom? Does the study of popular culture necessitate the trivializing of objects and texts important to students? Can the study of media take place without reinforcing existing hierarchies of taste and social stratification based on race, gender, and class? Just as importantly, many teachers wonder if their colleagues and administrators will see the pursuit of popular culture in the classroom as legitimate or valueless. One is hard pressed to think of another subject of teaching that is currently fraught with so many personal and professional dilemmas.[1]

Exploring the links between formal schooling and contemporary media culture is both an intellectual and political challenge for students and teachers. The challenge is intellectual because, as we have tried to show repeatedly throughout this book, media texts and artifacts do not always present simple, straightforward, unambiguous messages. Instead, the opposite is the norm. The study of media culture often means an abandonment of the search for some sort of singular, overarching, "truth" or "correct reading" in favor of multiple and competing interpretations. This is a positive attribute in the study of popular media culture, because it allows for experience in the practice of reasonable argumentation, the respectful differing of opinions, and the value of debate. There is often a sort of uncomfortableness on the part of students—and teachers—when a single, clear-cut answer does not emerge. Yet students and teachers should appreciate the evidence of ambiguity. The healthy voicing of differences of opinion is one sign of a democratic society, and the active participation of students and teachers in the voicing of difference is a crucial component in the development of critical citizenship.

The challenge becomes political in the need to defend or justify the examination of popular culture in the classroom. In the minds of many ensconced in positions of authority regarding educational policy in the United States, if the study of popular culture has any place in the curriculum whatsoever, it is a very low priority. For many educational policymakers, the study of popular culture is not the metaphoric low man on the totem pole; it is not even on the totem pole. The teacher who leads students upon the trail of investigation into popular culture implicitly goes against the grain of strongly entrenched conservative values over what is "right and wrong" in teaching. This is especially the case in the current social-political context of public education, including the fixation with quantified measurement of student achievement, national and international test-score comparisons (and bemoaning of the results of such comparisons in the American press), the drive for productivity in the educational system, the concerns of parents and citizens over the quality of public education (often exacerbated by local or regional manifestations of the "property tax revolt"), and the perceived dropoff of student skills in math and sciences.

This is not to argue against the importance of skills teaching, the information gleaned from mass-produced quantitative measurement techniques, or the value of math and science. Math and science training and skills measurement are extremely important; but equally important, and less easily quantifiable, is excellent teaching in the liberal arts, the humanities, and popular culture. The study of humanities by its very nature does not so readily lend itself to the unambiguous conclusions that are typical of the physical sciences. Nevertheless, the 1980s have witnessed a strong push by conservative forces to remove the unambiguity of humanities, including the advocacy of a standardized "cultural literacy."[2] Such a notion of a standardized cultural literacy is against the grain of everything a critical citizenship stands for, because the notions of change and dissent are part of the historical bedrock of the humanities. As Gerald Graff observes, universities have historically recruited faculty with a wide range of opinion, yet administrators and the press are perpetually surprised when those faculty cannot ever agree over what books and topics to teach and how to teach them. Having programmed the makings of ideological dissent into the system, everyone then wonders why there is so much dissent in the academy.[3]

Cultural conflict—in this case, the debate over popular culture in the classroom—should not be seen as a disease to be cured, but instead as part of the lifelong experience that students will face. Part of the teaching of media culture should include a discussion of why the teaching of media culture is perceived as controversial. Indeed, this is an excellent starting point for student discussion. Many students are likely to be surprised at the notion that the experiences of their everyday lives as bound up in media culture have no legitimate position as objects of study and debate in the classroom—at least, according to many involved in education policy.

The debate over cultural conflict is also an opportune occasion for students and teachers to begin considering the importance of developing a discourse of critical citizenship, a discourse that includes a language of resistance. Such a language provides students with the opportunity for their own empowerment and subsequent social and intellectual transformation. As Peter McLaren argues, a language of resistance also offers the potential for a new vision of the world.

> Such a language must also help to transform critical pedagogy into a pedagogy of hope. It must move beyond the divisiveness of sectarian interest groups.... We need to move beyond the great liberal Conversation and refuse to accept the constant deferral of meaning in any dialogue to the point where we choose only to speak to ourselves. The former position believes that by affirming difference unproblematically, liberation will ensue in a dance of pluralistic reverie. The latter believes that the tenuousness of all meaning inevitably places us in the thrall of never being capable of taking a position or speak from a space of authority or power. At its least dangerous extreme, the Great Conversation lapses into a silly relativism while the poststructuralist position becomes merely political foolishness. At their worst extremes, both positions lead to political inertia and moral cowardice where educators remain frozen in the zone of "dead" practice in which it is assumed that all voices are those which silence or which contain the "other" by a higher act of violence, and all passionate ethical stances are those built upon the edifices of some form of tyranny or

> another. Unable to speak with any certainty, or with an absolute assurance that his or her pedagogy is untainted by any form of domination, the "post-critical" educator refuses to speak at all. This distressing position that has been assumed by some critical educators reminds me of a form of philosophical detachment of some social critics who, by constantly criticizing and radicalizing themselves on their path to universality, often fail to form a concrete praxis based on their own principles.[4]

Critical citizenship can provide a language of empowerment that moves out of the dead zone of contemporary pedagogical debate and gives voice back to those who now feel compelled to silence.

Furthermore, education needs to be recognized as producing not only knowledge and discourse but also political subjects.[5] Students must begin to master the language of politics, and the politics of language, in order to eventually exercise power over their own lives and thereby challenge and transform existing and future social inequities and injustices. This concept of politics and language should not be couched in a single voice—a master narrative—but instead should build upon the values of difference and multiple points of view. Knowledge is not a "sacred text" but rather an ongoing engagement with a variety of narratives and discourses that need to be weighed and valued against each other. As a part of this process, a healthy and enlightening appreciation for the elements of a discourse that constitutes its strength and enduring values can promote better relations and a sense of egalitarianism among students with different social and cultural histories. As stated in the introduction, the texts and messages of media culture often have the possibility of multiple and competing readings. This absence of univocal meaning provides the perfect occasion for students to construct alternative discourses as a part of self-empowerment.

This process can also encourage the creation of new forms of knowledge by enhancing the abilities of students and teachers to cross traditional disciplinary boundaries with skill and ease. The ability to think in an interdisciplinary manner can produce new approaches and new knowledges; when these insights and perspectives are brought to bear on traditional disciplines, those traditional disciplines also stand to gain. The ability to transcend individual disciplines can also reveal to students that the "objective truths" supposedly upheld within individual disciplines often erode outside of the context of that discipline. Objectivity then comes to be recognized not as an unquestioned truth but rather as a historically and socially constructed position that empowers some and disempowers others. Moving beyond the traditional notions of objectivity can be a liberating phenomenon, as Henry Giroux has noted:

> ...critical pedagogy needs to explore in programmatic terms a language of possibility that is capable of thinking risky thoughts, that engages a project of hope, that points to the horizon of the "not yet." A language of possibility does not have to dissolve into a reified form of utopianism; instead, it can be developed as a precondition for nourishing convictions to summon up the courage to imagine a different and more just world and to struggle for it. A language of moral and political possibility is more than an outmoded vestige of humanist discourse. It is central to responding not only with compassion to human beings who suffer and agonize but also with a politics and a set of pedagogical practices that can refigure and change existing narratives of domination into images and concrete instances of a future which is worth fighting for.[6]

Teachers can make a real difference by encouraging students to speak the language of the "not yet" as part of the discourse of possibility; in helping students conceive of and fight for a better future, teachers transcend their role as disseminators of knowledge and become transformative intellectuals who occupy specifiable political and social locations.

For those teachers who have made the decision to include popular media culture in their pedagogical practice, the discussions and examples of analysis in the preceding chapters of this book are useful in two ways. First of all, the topics selected cut across the wide array of media forms and technologies: television entertainment programming, journalism and broadcasting, advertising, Hollywood films, and new communications technologies are all individual constellations in the galaxy of media culture. Of course, our list is nowhere near exhaustive. Such a goal would be impossible in a single book. But we do see our selections as broadly representative of the scope of topics students and teachers might choose for examination. Peter McLaren and Rhonda Hammer have pointed out that critical pedagogy must become a strategic and empowering response to the history of our everyday past, particularly in our engagement with texts and messages of popular culture.[7]

In addition to demonstrating the broad range of topics and subjects available for analysis, the preceding chapters have also demonstrated some of the important analytical questions and approaches that have been developed by scholars of media and popular culture over the past twenty years. The vast range of subject matter, along with the interdisciplinary nature of the world of popular media culture scholarship, has created a situation where there now exists a number of fruitful and productive approaches to media analysis.[8]

Some of thc questions and approaches developed in earlier chapters include the linking of questions concerning race and class to representations of citizens of racial and groups on evening news specials. This is only one way to discuss the representation of race and class on television; one other example that immediately comes to mind is race representation in prime time situation comedies. The questions of feminism and the Hollywood feature film are also applicable to television, or to popular fictional literature. Another chapter demonstrates the methods of close textual analysis of television advertising. Similar analysis can be accomplished for dramatic and nondramatic program fare. Other chapters have taken up the question of relationships between popular media culture and broad social and intellectual concerns such as questions concerning technology and history. This should not prevent readers from doing their own analysis concerning other major concerns, such as economic issues, or the representation of religion. While we realize that readers may not be familiar with each and every one of the programs, advertisements, films, or technologies we discuss, we believe that our methods of analysis are applicable to media texts and artifacts as a whole and not only to the individual objects discussed in the preceding chapters. The importance is not so much in viewing exactly what we have viewed to verify our findings; instead we advocate the viewing and analysis of new material with the application of methods, techniques, questions, and approaches we have raised.

Among the new material needing to be viewed and analyzed by teachers and students is the vast television and press coverage of the Persian Gulf War. During the time this manuscript was being prepared by SUNY Press for publication, war began in the Persian Gulf. The authors received the copyedited manuscript for proofreading the morning after the first night of American bombardment, and completed the final post-copyedited changes and revisions the day after announcement of a cease-fire and temporary halt in the ground war. Although the demands of publication schedules and deadlines allow us little more than initial comments and observations, we are nevertheless offering what we can at this moment as a means of encouraging further analysis of this conflict in the context of media culture.

At this moment, the duration of this conflict still remains unclear.

Despite a cease-fire, it already seems clear that the impact of this conflict on American culture will resonate for a long time. Nearly as big a story as the war itself is the story of reporting the war. Newspapers, magazines, television journalists at national and local levels, and radio talk shows regularly describe this as the first war covered live on television, and the early strategy of late-night bombardments and missile/antimissile engagements have had the peculiar function, thanks to the international system of time zones, of placing the bulk of early action squarely within the prime time hours of American television viewing. Many Americans have, these past weeks, been logging an unprecedented number of television viewing hours. The Presidential address delivered by George Bush on the first night of hostilities —approximately 10:00 pm EST—is estimated to have received the largest viewing audience of any single television broadcast in American history.[9]

The rapidity of escalation toward hostilities in the final weeks of December 1990 and the first days of January 1991 was remarkable, and also frightening. Indeed, one of the very few moments of shared American opinion took place the first night of conflict—a sense of stunned disbelief that an ultimatum had so quickly become a war. Within twenty-four hours, the political positions were laid out, and the television coverage of pro-war and anti-war demonstrations were to be found everywhere. However, that first night was one of shared disbelief. A part of that disbelief centered on the particularly unusual choice of a word to describe the action: euphoria. For the first time, the onset of war was described by national leaders as euphoric, at least for public airing. It is too early to do anything other than raise the specter of the implications of the use of this word to describe the onset of war.

From the perspective of broadcast journalism, the pivotal role of Cable News Network in coverage of the war, particularly the first night, deserves mention here. World leaders and military officials all acknowledged the importance of CNN coverage to their own decisionmaking and analysis, including Richard Cheney, U.S. Secretary of Defense. The most vivid coverage of the first night came from CNN's three reporters in Baghdad, describing the bombing by audio feed. Perhaps CNN should legitimately be viewed not as an American television news network, but rather as a global television news network that happens to be headquartered within the United States. Ed Turner, an executive of parent company Turner Broadcasting, confirmed this analysis of CNN by commenting on CNN's *Larry King Live!* that "we are a global network and serve many nations."[10]

The impact of new technology upon waging war has received major attention from television reporters and other journalists. Much of the new military technology utilizes complex information processing techniques and modes of computer visualization. The eye of the machine now seems the equivalent of the eye of the creator; television news has, on several occasions, shown how these machines see by showing tapes of bombing runs where laser guidance of bombs makes use of this imaging technology. In *The Mode of Information* Mark Poster observes that "A symbiotic merger between human and machine might literally be occurring, one that threatens the stability of our sense of the boundary of the human body in the world."[11] The elusiveness of Saddam Hussein, appearing only briefly on Iraqi television and radio broadcasts, has many Americans asking where he actually is. The integration of weapon and image—for example, the Tomahawk missile, programmed with a computer map and a photograph of the target it seeks—narrows the gap between human and mechanical vision. CNN's broadcasts are the recognized "eyes and ears" of every government involved in the conflict.

The representation of technology in the Persian Gulf War raises profound questions regarding the relationships between technology at both the social and individual levels. The metaphors of information processing and data control partially serve to neutralize the destructive and fatal effects of this technology. Such a rhetoric of neutralization has typified the American military-industrial complex during the 1980s. A prime example of this rhetorical strategy has been the Strategic Defense Initiative, commonly known as "Star Wars." Metaphors such as umbrellas or protective shields have commonly been employed to describe this technology to the public. In 1986, Secretary of State George Schultz commented that the Strategic Defense Initiative "is one dramatic example of the impact of intellectual and scientific change in our ways of dealing with the world. SDI can well be described, in fact, as a gigantic information processing system."[12]

Ultimately, an active and engaging viewership will not only have to take up the issue of benign technology, but also consider how the war and its media coverage are forcing us to come to grips with the increasing mechanization of our own corporeal bodies. Are we becoming dehumanized? Or is technology becoming more humane? How is this dialectic being worked out in contemporary society? What are the structures of power, and the avenues of liberation? What leads to war in the postmodern age, and what can promote peace? While we fervently hope the fighting has permanently ended by the time this book appears in print, these and other issues and questions this war has raised in the minds of Americans will need to be addressed for many years. This must be done in the context of critical citizenship if we have any hope of eventually transcending above the brutality with which we now are forced to live.

When it comes to teacher and student empowerment, we can only sketch out the paths to critical citizenship through readings in media culture. It is up to students and teachers to embark upon those paths and, in so doing, help blaze new trails to follow in the quest for greater understanding of the world in which we live. With this in mind, we close by stressing the value of the study of media and popular culture not only because of what students can learn from teachers, but just as importantly, what teachers can potentially learn from students. As Lawrence Grossberg has argued, if we expect students to genuinely learn from us, we must also genuinely expect to learn from our students.[13] From the vantage point we hold today at the end of the twentieth century—truly, the century of mass media culture—the potential for reciprocal education in the field of media studies is very fertile indeed. In the final analysis, such a reciprocal education is the byproduct of a critical citizenship—the creation of a society where teachers as well as students enjoy the benefits, equality, and freedom of a lifelong education and a critical community.

NOTES

NOTES TO FOREWORD

1. For a further discussion of these issues, see Henry Giroux and Peter McLaren, eds., *Critical Pedagogy, the State, and Cultural Struggle* (Albany: State University of New York Press, 1989), especially the introduction and chapter 13.

NOTES TO INTRODUCTION

1. Trinh T. Minh-ha, "Documentary Is/Not a Name," *October* 52, p. 76–100.
2. Susan Buck-Morss, *The Dialectics of Seeing: Walter Benjamin and the Arcades Project*, (Cambridge: MIT Press, 1989), p. 304.
3. Buck-Morss, *Dialectics*, p. 304.
4. Buck-Morss, *Dialectics*, p. 312.
5. Buck-Morss, *Dialectics*, p. 306.
6. Buck-Morss, *Dialectics*, p. 312.
7. James Carey, *Communication as Culture: Essays on Media and Society*, (Cambridge: Unwin Hyman, 1989), p. 86.
8. Stuart Hall, *The Hard Road to Renewal: Thatcherism and the Crisis of the Left*, (London: Verso, 1988), p. 142.
9. Hall, *The Hard Road*, p. 143.
10. Mark Poster, *Critical Theory and Poststructuralism: In Search of A Context*, (Ithaca: Cornell University Press, 1989), p. 129; also see Poster's *The Mode of Information: Poststructuralism and Social Context*, (Chicago: University of Chicago Press, 1990).

11. Minh-Ha, "Documentary,", p. 85.

12. Henry A. Giroux and Roger Simon, "Pedagogy, Popular Culture, and Public Life: An Introduction," in Giroux and Simon, eds., *Popular Culture, Schooling, and Everyday Life,* (South Hadley: Bergin and Garvey, 1989), p. 25.

13. Henry A. Giroux, *Schooling and the Struggle for Public Life,* (Minneapolis: University of Minnesota Press, 1988).

14. Stuart Hall, "New Ethnicities," *ICA Documents* 7 (London, 1988), p. 27–31.

15. Kobena Mercer, "Travelling Theory: The Cultural Politics of Race and Representation," *Afterimage* 18 (1990), p. 7–9.

16. A. S. Godeau, "Living With Contradictions: Critical Practices in the Age of Supply-Side Aesthetics," *Screen* (Summer, 1987), p. 2–21.

17. P. Redding, "Nietzchean Perspectivism and the Logic of Practical Reason," *The Philosophical Forum,* XXII:1 (Fall, 1990), p. 72–88.

18. Minh-Ha, "Documentary," p. 89.

19. Georg Lukacs, *The Theory of the Novel,* Anna Bostock, trans. (Cambridge: MIT Press, 1971).

20. Cathy Davidson, "Photographs of the Dead: Sherman, Daguerre, Hawthorne," *South Atlantic Quarterly* 89:4 (Fall, 1990), p. 667–701.

21. Stanley Aronowitz and Henry Giroux, *Postmodern Education: Politics, Culture, and Social Criticism,* (Minneapolis: University of Minnesota Press, 1991); Peter McLaren, *Decentering Pedagogy,* (London: Routledge, forthcoming).

22. David Trend, "Cultural Struggle and Educational Activism," *Afterimage* 17 (1989), p. 4–6.

23. David Trend, "Changing the Subject: From Reproduction to Resistance in Media Education," *Afterimage* 16 (1988), p. 10–13.

24. Peter McLaren, *Life in Schools,* (New York: Longman, 1989).

25. Minh-Ha, "Documentary," p. 96.

NOTES TO CHAPTER 1

1. *TV Guide,* 27 January 1987, p. 39.

2. Articles appear intermittently, but nonetheless regularly, on historically-

based movies and mini-series, as well as on made-for-TV movies based on real events. They tend to assess television's "fidelity" to reality in these dramatic formats, raising questions about dramatic license, entertainment versus instruction, the distortions of the medium, the excitement of the "reality" which is ignored in television's dramatizations, and so forth. According to these articles, when it comes to historical fiction (as opposed to documentary and compilation films, in particular), television drama almost always emerges as a lesser version of the "real story" it represents. Larry King (1987) commented on a movie about President Lyndon Johnson "I don't know what it cost to make, but in terms of its historical accuracy it's worth about 15 cents." Curiously enough, *TV Guide* itself tries to correct the historical inaccuracies on the made-for-TV movie in question by calling upon Theodore White to discuss the "real LBJ" in the same issue. (*TV Guide*, 31 January 1987).

3. A great deal of work has been done in a variety of theoretical and disciplinary contexts on the construction of history. It is impossible to offer an exhaustive account of this work. Some of the important influences include: Roland Barthes, "Historical Discourse," in Michael Lane, ed., *Introduction to Structuralism*, (New York: Basic Books, 1970); Emile Benveniste, "The Correlations of Tense in the French Verb," *Problems of General Linguistics*, Mary Elizabeth Meek, trans. (Coral Gables: University of Miami Press, 1971); Michel de Certeau, *L'Ecriture de l'Histoire*, (Paris: Gallimard, 1975) and *Heterologies*, Brian Massumi, trans. (Minneapolis: University of Minnesota Press, 1986); Michel Foucault, *The Archeology of Knowledge*, A. M. Sheridan Smith, trans. (New York: Basic Books, 1972.)

   In the context of film and television see Jean-Louis Commoli, "Historical Fiction—A Body Too Much," Ben Brewster, trans. *Screen*, 19 (Summer 1978), p. 41–53 ; Stephen Heath, "Contexts," *Edinburgh Magazine*, 2 (1977), p. 37–43; Colin McCarthur, *Television and History*, (London: British Film Institute, 1978); Christian Metz, "History/Discourse: A Note on Two Voyeurisms," Susan Bennet, trans. *Edinburgh Magazine*, 1 (1976), p. 21–25; Keith Tribe, "History and the Production of Memories", *Screen*, 18 (Winter 1977–78), p. 2–22.

4. Jean Baudrillard, *Simulations*, Paul Foss, Paul Patton, and Philip Beitchman, trans. (New York: Semiotext(e), 1983).

5. In addition to Baudrillard, *Simulations*, also see Frederic Jameson, "Postmodernism and Consumer Culture," in Hal Foster, ed., *The Anti-Aesthetic: Essays in Postmodern Culture*, (Port Townsend: Bay Press, 1983), p. 111–125; Jean-Francois Lyotard, *The Postmodern Condition: A Report on Knowledge*, (Minneapolis: University of Minnesota Press, 1984); Dana Polan, "Brief Encounters: Mass Culture and the Evacuation of Sense," in Tania Modleski, ed., *Studies in Entertainment: Critical Approaches to Mass Culture*, (Bloomington: Indiana University Press, 1986), p. 167–187; and

Andreas Huyssen, *After the Great Divide: Modernism, Mass Culture, Postmodernism,* (Bloomington: Indiana University Press, 1986).

6. de Certeau, *L'Ecriture;* Jane Feuer, "The Concept of Live Television: Ontology as Ideology," in E. Ann Kaplan, ed., *Regarding Television,* (Frederick: University Press of America, 1983), p. 12–22.

7. Benveniste, "The Correlations of Tense"; Metz, "History/Discourse"; Kaja Silverman, *The Subject of Semiotics,* (New York: Oxford University Press, 1983).

8. This distinction involves subject positionality as a function of discourse. A lucid discussion is provided by Silverman, *The Subject of Semiotics,* p. 45–53.

9. The ad appeared in *Broadcasting,* January 5, 1987, p. 43. The cited text is the headline on the first page of an eight page promotion for the series.

10. James Baughman, "Television and the Golden Age," *The Historian,* XLVII:2 (February 1985), p. 175–95; Michael Kerbel, "The Golden Age of TV Drama," *Film Comment,* 15 (July–August 1979), p. 12–19.

11. A good study that avoids the common historical pitfalls of writing about this period is William Boddy, *Fifties Television: The Industry and Its Critics,* (Urbana: University of Illinois Press, 1990).

12. A good technologically based account of this period is Joseph Udelson, *The Great Television Race 1925–1941,* (University: University of Alabama Press, 1982).

13. This question takes a cue from film studies which has typically included "precinematic" technologies as part of its historical perspective. Scientific and entertainment apparatuses involving illusion of motion, projection, and so forth are acknowledged stages in the story of film. Crucially, these are not construed merely as points of technological progress with cinema as the telos, but as the constituent elements of an ideological history of vision, perception, and representation in which the cinematic apparatus figures prominently. While I cannot offer this sort of "story" for television, I do hope to underscore how and why this sort of questioning can be important.

14. The papers of John Royal (NBC Vice President) hold the correspondence of one such study commissioned in 1944. Papers of John Royal, Box 111, Folder 24, NBC Collection, Mass Communications History Center of the State Historical Society of Wisconsin. In *NBC and You* (New York: NBC, 1945), an employee handbook, the network describes how they expanded their broadcast hours during the war years, from one to four evenings per week. Also see James Schwoch, "Selling the Sight/Site of

Sound: Broadcast Advertising and the Transition from Radio to Television," *Cinema Journal,* 30:1 (Fall 1990), p. 55–66.

15. This was the culmination of two decades of work towards developing an adequate system of program preservation. see Udelson, *The Great Television Race;* Brian Winston, *Misunderstanding Media,* (Cambridge: Harvard University Press, 1986); and Michael Beil, "The Making and Use of Broadcast Recordings Prior to 1936'" Ph. D. diss., Northwestern University, 1977. Some examples of early recordings include the Francis Jenkins "radio movies" from the 1920s in the Library of Congress, and the John Logie Baird disc recordings at the British Museum. Both of these processes represent low definition, small-image television based on mechanical systems. They have little in common with today's standards and technology for image reproduction. Significant documentation from the 1930s exists about the development of television, some of it humorous. In 1933, radio columnist Russell Nye saw a demonstration of the Don Lee TV system in Los Angeles with "all seven reels" of *The Texan,* reporting he could not distinguish Gary Cooper from the leading lady (*Los Angeles Times,* September 3, 1933). In the same year "What Is This Thing Called Television?" (*Los Angeles Times,* July 2, 1933) included a range of Hollywood opinions. The Marx Brothers responded with: 1) Chico, "Television? Is this vision a blonde or a brunette, and what am I supposed to tell her?" 2) Zeppo, "How big of a set will I have to buy to get Kate Smith? The only kind I could afford now wouldn't be big enough to get anything but Singer's midgets." and 3) Groucho, "Just think, when television is perfected, you'll be able to sit in your own home and watch a ball game, but until they invent a way of transmitting hot dogs with mustard through the air, it'll never mean a thing to me."

16. Jeanne Allen, "The Social Matrix of Television: Invention in the United States," *Regarding Television,* in E. Ann Kaplan, ed., (Frederick: University Press of America, 1983), p. 109–119, discusses a variety of potential avenues for television development advanced in the 1930s, and how and why the medium assumed the form it did in relation to these possibilities.

17. See Boddy, *Fifties Television.*

18. Jameson, "Postmodernism," p. 125.

19. Blooper shows, comprised largely of outtakes and on-air "mistakes," began as specials. For a while both the American Broadcasting Corporation (ABC) and NBC ran weekly shows that included bloopers as part of their regular fare.

20. The use of fictional characters as participant-observers at major historical events is a convention of historical narrative films. For two examples,

see Mimi White, "The Birth of A Nation: History as Pretext," *Enclitic*, 5 (1982), p. 17–24; and Mimi White, "Rehearsing Feminism: Women/History in *Rosie the Riveter* and *Swing Shift*," *Wide Angle*, 7 (1985), p. 34–43.

21. Lyotard, *The Postmodern Condition*, p. 75.

22. The time sequence is a bit more complicated than the description allows. Bobby Ewing/Patrick Duffy appeared in Pam's shower in the last thirty seconds of the final episode of the 1985–86 season. Pam awoke, went into the bathroom, and he turned around and said, "Good morning." This (his sudden appearance in her bathroom, apparently the morning after her marriage to Mark Graison) was the "cliffhanger" that generated extensive media publicity during the summer hiatus. This publicity focused on how Bobby's return would be resolved by the narrative—including the possibility that it was a Bobby impersonator. The program resumed at this point in the season opener in the Fall of 1986.

23. Pam's half-sister Katherine was driving the car and aiming at Pam. She hit Bobby instead when he pushed Pam out of the way of the oncoming vehicle. This was the resumption and culmination of plot developments from the previous seasons dealing with Katherine's attraction to Bobby, and her collusion with J.R. Ewing to secure Pam and Bobby's divorce. In the episode in which Bobby was hit, at the end of the 1984–85 season, Pam and Bobby had just reconciled and were planning to remarry. By Winter 1987, those plans had been fulfilled.

24. Reference to "Pam's Dream" became a running media joke. For example, on *Late Night With David Letterman*, comments on previous shows as dreams were common. A *TV Guide* article on outlandish plot developments in daytime soap operas concluded with the following observation: "And, lest we forget, even in soapland there are lines you don't cross. For in the convoluted history of daytime drama, no exhausted writer has ever been so stupid as to have a character wake up and find out that the last fifty-two weeks were simply a bad dream." Mary Alice Kellogg, "She Told the Gorilla Her Troubles And He Carried Her Off To Safety," *TV Guide*, 17 January 1987, p. 38.

25. For a perspective on the prime time soap using the practice of character substitution by multiple actors as a starting point, specifically the year in which Miss Ellie on *Dallas* was played by Donna Reed instead of Barbara Bel Geddes, see Rosalind Coward, "Come Back Miss Ellie: On Character and Narrative in Soap Operas," *Critical Quarterly*, 28 (Spring–Summer 1986), p. 171–178. It should be noted, however, that prior to this instance of actor substitution for an admittedly major character, *Dallas* had employed multiple actors for the (then minor) roles of Gary Ewing and Jenna Wade.

26. The idea of an "extra body" of knowledge posed by historical representation, and the potential threat it constitutes to the unity and coherence of the representation and attendant identification, is developed in relation to acting in Commoli, "Historical Fiction."

27. Of course this raises the whole question of ratings. In general *Dallas* and the other prime time soaps have slipped in the ratings since the 1986–87 season. *Dallas*, in particular, had regularly been in the top ten rated shows for a long time, usually in the top five. During the 1988–89 season it was usually in the top twenty rated shows, still the mark of a very large audience. 1989–90 and 1990–91 have shown continued declines in audiences. It consistently was the highest rated prime time soap in the 1986–87 season.

28. Heath, "Contexts."

29. Andrew Ross, *No Respect: Intellectuals and Popular Culture*, (New York: Routledge, 1989), p. 231–232.

30. Michael Rogin, *Ronald Reagan: The Movie and Other Episodes in Political Demonology*, (Berkeley: University of California Press, 1987).

NOTES TO CHAPTER 2

1. This analysis is based primarily on the 1988 television advertising campaigns of the following corporations: American Telephone and Telegraph (ATT); General Telephone and Electronics (GTE); Hewlett-Packard; BASF; Contel; MCI; New York Life; International Business Machines (IBM); Centel; Apple; Radio Shack (Tandy Corporation); NYNEX; Ameritech; International Telephone and Telegraph (ITT); McDonnell-Douglas; Prudential; Wang; and Martin Marietta. Analysis was in part done through extensive viewing, taping, and editing of air checks (i.e., broadcast and cable off-air taping) and assembly editing. Although these television commercials appeared at one time or another in virtually all dayparts and were aimed at virtually all demographic audiences, they most often aired during national news and public affairs programs (particularly Sunday morning network broadcasts), local news broadcasts in the Chicago television market, and nationally broadcast and cablecast sports events.

2. David Nye, *Image Worlds: Corporate Identities at General Electric*, (Cambridge: MIT Press, 1985), p. 112–60, contains an excellent discussion of the use of visual iconography and photographs in General Electric advertising and public relations. The concerns and questions raised by Nye will be important in my analysis of present day television advertising.

3. The concepts of social tableaux, parables, and visual cliches and icons are borrowed from Roland Marchand, *Advertising the American Dream: Making Way for Modernity, 1920–1940,* (Berkeley: University of California Press, 1985).

4. Edward Bellamy, *Looking Backward 2000–1887,* (1888; New York: Signet, 1960), p. 54–55. The speaker is Dr. Leete, who explains the future world to hero Julian West.

5. National Resources Committee of the United States, *Technological Trends and National Policy,* (Washington: Government Printing Office, 1937), p. 33.

6. *Time,* 3 January 1983, p. 1–15. This was the annual "Man of the Year" issue which for the first time selected a non-human: the computer.

7. John Naisbitt, *Megatrends: Ten New Directions Transforming Our Lives,* (New York: Warner, 1982), p. 283.

8. Howard Segal, *Technological Utopianism In American Culture,* (Chicago: University of Chicago Press, 1985), p. 21–22.

9. Important works on American consumer culture include Richard W. Fox and T.J. Jackson Lears, eds., *The Culture of Consumption: Critical Essays in American History 1880–1980,* (New York: Pantheon, 1983); Susan Porter Benson, *Counter Cultures: Saleswomen, Managers, and Customers in American Department Stores 1890–1940,* (Urbana: University of Illinois Press, 1986); Nye, *Image Worlds;* Marchand, *Advertising the American Dream;* Cecelia Tichi, *Shifting Gears: Technology, Literature and Culture in Modernist America,* (Chapel Hill: University of North Carolina Press, 1987); Jackson Lears, "The Concept of Cultural Hegemony: Problems and Possibilities", *American Historical Review* 90:3 (June 1985), p. 567–93.

10. Nye, *Image Worlds,* p. 148–56.

11. "...advertising had served as society's "green light," beckoning consumers to join in a cost-free progress toward modernity...it expressed in more material, technological terms the promise of an open road accessible to consumers who would run faster, stretch out their arms farther. Far from being "borne back ceaselessly into the past," consumers would retain every amenity of the smaller, more personal scale of life in the past as they accelerated forward into modernity." Marchand, *Advertising the American Dream,* p. 363. Although space does not here permit the digression, surely a wonderful paper could be written on corporate advertising's simultaneous uses of history as a value to be both scorned and cherished.

12. While this citation is not intended to be exhaustive, some of the major

works include John Brooks, *Telephone: The First One Hundred Years,* (New York: Harper and Row, 1976); N.R. Danielian, *ATT: Story of Industrial Conquest,* (New York: Vanguard, 1939); Alvin Harlow, *Old Wires and New Waves,* (New York: Appleton-Century, 1936); Frank Waldrop and Joseph Borkin, *Television: The Struggle for Control,* (New York: William Morrow, 1938); Leonard S. Reich, *The Making of Industrial Research: Science and Business at G.E. and Bell, 1876–1926,* (Cambridge: Cambridge University Press, 1985); Philip Abbott, *Seeking Many Inventions: The Idea of Community in America,* (Knoxville: University of Tennessee Press, 1987); Horace Coon, *American Tel and Tel,* (New York: Longman, Greens, 1939); James Schwoch, "The Information Age, the AT&T Settlement: Corporatism-in-the-making?" *Media Culture and Society* 6 (1984), p. 273–288.

13. See note below. Briefly, the "old" ATT system (before the divestiture) of long distance telephony worked on a switching network of five levels. Central offices were the fifth level and the first point of access for consumers into the long distance system. A central office used to represent one exchange (first three digits of a number.) Central offices were then tied into regional, sectional, and national switching stations. The advent of new switching technologies (such as PBXs and digital switching) in the 1970s and the rise of long distance competitors such as MCI or US Sprint are among the factors which have somewhat blurred the distinctions between switching centers. The recent emergence of the LATA (Local Access Transport Area) is an attempt to re-establish the technical distinction between local and long distance calling in terms of actual technical switching. Basically, the LATA is the point where local calling "ends" and various long distance companies begin to carry the signal.

14. I was first exposed to much of the information on current-day telecommunications policy discussed in this chapter when I attended a two-week postdoctoral seminar session for telecommunications scholars in Washington DC sponsored by the Annenberg School of Communications in June 1986. Unless otherwise indicated, information on ATT in this section is from these seminars. A good introduction to telephone technology (unencumbered by excessive technical jargon) is Herbert Dordick, *Understanding Modern Telecommunications,* (New York: Prentice-Hall, 1981).

15. An overview of early telephone advertising is Connie Lauermann, "Reaching Out, Touching Everyone," *Chicago Tribune Magazine,* 10 April 1988, p. 10. For an interesting discussion of the social reception of electric communications in the United States during the nineteenth century, see Carolyn Marvin, *When Old Technologies Were New,* (New York: Oxford University Press, 1988).

16. The discussion on ATT advertising strategies and the image of the tele-

phone in American advertising during this period is largely from Marchand, *Advertising the American Dream*, p. 117–284.

17. Marchand, *Advertising the American Dream*, p. 119.

18. This ad is reproduced in Marchand, *Advertising the American Dream*, p. 169.

19. This ad is reproduced in Marchand, *Advertising the American Dream*, p. 239.

20. This ad is reproduced in Marchand, *Advertising the American Dream*, p. 243.

21. Marchand recites this Western Union tale in *Advertising the American Dream*, p. 350–351.

22. Marchand, *Advertising the American Dream*, p. 350.

23. The following account of corporate promotion of electricity is based on Nye, *Image Worlds;* Reich, *The Making of American Industrial Research*, p. 88–111; Marvin, *When Old Technologies Were New;* and in the case of the United Kingdom, Adrian Forty, *Objects of Desire: Design and Society from Wedgewood to IBM*, (New York: Pantheon, 1986), p. 182–221. Forty's work reminds us that although this chapter is centered on American society, consumer culture is also a global phenomenon. I argue this point in the case of radio broadcasting in *The American Radio Industry and its Latin American Activities, 1900–1939*, (Urbana: University of Illinois Press, 1990).

24. For a discussion of the importance of "Yankee Ingenuity" in fostering the widespread experimentation with radio in the United States, see Susan Douglas, *Inventing American Broadcasting, 1899–1922*, (Baltimore: Johns Hopkins University Press, 1987). An older, more romanticized, yet still relevant account is Clinton DeSoto, *Two Hundred Meters and Down: The Story of Amateur Radio*, (West Hartford: American Radio Relay League, 1936).

25. Nye, *Image Worlds*, p. 144–145.

26. The use of Leonard Nimoy as a voiceover announcer provides the friendly voice of Mr. Spock from *Star Trek*, further reaffirming the benign and beneficial qualities of the product.

27. In his discussion of the history of technology Fernand Braudel has aptly noted the problems of analyzing technology out of a social context: "The history of inventions, taken by itself, is therefore a misleading hall of mirrors." *Civilization and Capitalism, 15th–18th Century: The Structures of Everyday Life*, (vol. 1), Sian Reynolds, trans. (New York: Harper and Row, 1984), p. 335.

28. Marchand, *Advertising the American Dream*, p. xvii.

NOTES TO CHAPTER 3

1. Michael Shudson, *Discovering the News,* (New York: Basic Books, 1978); Dan Schiller, *Objectivity and the News,* (Philadelphia: University of Pennsylvania Press, 1981). Also see John Hartley, *Understanding News,* (London: Methuen, 1983); Roger Silverstone, *The Message of Television,* (London: Heniemann Educational Books, 1981); Silverstone, "Television, Myth, and Culture," in J. W. Carey, ed., *Media, Myths and Narratives,* (Beverly Hills: Sage, 1988); S. L. Sperry, "Television News as Narrative," in R. Adler and D. Cater, eds., *Television as a Culture Force,* (New York: Praeger, 1976); Gaye Tuchman, "Television News and the Metaphor of Myth," *Studies in the Anthropology of Visual Culture* 5 (1978), p. 56–62; Robert Stam, "Television News and Its Spectator," (p. 23–43) and Margaret Morse, "Sport on Television: Replay and Display," (p. 44–66), both in E. Ann Kaplan, ed., *Regarding Television,* (Frederick: University Publications of America, 1983); in addition, see the recently published Roger Wallis and Stanley Baran, *The Known World of Broadcast News,* (London: Routledge, 1990).

2. For a discussion of this process in the newspaper industry, see Gary Atkins, "In Search of New Objectivity," in Leonard L. Sellers and William L. Rivers, eds., *Mass Media Issues,* (Englewood Cliffs: Prentice-Hall, 1977), p. 26–38.

3. Edward Jay Epstein, *News From Nowhere,* (New York: Random House, 1973). Also see Hal Himmelstein, *Television Myth and the American Mind,* (New York: Praeger, 1984).

4. *My Japan* was produced during the Second World War by the U.S. Office of War Information.

5. Herbert J. Gans, *Deciding What's News,* (New York: Pantheon, 1979).

6. William Appleman Williams, *Empire As A Way of Life,* (New York: Oxford University Press, 1980).

7. Gans, *Deciding What's News.* The next few paragraphs are built from Gans's analysis.

8. Todd Gitlin, *The Whole World Is Watching: Mass Media in the Making and Unmaking of the New Left,* (Berkeley: University of California Press, 1980).

9. As this book was in press, the Persian Gulf War broke out. U.S. Air Force General Colin Powell, an African-American and military commander of the war, may emerge as an exception to this tendency.

10. Doris A. Graber, *Processing the News,* (New York: Longman, 1988).

11. Stuart Hall, "Encoding and Decoding," in S. Hall et. al., eds., *Culture, Media, Language,* (London: Hutchinson, 1980).

12. Paulo Freire, *The Politics of Education,* (South Hadley: Bergin and Garvey, 1985).

13. *New York Times,* 3 July 1988.

14. William H. Taft, *American Journalism History,* (Columbia: Lucas Brothers, 1977).

15. A recently published study of communications and the American government during this period, centering on international shortwave broadcasting, is Holly Cowan Shulman, *The Voice of America: Propaganda and Democracy, 1941–1945,* (Madison: University of Wisconsin Press, 1990).

16. James F. Larson, "International Affairs Coverage on U.S. Evening Network News—1972–1979," in W. C. Adams, ed., *Television Coverage of International Affairs,* (Norwood: Ablex, 1982).

17. James Schwoch, "The American Radio Industry and International Communications Conferences, 1919–1927," *Historical Journal of Film, Radio and Television,* 7 (1987), p. 289–310.

18. A good analysis of contemporary broadcast journalism in an international context is Wallis and Baran, *The Known World of Broadcast News.*

19. David L. Altheide, *Media Power,* (Beverly Hills: Sage, 1985).

20. Thomas L. McPhail, *Electronic Colonialism,* (Beverly Hills: Sage, 1981).

21. Anthony Smith, *The Geopolitics of Information: How Western Culture Dominates the World,* (London: Oxford University Press, 1980).

22. Doris A. Graber, *Mass Media and American Politics,* (Washington: Congressional Quarterly Press, 1980).

23. David L. Paletz and Robert M. Entman, *Media, Power, Politics,* (New York: Macmillian, 1981). Also see Robert Entman, *Democracy Without Citizens: Media and the Decay of American Politics,* (New York: Oxford, 1989).

24. Graber, *Mass Media and American Politics.*

25. The rise of all-news cable stations such as Cable Network News (CNN), Headline News, and even the Weather Channel are, for the first time, providing millions of viewers the opportunity for multiple viewing of the same story. Cable is slowly changing American viewing habits in profound ways.

26. Walter Laqueur, "From Bad to Worse," *Washington Journalism Review*, June 1983.

27. Sperry, "Television News as Narrative."

28. Robert M. Batscha, *Foreign Affairs News and the Broadcast Journalist*, (New York: Praeger, 1975).

29. Mort Rosenblum, *Coups and Earthquakes*, (New York: Harper and Row, 1979).

30. Altheide, *Media Power.*

31. Rosenblum, *Coups and Earthquakes.*

32. Laqueur, "From Bad to Worse."

33. Rosenblum, *Coups and Earthquakes;* U.S. International Communications Agency, *The United States and the Debate on the World 'Information Order'*, (Washington: Government Printing Office, 1979).

34. Batscha, *Foreign Affairs News.* Additionally, the assumption that a "national mindset" or national public opinion is singular rather than pluralistic often undermines reporting.

35. Graber, *Mass Media and American Politics.*

36. Peter Dahlgren and Sumitra Chakrapani, "The Third World and TV News: Western Ways of Seeing the 'Other'," in W. C. Adams, ed., *Television Coverage of International Affairs*, (Norwood: Ablex, 1982).

37. Denise Kervin, "Reality According to Television News: Pictures from El Salvador," *Wide Angle* 7 (1985), p. 61–71.

38. Graber, *Mass Media and American Politics.*

39. Paletz and Entman, *Media, Power, Politics.*

40. William A. Dorman and Eshan Omeed, "Reporting Iran the Shah's Way," *Columbia Journalism Review*, 17:5 (Jan/Feb 1979); Hamid Naficy, "Mediawork's Representation of the Other: The Case of Iran," in Jim Pines and Paul Willemen, eds. *Questions of Third Cinema*, (London: BFI, 1989), p. 227–239.

41. Dorman and Omeed, "Reporting Iran"; Barry Rubin, *Paved With Good Intentions*, (New York: Oxford, 1980); Edward Said, "Iran," *Columbia Journalism Review*, 18:6 (March/April 1980); Cary Bazalgette and Richard Paterson, "Real Entertainment: The Iranian Embassy Siege," *Screen Edu-*

cation 37 (Winter 1980/81), p. 55–67.

42. James A. Bill, "Iran and the Crisis of '78," *Foreign Affairs*, 57:2 (Winter 1978/1979).

43. Rubin, *Paved With Good Intentions*.

44. Bill, "Iran and the Crisis"; David Schoenbaum, "The United States and Iran's Revolution," *Foreign Policy*, 34 (Spring 1979); Said, "Iran."

45. Said, "Iran."

46. Said, "Iran."

47. Myles Breen and Farrell Corocran, "Myth in the Television Discourse," *Communication Monographs*, 49:2 (June 1982).

48. Said, "Iran."

49. Bill, "Iran and the Crisis."

50. Hamid Mowlana, "Technology Versus Tradition: Communication in the Iranian Revolution," *Journal of Communication*, 29:3 (Summer 1981).

51. Mowlana, "Technology Versus Tradition."

52. Rubin, *Paved With Good Intentions*.

53. Bill, "Iran and the Crisis."

54. Alexis DeTocqueville, "Political Functions of Education," in J. Stone and S. Mennel, eds., *DeTocqueville on Democracy, Revolution and Society*, (Chicago: University of Chicago Press, 1980).

NOTES TO CHAPTER 4

1. David F. Musto, *The American Disease: Origins of Narcotic Control*, (New York: Oxford University Press, 1987).

2. Troy Duster, *The Legislation of Morality: Law, Drugs, and Moral Judgement*, (New York: Free Press, 1970).

3. An excellent examination of this "blame-the-victim" mentality in legal discourse is found in Patricia Williams, "Comment: Metro Broadcasting, Inc. v. FCC: "Regrouping in Singular Times," *Harvard Law Review* 104 (December, 1990), p. 525–47; also see her book, *The Alchemy of Race and Rights*, (Cambridge: Harvard University Press, 1991) for an illuminating

discussion of the roots of contemporary contract laws in early American laws governing the ownership and sale of slaves.

4. In previous ABC programs, the widespread use of drugs was portrayed in news specials titled *Drugs, A Plague Upon the Land* (April 1988) and *Drugs, Why This Plague?* (July 1988).

5. Later on in this program, statistics are presented by a former director of the National Institute on Drug Abuse to suggest that blacks account for less than twenty percent of all addicts in the USA. However, the overwhelming majority of images associated with drug use in this program depict black users.

6. Analyses of the representation of African-Americans in American media include Donald Bogle, *Brown Sugar: Eighty Years of American Black Superstars,* (New York: Harmony, 1983); Bogle, *Toms, Coons, Mulattoes, Mammies, and Bucks: An Interpretive History of Blacks in American Films,* (New York: Viking, 1973); Thomas Cripps, *Slow Fade to Black: The Negro in American Film, 1900–1942,* (New York: Oxford University Press, 1977); J. Fred MacDonald, *Blacks and White TV: Afro-Americans in Television Since 1948,* (Chicago: Nelson-Hall, 1983).

7. Statistical information in this section is from the 1980 U.S. Government Census; the 1987 National Drug and Alcoholism Treatment Survey; and the 1988 National Institute on Drug Abuse National Household Survey on Drug Abuse.

8. Stuart Hall, *Policing the Crisis: Mugging, the State, and Law and Order,* (London: Macmillian, 1978).

NOTES TO CHAPTER 5

1. Among the major works are: Mary Ann Doane, *The Desire to Desire: The Woman's Film of the 1940s,* (Bloomington: Indiana University Press, 1987); Lorraine Gamman and Margaret Marshmont, eds., *The Female Gaze: Women as Viewers of Popular Culture,* (Seattle: The Real Comet Press, 1989); Christine Gledhill, ed., *Home is Where the Heart Is: Studies in Melodrama and the Woman's Film,* (London: BFI Books, 1987); E. Ann Kaplan, *Women and Film: Both Sides of the Genre,* (New York: Methuen, 1983); Annette Kuhn, *Women's Pictures: Feminism and Cinema,* (Boston: Routledge and Kegan Paul, 1982); Annette Kuhn, *The Power of the Image: Essays on Representation and Sexuality,* (Boston: Routledge and Kegan Paul, 1985); Judith Mayne, *Private Novels, Public Films,* (Athens: University of Georgia Press, 1988); Angela McRobbie and Trisha McCabe, *Femi-*

nism for Girls, (Boston: Routledge and Kegan Paul, 1981); Tania Modleski, *Loving With A Vengeance: Mass-Produced Fantasies for Women,* (Hamden: Archon, 1982); Laura Mulvey, *Visual and Other Pleasures,* (Bloomington: Indiana University Press, 1989); E. Diedre Pribram, ed., *Female Spectators: Looking at Film and Television,* (New York: Verso, 1988); June Sochen, *Enduring Values: Women in Popular Culture,* (New York: Praeger, 1987); Carol Thurston, *The Romance Revolution: Erotic Novels for Women and the Quest for New Sexual Identity,* (Urbana: University of Illinois Press, 1987); Judith Williamson, *Consuming Passions: The Dynamics of Popular Culture,* (London: M. Boyars, 1986); Janice Winship, *Inside Women's Magazines,* (New York: Pandora, 1987).

2. Modleski, *Loving With A Vengeance,* is exemplary here.

3. There is a growing body of literature on these genres. The most important background texts for my argument include Charlotte Brunsdon, "A Subject for the Seventies," *Screen,* 32:3–4 (September/October 1982), pp. 20–29; Mary Ann Doane, "The 'Woman's Film': Possession and Address," in *Re-Vision,* ed. Mary Ann Doane, Patricia Mellencamp, and Linda Williams, American Film Institute Monograph Series, vol. 3 (Frederick: University Publications of America, 1984), pp. 67–82; Doane, *The Desire to Desire;* Molly Haskell, *From Reverence to Rape,* (New York: Penguin, 1973), especially chap. 4; Modleski, *Loving With A Vengeance;* Janice Radaway, *Reading the Romance,* (Chapel Hill: University of North Carolina Press, 1984); and Thurston, *The Romance Revolution.*

4. Brunsdon, "A Subject for the Seventies," p. 22 (emphasis added).

5. Ibid., p. 20.

6. Ibid., p. 29.

7. This would include, for example, such films as *Stella Dallas* (1937), *Mildred Pierce* (1945), and *Interlude* (1957), among many others.

8. Modleski, *Loving With A Vengeance;* Radaway, *Reading the Romance;* Thurston, *Romance Revolution;* and Ann Barr Snitow, "Mass Market Romance: Pornography for Women is Different," in *Powers of Desire,* ed. Ann Snitow, Christine Stansell, and Sharon Thompson (New York: Monthly Review Press, 1983), pp. 245–63.

9. Elizabeth Cowie, "Fantasia," *m/f,* 9 (1984), pp. 71–104.

10. Ibid., p. 80.

11. For an excellent analysis of the women's picture in an historical context, see Lea Jacobs, *The Wages of Sin,* (Madison: University of Wisconsin Press, 1991.)

12. Cowie, "Fantasia," pp. 87, 101.

13. Ibid., p. 102.

14. Modleski, *Loving With A Vengeance*, pp. 35–36, 85–87; Radway, *Reading the Romance*, pp. 25–45; Thurston, *Romance Revolution*, pp. 46–66.

15. The social and historical background of this division is discussed in Judith Mayne, "Mediation, the Novelistic, and Film Narrative," in *Narrative Strategies*, ed. Syndy M. Conger and Janice R. Welsch (Macomb: Western Illinois University, 1980), pp. 79–92. Additional perspectives on women as producers and consumers of novels are provided by Terry Lovell, *Consuming Fiction*, (London: Verso, 1987).

16. This process is extended and reduplicated in the novelization for both *Romancing the Stone* and *Jewel of the Nile*, subsequent to the release of each film, under the name "Joan Wilder." On the inside title page, this is respecified as "Catharine Lanigan writing as Joan Wilder." *Romancing the Stone*, (New York: Avon, 1984); *Jewel of the Nile* (New York: Avon, 1985). To further complicate the questions of authorship, who writes and who reads, and who is affected by these narratives, the books clearly indicate that they are based on screenplays by third parties, and *Romancing the Stone* ends with two letters, one to the reader signed by Catherine Lanigan, the other to Cathy signed by Michael (Douglas, the producer and male star of both films) explaining how deeply affected and transformed they *both* were by involvement in the production of the film, and the novel.

17. For a more sustained assessment of these issues in *Desperately Seeking Susan* see Jackie Stacey, "Desperately Seeking Difference," *Screen*, 28:1 (Winter 1987), pp. 48–61.

18. Doane, *The Desire to Desire*; E. Ann Kaplan, *Women and Film*, (New York: Methuen, 1983); and Laura Mulvey, "Visual Pleasure and Narrative Cinema," *Screen*, 16:3 (Autumn 1975), pp. 6–18.

19. The idea of simulation as the mode of signification characteristic of contemporary culture is formulated in Jean Baudrillard, *Simulations*, trans. Paul Foss, Paul Patton, and Philip Beitchman (New York: Semiotext(e), 1983).

20. The foundation for these approaches in literary theory is developed in Rene Girard, *Deceit, Desire, and the Novel*, trans. Yvonne Freccero (Baltimore: Johns Hopkins University Press, 1965) and Marthe Robert, *Origins of the Novel*, trans. Sacha Rabinovitch (Bloomington: Indiana University Press, 1980).

NOTES TO CHAPTER 6

1. Fernand Braudel, *Afterthoughts on Material Civilization and Capitalism,* Patricia M. Ranum, trans. (Baltimore: Johns Hopkins University Press, 1977), pp. 7–8.

2. Colin Cherry, *The Age of Access: Information Technology and Social Revolution,* (posthumous papers), ed. William Edmondson (London: Croon Helm, 1985), p. 85.

3. For studies of the ATT divestiture, see Robert W. Crandall and Kenneth Flamm, eds., *Changing the Rules: Technological Change, International Competition, and Regulation in Communications,* (Washington: Brookings Institution, 1989); Paul Teske, *After Divestiture: The Political Economy of State Telecommunications Regulation,* (Albany: State University of New York Press, 1990); Harry Shooshan, ed., *Disconnecting Bell: The Impact of the AT&T Divestiture,* (New York: Permagon, 1984); Barry G. Cole, *After the Breakup: Assessing the New Post-AT&T Divestiture Era,* (New York: Columbia University Press, 1991); David S. Evans, ed., *Breaking Up Bell: Essays on Industrial Organization and Regulation,* (New York: North-Holland, 1983); Fred Henck and Bernard Strassburg, *A Slippery Slope: The Long Road to the Breakup of AT&T,* (New York: Greenwood, 1988); U.S. National Telecommunications Information Administration, *NTIA Trade Report: Assessing the Effects of Changing the AT&T Antitrust Consent Decree,* NTIA 87–119, (Washington: Government Printing Office, 1987); Steve Coll, *The Deal of the Century,* (New York: Atheneum, 1986); W. Brooke Tunstall, *Disconnecting Parties,* (New York: McGraw-Hill, 1985); Albert L. Danielsen and David R. Kamerschen, eds., *Telecommunications in the Post-Divestiture Era,* (Lexington: Lexington Books, 1986); Peter Temin and Louis Galambos, *The Fall of the Bell System: A Study in Prices and Politics,* (Cambridge: Cambridge University Press, 1987); Allan Stone, *Wrong Number: The Breakup of AT&T,* (New York: Basic Books, 1989); Gerald R. Faulhaber, *Telecommunications in Turmoil: Technology and Public Policy,* (Cambridge: Ballinger, 1987).

4. As a footnote to the opening paragraph, one night we discovered our neighbors had the same brand of baby monitor as we had, when our monitor was on and our son peacefully sleeping in plain sight and we heard a baby crying over the monitor. Other parents have related similar stories to us.

5. James Schwoch, "The American Radio Industry and International Communications Conference, 1919–1927," *Historical Journal of Film, Radio and Television,* 7 (October 1987), p. 289–310.

6. James Schwoch, *The American Radio Industry and Its Latin American Activities 1900–39,* (Urbana: University of Illinois Press, 1990), pp. 159–64.

7. Department of Commerce, *Report of the Interdepartmental Radio Advisory Committee (IRAC)*, period July 1, 1985–December 31, 1985, (Washington: Government Printing Office, 1985), pp. 43–44.

8. Schwoch, *The American Radio Industry*, pp. 7–8; Daniel R. Headrick, *The Tentacles of Progress: Technology Transfer in the Age of Imperialism, 1850–1940*, (New York: Oxford University Press, 1988), pp. 97–144.

9. While this book was in press, disagreements between *Prodigy* subscribers and the company broke out over censorship on bulletin board services offered on *Prodigy*. This dispute continued as the manuscript was copyedited.

10. Richard E. Low, "The Ownership of Unforeseen Rights," *Pennsylvania State University Studies*, no. 16 (1964).

11. Online data bases are also being developed primarily for the use of senior citizens, such as the SeniorNet system under development at the University of San Fransisco. See U.S. Congress, Office of Technology Assessment, *Critical Communications: Communication for the Future*, OTA–CIT–407 (Washington: Government Printing Office, January 1990), p. 229.

12. Joel Swerdlow, *Matching Needs, Saving Lives: Building a Comprehensive Network for Transplantation and Biomedical Research*, report, (Washington: Annenberg Program on Communication Policy Studies of Northwestern University, 1989).

13. The former is from Erik Bergaust and William Beller, *Satellite!*, (New York: Hanover House, 1956); the latter from Headrick, *The Tentacles of Progress*. Both were selected because I could reach them without getting up from my desk.

14. Andrew Ross, "Techno-Ethics and Tele-Ethics: Three Lives in the Day of *Max Headroom*," *Working Papers of the Center for Twentieth Century Studies*, no. 8, Fall 1988; also published in Patricia Mellencamp, ed., *Logics of Television*, (Bloomington: Indiana University Press, 1990).

15. U.S. Congress, Office of Technology Assessment, *Intellectual Property Rights in an Age of Electronics and Information*, OTA–CIT–302 (Washington: Government Printing Office, 1986), chap. 8.

16. U.S. General Accounting Office, *International Trade: Strengthening Worldwide Protection of Intellectual Property Rights*, GAO/NSIAD–87–65 (Washington: Government Printing Office, 1987), pp. 42–44. Also see U.S. Senate, Committee on Foreign Relations, *International Telecommunications and Information Policy: Selected Issues for the 1980s*, 96th Congress, 1st sess., (Washington: Government Printing Office, 1983).

17. David F. Linowes, *Privacy in America,* (Urbana: University of Illinois Press, 1989). This book, written in a style to be accessible to mass audiences, is one of the best contemporary treatments of the privacy issue in modern American society. In 1977, Linowes chaired a Presidential Commission investigating the relationships between privacy, the workplace, and telecommunications services. For another view centering on domesticity, see Kevin Wilson, *Technologies of Control: The New Interactive Media for the Home,* (Madison: University of Wisconsin Press, 1988). Also see Mark Poster, *The Mode of Information: Poststructuralism and Social Context,* (Chicago: University of Chicago Press, 1990); and Timothy Luke, *Screens of Power: Ideology, Domination, and Resistance in Informational Society,* (Urbana: University of Illinois Press, 1989).

18. Linowes, *Privacy in America,* pp. 6–7; Communication Workers of America, "Secret Monitoring in the Workplace: Information Packet," 1987.

19. Linowes, *Privacy in America,* details (p. 27) how one individual lost out on a promotion because other individuals at the company violated the confidentiality of a doctor's insurance reports held in personnel files.

20. Linowes, *Privacy in America,* pp. 81–82.

21. Linowes, *Privacy in America,* pp. 84–85.

22. Robert G. Meadow, ed., *New Communication Technologies in Politics,* (Washington: Annenberg Program on Telecommunications, 1985).

23. "Hacker in trouble: loner gone astray?" *Chicago Tribune,* 21 January 1990.

24. "Computer revolution of the '90s may hit home over phone lines," *Chicago Tribune,* 3 December 1989.

25. "Sponsors, callers hooked to new 900 phone lines," *Chicago Tribune,* 3 December 1989.

26. "Hostile beams target where-you're-at device," *Chicago Tribune,* 7 November 1989.

NOTES TO CONCLUSION

1. Henry Giroux and Roger Simon, "Popular Life and Critical Pedagogy: Everyday Life as a Basis for Curriculum Knowledge," in Giroux and Peter McLaren, eds., *Critical Pedagogy, the State, and Cultural Struggle,* (Albany: State University of New York Press, 1989), p. 236–52, develops these questions in detail.

2. Among the studies of this debate drawing considerable attention are E. D. Hirsch, *Cultural Literacy: What Every American Needs to Know,* (Boston: Houghton Mifflin, 1987); Allan Bloom, *The Closing of the American Mind,* (New York: Simon and Schuster, 1987); and Gerald Graff, *Professing Literature: An Institutional History,* (Chicago: University of Chicago Press, 1987).

3. Gerald Graff, "Cultural conflict is part of what students have to know," *Chronicle of Higher Education,* 2 May 1990, p. B4. A complete elaboration of Graff's position is found in *Professing Literature.*

4. Peter McLaren, "Schooling the Postmodern Body: Critical Pedagogy and the Politics of Enfleshment," *Boston University Journal of Education,* 170:3 (1988), p. 71–72. Capitalizations ("Conversation," "Great Conversation") in original.

5. The positions over the next few paragraphs are built upon recommendations advanced in Henry Giroux, "Postmodernism as Border Pedagogy: Redefining the Boundaries of Race and Ethnicity" and Henry Giroux, "Rethinking the Boundaries of Educational Discourse: Modernism, Postmodernism, and Feminism," both in Henry A. Giroux, ed., *Postmodernism, Feminism, and Cultural Practice: Rethinking Educational Boundaries,* (Albany: State University of New York Press, 1991).

6. Giroux, "Rethinking the Boundaries of Educational Discourse."

7. Peter McLaren and Rhonda Hammer, "Critical Pedagogy and the Postmodern Challenge: Toward a Critical Postmodernist Pedagogy of Liberation," *Educational Foundations,* Fall 1989, p. 37.

8. See the notes and bibliography of this book for a representative sampling of many of the scholars and approaches to the analysis of media and popular culture.

9. As of this writing, precise audience measurement figures were unavailable. The estimate was based on overnight surveys of major media markets, and widely reported in broadcast and print journalism.

10. This interview was cablecast on 30 January 1991.

11. Mark Poster, *The Mode of Information,* (Chicago: University of Chicago Press, 1990), p. 4. See also Jean Baudrillard, *Simulations,* trans. Paul Foss, Paul Patton, and Philip Beitchman, (New York: Semiotext(e), 1983); Paul Virilio and Sylvere Lotringer, *Pure War,* trans. Mark Polizotti, (New York: Semiotext(e), 1983); Virilio, *Speed and Politics,* trans. Mark Polizotti, (New York: Semiotext(e), 1986); Virilio, *War and Cinema: The Logistics of Perception,* Patrick Camiller, trans. (London: Verso, 1989); and Gilles Deleuze and Felix Guattari, *Nomadology: The War Machine,* Brian Massumi, trans. (New York: Semiotext(e), 1986).

12. "The Shape, Scope and Consequences of the Age of Information," address by George P. Schultz to the Stanford Alumni Association's First International Conference, Paris, 21 March 1986; for an analysis of the rhetoric of military-industrial discourse, see James Schwoch, *The American Radio Industry and Its Latin American Activities, 1900–1939,* (Urbana: University of Illinois Press, 1990), pp. 42–48.

13. Lawrence Grossberg, "Pedagogy in the Present: Politics, Postmodernity, and the Popular," in Henry Giroux and Roger Simon, eds., *Popular Culture: Schooling and Everyday Life,* (Granby: Bergin and Garvey, 1989), p. 91–116.

BIBLIOGRAPHY

Abbott, Philip. *Seeking Many Inventions: The Idea of Community in America.* Knoxville: University of Tennessee Press. 1987.

Allen, Jeanne. "The Social Matrix of Television: Invention In the United States." in E. Ann Kaplan, ed. *Regarding Television.* Frederick: University Press of America. 1983.

Altheide. David L. *Media Power.* Beverly Hills: Sage. 1985.

Atkins, Gary. "In Search of New Objectivity." in Leonard L. Sellers and William L. Rivers, eds. *Mass Media Issues.* Englewood Cliffs: Prentice-Hall. 1977.

Barthes, Roland. "Historical Discourse." in Michael Lane, ed. *Introduction to Structuralism.* New York: Basic Books. 1970.

Batscha, Robert M. *Foreign Affairs News and the Broadcast Journalist.* New York: Praeger. 1975.

Baudrillard, Jean. *Simulations.* Trans. Paul Foss, Paul Patton, and Philip Beitchman. New York: Semiotext(e). 1983.

Baughman, James. "Television and the Golden Age." *The Historian* XLVII:2 (February 1985): 175–95.

Bazalgette, Cary and Richard Paterson. "Real Entertainment: The Iranian Embassy Seige." *Screen Education* 37 (Winter 1980/81): 55–67.

Bellamy, Edward. *Looking Backward 2000–1887.* pub. 1888. Reprint. New York: Signet. 1960.

Benson, Susan Porter. *Counter Cultures: Saleswomen, Managers, and Customers in American Department Stores 1890–1940*. Urbana: University of Illinois Press. 1986.

Benveniste, Emile. "The Correlations of Tense in the French Verb." in *Problems of General Linguistics*. Mary Elizabeth Meek, trans. Coral Gables: University of Miami Press. 1971.

Bill, James A. "Iran and the Crisis of '79." *Foreign Affairs* 57:2 (Winter 1978/1979).

Bloom, Allan. *The Closing of the American Mind*. New York: Simon and Schuster. 1987.

Boddy, William. *Fifties Television: The Industry and its Critics*. Urbana: University of Illinois Press. 1990.

Bogle, Donald. *Brown Sugar: Eighty Years of American Black Superstars*. New York: Harmony. 1980.

Bogle, Donald. *Toms, Coons, Mulattoes, Mammies, and Bucks: An Interpretive History*. New York: Viking. 1973.

Braudel, Fernand. *Afterthoughts on Material Civilization and Capitalism*. Baltimore: Johns Hopkins University Press. 1977.

Braudel, Fernand. *Civilization and Capitalism, 15th–18th Centuries*. 3 vol. (*The Structures of Everyday Life; The Wheels of Commerce; The Perspective of the World*.) Sian Reynolds, trans. New York: Harper and Row. 1984.

Breen, Myles and Farrell Corocran. "Myth in the Television Discourse." *Communication Monographs* 49:2 (June 1982).

Brooks, John. *Telephone: The First One Hundred Years*. New York: Harper and Row. 1976.

Brundson, Charlotte. "A Subject for the Seventies." *Screen* 32:3–4 (September/October 1982): 20–29.

Cherry, Colin. *The Age of Access: Information Technology and Social Revo-*

lution. (posthumous papers) William Edmonson, ed. London: Croon Helm. 1985.

Cole, Barry. *After the Breakup: Assessing the New Post–AT&T Divestiture Era*. New York: Columbia University Press. 1991.

Coll, Steve. *Deal of the Century*. New York: Antheneum. 1986.

Commoli, Jean-Louis. "Historical Fiction—A Body Too Much." Ben Brewster, trans. *Screen* 19 (Summer 1978): 41–53.

Coon, Horace. *American Tel and Tel*. New York: Longman, Greens. 1939.

Coward, Rosalind. "Come Back Miss Ellie: On Character and Narrative in Soap Opera." *Critical Quarterly* 28 (Spring–Summer 1986): 171–78.

Cowie, Elizabeth. "Fantasia." *m/f* 9 (1984): 71–104.

Crandall, Robert W. and Kenneth Flamm, eds. *Changing the Rules: Technological Change, International Competition, and Regulation in Communications*. Washington: Brookings Instituion. 1989.

Cripps, Thomas. *Slow Fade to Black: The Negro in American Film, 1900–1942*. New York: Oxford. 1977.

Dahlgren, Peter and Sumitra Chakrapani. "The Third World and TV News: Western Ways of Seeing the `Other'." in W. C. Adams, ed. *Television Coverage of International Affairs*. Norwood: Ablex. 1982.

Danielean, N. R. *ATT: Story of Industrial Conquest*. New York: Vanguard. 1939.

Danielsen, Albert L. and David R. Kamerschen, eds. *Telecommunications in the Post-Divestiture Era*. Lexington: Lexington Books. 1986.

de Certeau, Michel. *Heterologies*. Brian Massumi, trans. Minneapolis: University of Minnesota Press. 1986.

de Certeau, Michel. *L'Ecriture de l'Histoire*. Paris: Gallimard. 1975.

Deleuze, Gilles, and Felix Guattari. *Nomadology: The War Machine.* Brian Massumi, trans. New York: Semiotext(e). 1986.

Doane, Mary Ann. "The `Woman's Film': Possession and Address." in Mary Ann Doane et. al., eds. *Re-Vision.* AFI Monograph Series, vol. 3. Frederick: University Press of America. 1984.

Doane, Mary Ann. *The Desire to Desire: The Woman's Film of the 1940s.* Bloomington: Indiana University Press. 1987.

Dordick, Herbert. *Understanding Modern Telecommunications.* New York: Prentice-Hall. 1981.

Dorman, William A. and Eshan Omeed. "Reporting Iran the Shah's Way." *Columbia Journalism Review* 17:5 (Jan/Feb 1979).

Douglas, Susan. *Inventing American Broadcasting 1899–1922.* Baltimore: Johns Hopkins University Press. 1987.

Duster, Troy. *The Legislation of Morality: Law, Drugs and Moral Judgement.* New York: Free Press. 1970.

Entman, Robert. *Democracy Without Citizens.* New York: Oxford. 1989.

Epstein, Edward Jay. *News From Nowhere.* New York: Random House. 1973.

Evans, David S. ed. *Breaking Up Bell: Essays on Industrial Organization and Regulation.* New York: North-Holland. 1983.

Faulhaber, Gerald R. *Telecommunications in Turmoil: Technology and Public Policy.* Cambridge: Ballinger. 1987.

Feuer, Jane. "The Concept of Live Television: Ontology as Ideology." in E. Ann Kaplan, ed. *Regarding Television.* Frederick: University Press of America. 1983: 12–22.

Forty, Adrian. *Objects of Desire: Design and Society From Wedgewood to IBM.* New York: Pantheon. 1986.

Foucault, Michel. *The Archeology of Knowledge.* A. M. Sheridan Smith, trans. New York: Basic Books. 1972.

Fox, Richard W. and T. J. Jackson Lears, eds. *The Culture of Consumption: Critical Essays in American History, 1880–1980.* New York: Pantheon. 1983.

Friere, Paulo. *The Politics of Education.* South Hadley: Bergin and Garvey. 1985.

Gamman, Lorraine and Margaret Marshmont, eds. *The Female Gaze: Women as Viewers of Popular Culture.* Seattle: The Real Comet Press. 1989.

Gans, Herbert J. *Deciding What's News.* New York: Pantheon. 1979.

Girard, Rene. *Deceit, Desire, and the Novel.* Yvonne Freccero, trans. Baltimore: Johns Hopkins University Press. 1965.

Giroux, Henry and Peter McLaren, eds. *Critical Pedagogy, the State, and Cultural Struggle.* Albany: State University of New York Press. 1989.

Giroux, Henry and Roger Simon. "Popular Life and Critical Pedagogy: Everyday Life as a Basis for Curriculum Knowledge." in Giroux and Peter McLaren, eds. *Critical Pedagogy, the State, and Cultural Struggle.* Albany: State University of New York Press. 1989.

Giroux, Henry. "Postmodernism as Border Pedagogy: Redefining Boundaries of Race and Ethnicity" and "Rethinking the Boundaries of Educational Discourse: Modernism, Postmodernism, and Feminism." in Henry A. Giroux, ed., *Postmodernism, Feminism, and Cultural Practice: Rethinking Educational Boundaries.* Albany: State University of New York Press. 1991.

Gitlin, Todd. *The Whole World is Watching: Mass Media in the Making and Unmaking of the New Left.* Berkeley: University of California Press. 1980.

Gledhill, Christine ed. *Home is Where the Heart Is: Studies in Melodrama and the Woman's Film.* London: BFI. 1987.

Graber, Doris A. *Mass Media and American Politics.* Washington: Congressional Quarterly Press. 1980.

Graber, Doris A. *Processing the News*. New York: Longman. 1988.

Graff, Gerald. *Professing Literature: An Institutional History*. Chicago: University of Chicago Press. 1987.

Grossberg, Lawrence. "Pedagogy in the Present: Politics, Postmodernity, and the Popular." in Henry Giroux and Roger Simon, eds. *Popular Culture: Schooling and Everyday Life*. Granby: Bergin and Garvey. 1989.

Hall, Stuart. "Encoding and Decoding." in S. Hall et. al., eds. *Culture, Media, Language*. London: Hutchinson. 1980.

Hall, Stuart. *Policing the Crisis: Mugging, the State, and Law and Order*. London: Macmillian. 1978.

Harlow, Alvin. *Old Wires and New Waves*. New York: Appleton-Century. 1936.

Hartley, John. *Understanding News*. London: Methuen. 1983.

Haskell, Molly. *From Reverence to Rape*. New York: Penguin. 1973.

Headrick, Daniel R. *The Tentacles of Progress: Technology Transfer in the Age of Imperialism, 1850–1940*. New York: Oxford University Press. 1988.

Heath, Stephen. "Contexts." *Edinburgh Magazine* 2 (1977): 37–43.

Henck, Fred and Bernard Strassberg. *A Slippery Slope: The Long Road to the Breakup of AT&T*. New York: Greenwood. 1988.

Himmelstein, Hal. *Television Myth and the American Mind*. New York: Praeger. 1984.

Hirsch, E. D. *Cultural Literacy: What Every American Needs to Know*. Boston: Houghton Mifflin. 1987.

Huyssen, Andreas. *After the Great Divide: Modernism, Mass Culture, Postmodernism*. Bloomington: Indiana University Press, 1986.

Jacobs, Lea. *The Wages of Sin*. Madison: University of Wisconsin Press. 1991.

Jameson, Frederic. "Postmodernism and Consumer Culture." in Hal Foster, ed. *The Anti-Aesthetic: Essays in Postmodern Culture*. Port Townsend: Bay Press, 1983.

Kaplan, E. Ann. *Women and Film: Both Sides of the Genre*. New York: Methuen. 1983.

Kerbel, Michael. "The Golden Age of TV Drama." *Film Comment* 15 (July–August 1979): 12–19.

Kervin, Denise. "Reality According to Television News: Pictures From El Salvador." *Wide Angle* 7 (1985): 61–71.

Kuhn, Annette. *The Power of the Image: Essays on Representation and Sexuality*. Boston: Routledge and Kegan Paul. 1985.

Kuhn, Annette. *Women's Pictures: Feminism and Cinema*. Boston: Routledge and Kegan Paul. 1982.

Laqueur, Walter. "From Bad to Worse." *Washington Journalism Review* June 1983.

Larson, James F. "International Affairs Coverage on U.S. Evening Network News—1972–1979." in W. C. Adams, ed. *Television Coverage of International Affairs*. Norwood: Ablex. 1982.

Lears, Jackson. "The Concept of Cultural Hegemony: Problems and Possibilities." *American Historical Review* 90:3 (June 1985): 567–93.

Linowes, David F. *Privacy in America*. Urbana: University of Illinois Press. 1989.

Lovell, Terry. *Consuming Fiction*. London: Verso. 1987.

Low, Richard E. "The Ownership of Unforeseen Rights." *Pennsylvania State University Studies* 16 (1964).

Luke, Timothy. *Screens of Power: Ideology, Dominance and Resistance in Informational Society*. Urbana: University of Illinois Press. 1989.

Lyotard, Jean-François. *The Postmodern Condition: A Report On Knowledge*. Minneapolis: University of Minnesota Press. 1984.

MacDonald, J. Fred. *Blacks and White TV: Afro-Americans in Television Since 1948*. Chicago: Nelson-Hall. 1983.

Marchand, Roland. *Advertising the American Dream: Making Way For Modernity, 1920–1940*. Berkeley: University of California Press. 1985.

Marvin, Carolyn. *When Old Technologies Were New*. New York: Oxford University Press. 1988.

Mayne, Judith. "Mediation, the Novelistic, and Film Narrative." in Sydny M. Conger and Janice R. Welsch, eds. *Narrative Strategies*. Macomb: Western Illinois University. 1980.

Mayne, Judith. *Private Novels, Public Lives*. Athens: University of Georgia Press. 1988.

McCarthur, Colin. *Television and History*. London: British Film Institute. 1978.

McLaren, Peter and Rhonda Hammer. "Critical Pedagogy and the Postmodern Challenge: Toward a Critical Postmodernist Pedagogy of Liberation." *Educational Foundations* Fall 1989: 29–62.

McLaren, Peter. "Schooling the Postmodern Body: Critical Pedagogy and the Politics of Enfleshment." *Boston University Journal of Education* 170:3 (1988): 53–83.

McPhail, Thomas L. *Electronic Colonialism*. Beverly Hills: Sage. 1981.

McRobbie, Angela and Trisha McCabe. *Feminism for Girls*. Boston: Routledge and Kegan Paul. 1981.

Meadow, Robert G. ed. *New Communication Technologies in Politics*. Washington: Annenberg Program on Telecommunications. 1985.

Mellencamp, Patricia ed. *Logics of Television.* Bloomington: Indiana University Press. 1990.

Metz, Christian. "History/Discourse: A Note on Two Voyeurisms." Susan Bennet, trans. *Edinburgh Magazine* 1 (1976): 21–25.

Modleski, Tania. *Loving With a Vengeance: Mass-Produced Fantasies for Women.* Hamden: Archon. 1982.

Morse, Margaret. "Sport on Television: Replay and Display." in E. Ann Kaplan, ed. *Regarding Television.* Frederick: University Press of America. 1983: 44–66.

Mowlana, Hamid. "Technology Versus Tradition: Communication in the Iranian Revolution." *Journal of Communication* 29:3 (Summer 1981).

Mulvey, Laura. "Visual Pleasure and Narrative Cinema." *Screen* 16:3 (Autumn 1975): 6–18.

Mulvey, Laura. *Visual and Other Pleasures.* Bloomington: Indiana University Press. 1989.

Musto, David F. *The American Disease: Origins of Narcotic Control.* New York: Oxford University Press. 1987.

Naficy, Hamid. "Mediawork's Representation of the Other: The Case of Iran." in Jim Pines and Paul Willemen, eds. *Questions of Third Cinema.* London: BFI. 1989: 227–239.

Naisbitt, John. *Megatrends: Ten New Directions Transforming Our Lives.* New York: Warner. 1982.

Nye, David. *Image Worlds: Corporate Identities at General Electric.* Cambridge: MIT Press. 1985.

Paletz, David L. and Robert M. Entman. *Media, Power, Politics.* New York: Macmillian. 1981.

Polan, Dana. "Brief Encounters: Mass Culture and the Evacuation of Sense." in Tania Modleski, ed. *Studies In Entertainment: Critical*

Approaches to Mass Culture. Bloomington: Indiana University Press. 1986.

Poster, Mark. *The Mode of Information.* Chicago: University of Chicago Press.

Pribram, E. Diedre ed. *Female Spectators: Looking at Film and Television.* New York: Verso. 1988.

Radaway, Janice. *Reading the Romance.* Chapel Hill: University of North Carolina Press. 1984.

Reich, Leonard S. *The Making of Industrial Research: Science and Business at G. E. and Bell, 1876–1926.* Cambridge: Cambridge University Press. 1985.

Robert, Marthe. *Origins of the Novel.* Sacha Rabinovitch, trans. Bloomington: Indiana University Press. 1980.

Rogin, Michael. *Ronald Reagan: The Movie and Other Episodes in Political Demonology.* Berkeley: University of California Press. 1987.

Rosenblum, Mort. *Coups and Earthquakes.* New York: Harper and Row. 1975.

Ross, Andrew. "Techno-Ethics and Tele-Ethics: Three Lives in the Day of *Max Headroom.*" in Patricia Mellencamp, ed. *Logics of Television.* Bloomington: Indiana University Press. 1990.

Ross, Andrew. *No Respect: Intellectuals and Popular Culture.* New York: Routledge. 1989.

Rubin, Barry. *Paved With Good Intentions.* New York: Oxford University Press. 1980.

Said, Edward. "Iran." *Columbia Journalism Review* 18:6 (March/April, 1980).

Schiller, Dan. *Objectivity and the News.* Philadelphia: University of Pennsylvania Press. 1981.

Schoenbaum, David. "The United States and Iran's Revolution." *Foreign Policy* 34 (Spring 1979).

Schwoch, James. "Selling the Sight/Site of Sound: Broadcast Advertising and the Transition from Radio to Television." *Cinema Journal* 30:1 (Fall 1990): 55–66.

Schwoch, James. "The American Radio Industry and International Communications Conferences, 1919–1927." *Historical Journal of Film, Radio and Television* 7 (1987): 289–310.

Schwoch, James. "The Information Age, the AT&T Settlement: Corporatism-in-the-making?" *Media Culture and Society* 6 (1984): 273–88.

Schwoch, James. *The American Radio Industry and its Latin American Activities, 1900–1939*. Urbana: University of Illinois Press. 1990.

Segal, Howard. *Technological Utopianism in American Culture.* Chicago: University of Chicago Press. 1985.

Shosshan, Harry ed. *Disconnecting Bell: The Impact of the AT&T Divestiture.* New York: Permagon. 1984.

Shudson, Michael. *Discovering the News.* New York: Basic Books. 1978.

Shulman, Holly Cowan. *The Voice of America: Propaganda and Democracy, 1941–1945.* Madison: University of Wisconsin Press. 1990.

Silverman, Kaja. *The Subject of Semiotics.* New York: Oxford University Press. 1983.

Silverstone, Roger. "Television, Myth, and Culture." in J.W. Carey, ed. *Media, Myths, and Narratives.* Beverly Hills: Sage. 1988.

Silverstone, Roger. *The Message of Television.* London: Heinemann Educational Books. 1981.

Smith, Anthony. *The Geopolitics of Information: How Western Culture Dominates the World.* London: Oxford University Press. 1980.

Snitow, Ann Barr. "Mass Market Romance: Pornography for Women is Different." in Ann Snitow et. al., eds. *Powers of Desire.* New York: Monthly Review Press. 1983.

Sochen, June. *Enduring Values: Women in Popular Culture.* New York: Praeger. 1987.

Sperry, S. L. "Television News as Narrative." in R. Adler and D. Cater, eds. *Television as a Culture Force.* New York: Praeger. 1976.

Stacey, Jackie. "Desparately Seeking Difference." *Screen* 28:1 (Winter 1987): 48–61.

Stam, Robert. "Television News and Its Spectator." in E. Ann Kaplan, ed. *Regarding Television.* Frederick: University Press of America. 1983: 23–44.

Stone, Allan. *Wrong Number: The Breakup of AT&T.* New York: Basic Books. 1989.

Swerdlow, Joel. *Matching Needs, Saving Lives: Building a Comprehensive Network for Transplantation and Biomedical Research.* Washington: Annenberg Program on Communication Policy Studies of Northwestern University. 1989.

Taft, William H. *American Journalism History.* Columbia: Lucas Brothers. 1977.

Temin, Peter and Louis Galambos. *The Fall of the Bell System: A Study in Prices and Politics.* Cambridge: Cambridge University Press. 1987.

Teske, Paul. *After Divestiture: The Political Economy of State Telecommunications Regulation.* Albany: State University of New York Press. 1990.

Thurston, Carol. *The Romance Revolution: Erotic Novels for Women and the Quest for New Sexual Identity.* Urbana: University of Illinois Press. 1987.

Tichi, Cecelia. *Shifting Gears: Technology, Literature and Culture in Modernist America.* Chapel Hill: University of North Carolina Press. 1987.

Tribe, Keith. "History and the Production of Memories." *Screen* 18 (Winter 1977–78): 2–22.

Tuchman, Gaye. "Television News and the Metaphor of Myth." *Studies in the Anthropology of Visual Culture* 5 (1978): 56–62.

Tunstall, W. Brooke. *Disconnecting Parties.* New York: McGraw-Hill. 1985.

U.S. Congress, Office of Technology Assessment. *Critical Connections: Communication for the Future.* OTA–CIT–407. Washington: Government Printing Office. 1990.

U.S. Congress, Office of Technology Assessment. *Intellectual Property Rights in an Age of Electronics and Information.* OTA–CIT–302. Washington: Government Printing Office. 1986.

U.S. Department of Commerce. *Report of the Interdepartmental Radio Advisory Committee (IRAC).* period July 1, 1985–December 31, 1985. Washington: Government Printing Office. 1985.

U.S. General Accounting Office. *International Trade: Strengthening Worldwide Protection of Intellectual Property Rights.* GAO/NSIAD–87–65. Washington: Government Printing Office. 1986.

U.S. International Communications Agency. *The United States and the Debate on the World 'Information Order'.* Washington: Government Printing Office. 1979.

U.S. National Telecommunications Information Administration. *NTIA Trade Report: Assessing the Effects of Changing the AT&T Antitrust Consent Decree.* NTIA 87–119. Washington: Government Printing Office. 1987.

U.S. Senate, Committee on Foreign Relations. *International Telecommunications and Information Policy: Selected Issues for the 1980s.* 96th Congress, 1st session. Washington: Government Printing Office. 1983.

Udelson, Joseph. *The Great Television Race 1925–1941.* University: University of Alabama Press. 1982.

Virilio, Paul, and Sylvere Lotringer. *Pure War.* Mark Polizotti, trans. New York: Semiotext(e). 1983.

Virilio, Paul. *Speed and Politics.* Mark Polizotti, trans. New York: Semiotext(e). 1986.

Virilio, Paul. *War and Cinema: The Logistics of Perception.* Patrick Camiller, trans. London: Verso. 1989.

Waldrop, Frank and Joseph Borkin. *Television: The Struggle For Control.* New York: William Morrow. 1938.

Wallis, Roger and Stanley Baran. *The Known World of Broadcast News.* London: Routledge. 1990.

White, Mimi. "Rehearsing Feminism: Women/History in *Rosie the Riveter* and *Swing Shift.*" *Wide Angle* 7 (1985): 34–43.

White, Mimi. "*The Birth of A Nation:* History as Pretext." *Enclitic* 5 (1982): 17–24.

Williams, Patricia. "Comment: Metro Broadcasting, Inc. v. FCC: Regrouping in Singular Times." *Harvard Law Review* 104 (December 1990): 525–47.

Williams, Patricia. *The Alchemy of Race and Rights.* Cambridge: Harvard University Press. 1991.

Williams, William Appleman. *Empire as a Way of Life.* New York: Oxford University Press. 1980.

Williamson, Judith. *Consuming Passions: The Dynamics of Popular Culture.* London: M. Boyars. 1986.

Wilson, Kevin. *Technologies of Control: The New Interactive Media in the Home.* Madison: University of Wisconsin Press. 1988.

Winship, Janice. *Inside Women's Magazines.* New York: Pandora. 1987.

Winston, Brian. *Misunderstanding Media.* Cambridge: Harvard University Press. 1986.

INDEX